Maritime archaeology

To the memory of my Father,
and of Dr D. L. Clarke

KEITH MUCKELROY

Maritime archaeology

CAMBRIDGE UNIVERSITY PRESS

CAMBRIDGE

LONDON · NEW YORK · MELBOURNE

Published by the Syndics of the Cambridge University Press
The Pitt Building, Trumpington Street, Cambridge CB2 1RP
Bentley House, 200 Euston Road, London NW1 2DB
32 East 57th Street, New York, NY 10022, USA
296 Beaconsfield Parade, Middle Park, Melbourne 3206, Australia

© Cambridge University Press 1978

First published 1978

Filmset in 'Monophoto' Imprint by
Servis Filmsetting Ltd, Manchester

Printed in Great Britain at the
University Press, Cambridge

Library of Congress Cataloguing in Publication Data

Muckelroy, Keith, 1951–
Maritime archaelogy.

(New studies in archaeology)
Bibliography: p.
Includes index.
1. Underwater archaeology. 2. Ship-building –
History. 3. Naval art and science – History.
4. Shipwrecks. I. Title. II. Series.
CC77.U5M83   930'.1'02804   78–5693
ISBN 0 521 22079 3 hard covers
ISBN 0 521 29348 0 paperback

CONTENTS

Preface vii *Acknowledgments* x

Part One
The scope of maritime archaeology

1.   Introducing maritime archaeology 3
1.1   General introduction and definitions 3
1.2   The development of maritime archaeology 10
1.3   Summary and prospectus 22

2   The constraints of work under water 24
2.1   The organisation of work under water 24
2.2   Some problems in work under water 36
2.3   The advantages of excavation under water 49

3   The contribution of current work under water 59
3.1   Mediterranean shipbuilding in classical times 59
3.2   Mediterranean trade in pre-classical and classical times 69
3.3   Early Mediterranean harbours 75
3.4   Ships of the early medieval period in north-west Europe 84
3.5   Post-medieval ship construction 91
3.6   The Spanish Armada, 1588 98
3.7   The expansion of Europe, sixteenth to nineteenth centuries 105
3.8   The annexation of the New World 111
3.9   Navigational instruments 118

4   The unrealised potential of maritime archaeology 127
4.1   Prehistoric craft 127
4.2   Medieval shipbuilding in north-west Europe 131
4.3   Shipbuilding in Asia 135
4.4   Inland craft 138
4.5   Pre-1500 trade outside the Mediterranean 141
4.6   Anchors and anchorages 146
4.7   Deep-water archaeology 149

Part Two
Towards a theory of maritime archaeology 155

5   The archaeology of shipwrecks 157
5.1   Introduction 157
5.2   Wreck-sites and their environments 160

Contents

5.3 Extracting filters 165
5.4 Scrambling devices A
    The process of wrecking 169
5.5 Scrambling devices B
    Sea-bed movement 175
5.6 The analysis of sea-bed distributions A
    Continuous sites 182
5.7 The analysis of sea-bed distributions B
    Discontinuous sites 196

6   The archaeology of ships 215
6.1   Introduction 215
6.2   The ship as a machine 216
6.3   The ship as an element in a military or economic system 219
6.4   The ship as a closed community 6.4

7   The archaeology of maritime cultures 226
7.1   Introduction 226
7.2   Nautical technology 230
7.3   Naval warfare and maritime trade 237
7.4   Shipboard societies 240
7.5   Incidental contributions to archaeology in general 242
7.6   Conclusions 246

8   Theory and practice 248

      Bibliography 255

      Index 268

PREFACE

The emergence of archaeology from the antiquarian amusements of leisured Victorian gentlemen and clergymen into the highly complex and scientific discipline that it is today was accompanied, in the first half of this century, by a serious consideration of the value and purpose of this new study. This movement was associated with the work of Professors Gordon Childe, Grahame Clark, Sir Mortimer Wheeler, and other members of the first generation of professional archaeologists. Together, they established a theoretical basis from which the discipline has subsequently evolved. Maritime archaeology, however, has been a late developer within even this short lifespan, its appearance having followed from the wartime invention of the aqualung. Furthermore, it has arisen from a background of lucrative salvage operations and the tentative endeavours of amateur divers, so that it is only just beginning to achieve some kind of internal cohesion. Nevertheless, the volume of material now coming from underwater investigations, and the recent appearance of a few full-time professional maritime archaeologists, suggest that the moment has come to consider similarly the value and purpose of this sub-discipline, as an aid to the planning of future research and as a statement of the case for according it wider academic recognition and greater support from public funds. With a clear definition of its scope and potential, it will have come of age and can take its place within the modern discipline of archaeology. This book seeks to fulfill these objectives.

It may be as well to state from the start what this book is not about. It is not a manual on how to practise archaeology under water; guidance in this can be found in several widely available works, although full competence can only be achieved through thorough practical training and widespread on-site experience. Neither is it an attempt to summarise the results of every underwater investigation ever undertaken, or even of every important investigation; where recent work is discussed, as in chapter 3, it is solely in an attempt to highlight some significant contributions made to certain aspects of maritime studies. Finally, it is most definitely not a wreck-hunters' guide to untapped wealth on the sea-floor; it is the principal thesis of this book that interference with the submerged remains of past ships and seafaring is irresponsible and destructive unless it is solely and consciously undertaken with a view to solving specific problems in maritime research. This book is a statement (of necessity a tentative one at this stage) of which problems constitute the proper concern of maritime archaeology, the extent to which recent work has tackled such matters, and the directions in which future studies might profitably proceed. Naturally it reflects in detail the attitudes and ideas of one individual maritime archaeologist studying in Britain in the second half of the 1970s, but it is intended that the framework proposed should be applicable to all responsible and scientific archaeological investigations under water, wherever and whenever they may be undertaken.

Inevitably, an essay in synthesis such as this owes a great deal to the work of others. Above all, I must personally thank all those listed in the acknowledgements for so freely making available their illustrations and other material for use in this book. My own involvement in the field would never have come about without the exceptional tradition of solid scientific work under water maintained by the Cambridge University Underwater Exploration Group, whose members, past and present, have supported and assisted me in many ways; particular mention should be made of Dr Nic Flemming, one of the founders of the Group, and Mr Jeff Dubery, who was the Diving Officer brave enough to try to teach me to dive. On various expeditions, I have particularly benefitted from the guidance and advice of Mrs Margaret Rule (Archaeological Director of the *Mary Rose* Project), Mr Tom Henderson (Curator of the Shetland County Museum), and Mr Bob Yorke (leader of the Maghreb and Carthage underwater surveys). In this context, I must especially acknowledge the debt I owe to Mr Richard Price, who has organised, equipped, and led the excavations in the Out Skerries since 1973, who was kind enough to invite me to participate in them initially, and who has since then endured my theorising and archaeological rigour with patience and good humour, tempered by much critical common-sense. As with so many other workers in this field, I am particularly grateful to Dr Joan du Plat Taylor, the editor of the *International Journal of Nautical Archaeology*, for all she has done to lay the foundations of this sub-discipline in Britain and elsewhere, and for her never-failing encouragement and support for me personally.

The structure and scope of this book was conceived on a rocky islet in the Sound of Mull called Eilean Rudha an Ridire, in the summer of 1974, shortly after I had taken up the post of Research Assistant at the newly formed St Andrews Institute of Maritime Archaeology. It was researched and written over the remaining three years of my stay there, so I owe an immeasurable debt to the Council and sponsors of that Institute, and especially its principal benefactor, the Leverhulme Trust. My colleagues on the staff there, Mr and Mrs Colin Martin (Director and Research Assistant), Mr Tony Long (Technician), and Mr Andy Fielding (Research Student), provided the intellectual framework within which these ideas have grown, and have read through and discussed much of the resulting text with me; I hope they can find in the final product some recompense for their kindness and consideration. In addition, earlier drafts of the script have been considered by Mrs Margaret Rule, Professor George Bass, and Dr Ian Hodder, whose helpful comments and criticisms have been greatly appreciated. Similarly, the book in its present form owes an enormous amount to the judgement and skills of the staff of the Cambridge University Press, whose patience in the face of the unusual demands of a specialist in this unfamiliar field was well-nigh unbelievable. Finally, the overall approach here bears the marks of one who graduated from that hothouse of academic archaeology, the Department of Archaeology at Cambridge University under Professors Grahame Clark and, more recently, Glyn Daniel; I must express my gratitude to all the lecturers and supervisors there who were prepared to devote time and energy to my education. despite my addiction to a specialism of dubious respectability and uncertain validity. Above all, I must mention the late Dr David Clarke, to whose memory this book is conjointly dedicated, who inspired me and my fellow students with a breadth of understanding and an intellectual vitality which we shall never forget; it is sad that this work, which he had the courage to commission, must now be offered as an inadequate tribute to that inspiration.

December 1977   K.M.

ACKNOWLEDGMENTS

Society of Antiquaries of Scotland, Queen Street, Edinburgh, Scotland: fig. 1.2.

G. Ucelli: fig. 1.3 (from *Le nave de Nemi* (1950), p. 74, fig. 75, Istituto Poligrafico dello Stato, Rome, Italy).

G. Bass: figs. 1.4, 3.7, 3.8, 5.13, 6.2.

The National Maritime Museum, Stockholm, Sweden: figs. 1.5, 3.18.

The National Maritime Museum, Greenwich, England: figs. 1.6, 3.29, 4.1, 6.1, 7.3.

P. E. Baker/Western Australian Museum, Australia: figs. 1.8, 3.28.

C. Martin: figs. 2.4, 2.6 2.12, 2.17, 3.20, 3.21, 3.22, 5.5, 5.10, 5.14, 5.16, 8.2.

C. Martin and A. Long. fig. 3.19.

J. Cassils: fig. 2.10.

M. Rule and the *Mary Rose* (1967) Committee: figs. 2.11, 3.17.

Shetland Museum, Lerwick, Shetland, Scotland: figs. 2.14, 7.2.

Royal Ontario Museum, Ontario, Canada: fig. 2.15.

Institut d'Archéologie Mediterranéenne, Chéné, France: figs. 2.16, 3.3.

F. H. van Doorninck: figs 3.1, 5.12.

F. Benoit: figs. 3.2 (from *L'Epave du Grand Congloué* à Marseilles, XIVe supplément à *Gallia*, plates XXVI and XXIII), 3.9 (from *ibid.*, plate III).

Mansell Collection, Istituto di Edizioni Artistiche, Florence, Italy: fig. 3.4.

P. Throckmorton: fig. 3.5.

H. Frost: figs. 3.6. 3.10, 3.11, 4.11 (from *Under the Mediterranean* (1963), pp. 39–40, figs. 2 and 3, Routledge and Kegan Paul, London).

R. A. Yorke: figs. 3.12, 3.13.

University Museum of National Antiquities, Oslo, Norway: fig. 3.14.

The Viking Ship Museum, Roskilde, Denmark: figs. 3.15, 3.16.

M. Peterson: fig. 3.25 (from *A History of seafaring* (1972), ed. G. Bass, p. 255, fig. 1, Thames and Hudson, London).

Texas Archaeological Research Laboratory, Antiquities Conservation Facility, The University of Texas at Austin, USA: fig. 3.26.

V. Barber: fig. 3.27.

National Museum of Antiquities, Edinburgh, Scotland: figs. 3.33, 6.3.

P. Johnstone: fig. 4.2.

Folke-Museum, Bremen, W. Germany: fig. 4.3.

B. Greenhill: fig. 4.4.

J. Needham: fig. 4.5 (from *Science and civilisation in China* (1971), vol. 4, part 3, plate CDX, fig. 979, Cambridge University Press, London).

Musée d'Archéologie, Neuchàtel, Switzerland: fig. 4.6.

The Trustees of the British Museum, London, England: figs. 4.8, 4.9.

National Museum, Bangkok, Thailand: fig. 4.10.

Dorset Natural History and Archaeological Society, Dorchester, England: fig. 4.12.

W. Bascom: fig. 4.13 (from *Deep water, ancient ships* (1976), fig. 16, Doubleday, New York).

F. Dumas: fig. 5.14 (from *Deep water archaeology* (1962), p. 10, fig. 2, Routledge and Kegan Paul, London).

R. Piercy: fig. 5.11.

Crown Copyright: fig. 7.4 (from Ministry of Public Buildings and Works, *Guide to Deal Castle, Kent* (1966), p. 21, fig. 1, HMSO, London).

Several of the figures listed above have appeared in issues of the *International Journal of Nautical Archaeology* (published for the Council for Nautical Archaeology by Academic Press), and are reproduced with the approval and co-operation of its editor, Dr Joan du Plat Taylor.

PART ONE

The scope of maritime archaeology

1

Introducing maritime archaeology

1.1 General introduction and definitions

In any pre-industrial society, from the upper palaeolithic to the nineteenth century A.D., a boat or (later) a ship was the largest and most complex machine produced. At Star Carr, the mesolithic site in Yorkshire excavated by Professor Grahame Clark, none of the artefacts discussed in the report would have rivalled in terms of size, variety of materials, or construction time the skin-craft whose existence the excavator has postulated (Clark 1954, 23). At the other end of that timespan, the eighteenth-century First-Rate naval ship, with its hundred-plus guns and crew of over 800, exceeded several times over, in numbers of constituent artefacts and in quantity of power harnessed, the largest machines used on land for transport, manufacture, or mining. Even the Roman Empire, with its development of large-scale systems in military, mining, and food-processing technology is not exempt, since these operations were paralleled by a gigantism in shipbuilding which reached its peak with the grain ships running between Egypt and Rome (Casson 1971, 184–9). But such a dominating position for maritime activities has not been limited to the technical sphere; in many societies it has pervaded every aspect of social organisation. The political importance of these same grain ships, in giving the ruling Emperor the whiphand over the Roman populace, constituted an important part of his power-base (Lewis & Reinhold 1955, 138–42). In fifth-century B.C. Athens, the political power of the *Demos* owed a great deal to its role as the motive force for the Athenian galleys, on which in turn the security of the state was thought to depend (Ehrenberg 1967, 216). And in eighteenth-century England, the Admiralty was the biggest single employer of labour in manufacturing, and played no small role in determining the level of economic activity, and stimulating industrial innovation. At a different level, in many societies past and present, seafaring and fishing folk have formed a distinct sub-culture, alongside the more generally recognised urban and rural groups (Hasslöf 1972, 15–17). In these ways, and countless others besides, the course of human history has owed not a little to maritime activities, and their study must constitute an important element in the search for a greater understanding of man's past.

When considering any aspect of the past, there are several different approaches which may be used, the principal distinction between them being the type of evidence they are designed to utilise. The longest established and most highly developed of these disciplines, in the study of seafaring as in the study of most other activities, is the historical one, in which the primary concern is with the uncovering and interpretation of surviving documentary evidence for past events, and by which the researcher seeks to understand not only the precise course of events but also the reasons, causes, or motives behind them. Another approach, the development of which has proceeded furthest in the Scandinavian countries, is ethnological – the systematic study of surviving indigenous practices, traditions, and customs, in this case within specialised fishing and seafaring communities. Finally, one can study the objects which have survived from past activities on and around the sea, and from them derive insights into the men and societies which produced them; this is essentially an archaeological study. The information and ideas contributed by these various approaches sometimes duplicate and sometimes contradict each other, but above all they should be viewed as complementary in the overall field of maritime studies. In the present work, attention is focussed on the special characteristics of the last of these, maritime archaeology, which can be defined as 'the scientific study of the material remains of man and his activities on the sea'.

Some of the ideas implicit within this statement are worth elaborating. Above all, it should be noted that the primary object of study is man, as asserted in the first half of the formula, and not the ships, cargoes, fittings, or instruments with which the researcher is immediately confronted. Archaeology is not the study of objects simply for themselves, but rather for the insight they give into the people who made or used them, a sentiment summed up in Sir Mortimer Wheeler's trenchant dictum 'the archaeologist is digging up, not things, but people' (Wheeler 1954a, 13). Thus the first part of this definition simply defines archaeology, while the second part accounts for the qualification 'maritime'. With respect to this latter phrase, it is worth noting that there is no mention of boats or ships, but rather of everything that is connected with seafaring in its broadest sense. As considered in this book, maritime archaeology is concerned with all aspects of maritime culture; not just technical matters, but also social, economic, political, religious, and a host of other aspects. It is this fact which distinguishes the sub-discipline from the closely allied subject of nautical archaeology, which is here taken to mean the specialised study of maritime technology – in other words, ships, boats, and other craft, together with the ancilliary equipment necessary to operate them. It is thus a speciality within maritime archaeology, in just the same way as, for example, the study of town-houses can be regarded as a speciality within urban archaeology.

The adjective 'scientific' has been inserted at the start of the definition to show that this study is aimed at generating new insights and ideas through systematic research, and not as a tendentious contribution to the worn-out debate as to whether archaeology is a science or not. The reference here is to science in its widest sense, the disciplined search for knowledge (cf. latin *scire*: 'to know') as opposed to the aimless delight in 'curiosities'. It carries with it the implication that archaeological research in any field must be problem orientated; in other words, to ensure the maximum return from the available material, the researcher must always have in mind the questions outstanding in the current state of his discipline towards which that evidence might be expected to contribute some of the answers. It is only by this steady accretion of data within a systematic framework that any real advances in knowledge or understanding can be made; without it, each worker is essentially starting from scratch, and it is as if all previous workers had not existed, the same basic questions being considered over and over again. It can thus truly be said that the sign of a really successful piece of research in any discipline is a statement in the worker's conclusions to the effect that his studies 'have raised more questions than they have solved'. Real progress has been made, since his successors can study new material from a more advanced viewpoint. From this approach flows the implication that a discipline can be most effectively described by considering the problems towards which research is currently directed, the specific questions being raised, and the ways in which workers are seeking to answer them. Hence the main body of this book is concerned with problems rather than with artefacts, with questions rather than with treasure.

Turning now to what this definition does not say, some of the principal implications of this 'scientific' approach will be made explicit. Some readers will be surprised that it gives no time limits either before or after which the study of the material remains ceases to be archaeology. In fact, the requirement that the principal concern of any study must be man effectively defines a starting date, at the point at which the first hominids can be recognised. However, no terminal date is specified, even by implication, and none is intended. It is necessary though that scientific research should be contributing new knowledge, so that there is an effective closing date at the moment when other sources of information give the required data more readily and directly than an archaeological approach. This date will vary according to the question concerned, and for certain topics may be only a few years ago, while for others it may be several thousand of years back; any attempt to name a general closing date for the whole of maritime archaeology would thus be impossible, and contrary to its scientific nature.

The other outstanding omission from the above definition is the fact that it does not include the further phrase 'together with related objects on shore'. Concern with coastal communities which derive their livelihoods predominantly from the sea is excluded since, being primarily terrestrial settlements, they will be more closely related to surrounding communities in their material culture, and will display their maritime connections only marginally. Many of the objects used in seafaring are rarely brought ashore, and any artefact collection made there will represent very poorly the seafaring community itself. This exclusion is made in full consciousness that maritime ethnologists and anthropologists have included such communities in their brief; their case is somewhat different since they rely very heavily on such communities for their material, and can readily sort it into maritime and regionally orientated elements, according to the contexts within which it was gathered. With excavated finds, the distinction is often less clear and there will always be a grey area of uncertainty, defeating any attempt to separate out the two elements. Where there is no doubt, as with installations directly servicing ships and seafarers, such as harbours or wharves, then their study can properly be said to come within the scope of this sub-discipline. To sum up, therefore, maritime archaeology is the scientific study, through the surviving material evidence, of all aspects of seafaring: ships, boats, and their equipment; cargoes, catches, or passengers carried on them, and the economic systems within which they were operating; their officers and crew, especially utensils and other possessions reflecting their specialised lifestyle. Reference to current work in maritime history will show that this definition of the field of research mirrors the concerns of that discipline as well; only the sources of information tapped are different.

The relationship between these two disciplines, the historical and the archaeological, is a complex one, and must be explored a little further. 'Archaeology, is archaeology, is archaeology', wrote Dr David Clarke (1968, 13), and this applies in the present field as in any other; the aim is not simply to produce 'counterfeit' maritime history. The danger of accepting a role little better than that of an academic maid-servant, collecting interesting facts for historians to interpret, is a particularly insidious one, since it has the superficial attraction of association with an established and reputable discipline. As indicated above, both specialists have their own sets of evidence, and their own questions to answer, and with both disciplines becoming ever more sophisticated and specialised, it is increasingly difficult for one man to be an expert in both of them. He will either be a good historian and a bad archaeologist, or vice-versa. This is not to say, of course, that either should ignore the results of the other's work, where it contributes towards a topic under discussion, but rather that each should consider critically the conclusions of the other's work, integrate them within their own conclusions where possible, and indicate to their colleagues where a dichotomy exists. Thus problems can be tossed backwards and forwards between specialists in different disciplines to their mutual advantage, without any one of them asserting a general primacy. Unfortunately, because of the way academic research has developed in recent centuries, there is still a general tendency to assume a priority for the results of historical studies where conclusions conflict; this is certainly true at present with maritime history, and will probably continue to be so until maritime archaeology can evolve an ordered and coherent structure.

There is a similar confusion of aims and ideas between this subject and maritime ethnology, based on the fact that both proceed, at least in part, by the investigation of material evidence. However, the essence of ethnology is to view this evidence in the context of social forms, economic systems, etc., which themselves can also be recorded, while archaeology has only the material evidence to study. Thus, from the point of view of the archaeologist, ethnological studies are just a part of the wide range of sources from which inferences and parallels can be gathered when seeking to interpret the remains on a par with historical evidence, the results of experimental archaeology, or theories produced by logical processes. For various reasons to be considered further in Part Two, resort to ethnological parallels has been more popular in maritime archaeology than in almost any other archaeological sub-discipline, with many exceedingly fruitful results. However, the point to be emphasised at present is that, despite this close relationship, the two disciplines are essentially distinct, and any fudging of the boundary between them can only lead to both bad ethnology and bad archaeology.

So far, the subject has been defined in terms of the problems to be investigated, and the types of evidence used, thus distinguishing it from other branches of archaeology or allied specialities. However, it possesses one further attribute which fundamentally affects the procedures used, and which separates it markedly from all other archaeological sub-disciplines – almost all the fieldwork in maritime archaeology is carried out under water. Since this is a direct consequence of the type of material studied, it is not properly part of the definition of the subject; nevertheless, it is probably its most striking characteristic. A ship undertaking a voyage leaves absolutely no imprint on the archaeological record, and, if all goes well, the evidence will be effectively dispersed at the end of the voyage, when the cargo is sold, the crew go to their homes, and the ship is taken on for a new enterprise or broken up. It is only if disaster strikes during the voyage, and the whole unit – ship, cargo, and shipboard community – is deposited on the sea-bed, that there is any chance of a permanent material record which is archaeologically re-coverable. The actual quality of the remains will, of course, depend on a number of factors, such as the manner in which the vessel was wrecked, or the nature of the sea-bed on which it landed. Thus the scope of this sub-discipline as actually practised is largely determined by the potential and limitations of the underwater environment, both as a medium for the preservation of remains, and as the situation in which fieldwork has to be undertaken. Similarly, the modes of analysis appropriate to the material evidence are closely associated with an understanding of the process of a shipwreck.

An objection to this assertion of the dominance of underwater remains in these studies might be raised on the grounds that a considerable number of boats and ships have been excavated above water, ranging in date from the Ferriby boats (*c.* 2000 B.C.) through the Nydam boat (fourth century A.D.) or the Graveney boat (ninth century A.D.) to the *Amsterdam* (1749). However, while not denying the value or validity of the evidence gleaned from these sources, it should be recognised that they all represent special cases. Probably the largest group among these terrestrial finds consists of maritime equipment, above all boats, which has been deposited in graves; for example, Herr Müller-Wille has identified over 420 boat-burials of the Iron Age and early medieval period in Northern Europe (Müller-Wille 1974). At the moment of deposition these craft were not engaged in maritime activities; they were usually stripped of their sailing gear, and often otherwise structurally modified. For example, the Sutton Hoo boat (sixth century A.D.) had a substantial wooden chamber erected amidships to house the grave treasure (Bruce-Mitford 1975, 176–80). While such finds can obviously contribute considerable evidence, their total interpretation involves many considerations apart from the purely maritime; so these sites must be regarded as peripheral in the present context, and their special demands and features will not be considered further. Another terrestrial group is the remains of craft which have been deliberately beached and abandoned, usually after everything useful had been stripped from them; notable examples of this situation include the Graveney boat (Fenwick 1972) and the Bursledon ship (fifteenth century A.D.; Prynne 1968). Whilst undoubtedly falling in the mainstream of this sub-discipline, these remains are a special category because they too have been preserved at a time when not involved in a maritime activity, so that they betray little concerning their original economic and social roles. Finally, a substantial group within this category is in fact only terrestrial in a limited sense; it comprises sites originally under water which have been artificially drained, or otherwise removed from a marine environment. Occasionally, this removal has been at the instance of the archaeologists, as with the Roskilde Viking boats (Olsen & Crumlin-Pedersen 1967), but more usually it is the consequence of some other human activity, as with the Blackfriars Roman boat (Marsden 1966) or the hundreds of vessels discovered on the reclaimed lands of the Zuider Zee (van der Heide 1976). In these instances, a considerable number of the special considerations imposed by the underwater environment still apply, and it is principally in the techniques of fieldwork that distinctions must be made. Ultimately, it is only at sea that seafaring disasters can occur, so that it is under the surface of the sea that the bulk of the evidence must lie.

To clarify and summarise the import of this discussion, the relationship between maritime archaeology and the two allied topics of nautical archaeology and archaeology under water is represented diagrammatically in fig. 1.1. The area of concern in this book is outlined by the double circle, and thus excludes small sections of each of the other topics. In the case of nautical archaeology it is those boat and ship finds which are in a totally non-maritime context, notably grave finds (area A). In the case of archaeology under water, it is those sites which are not concerned directly with maritime activities, notably submerged ancient land surfaces (area F). But this covers only a very small section of underwater work; the bulk of it is concerned with maritime affairs, being relevant both to the study of maritime technology (area D) and to the many other aspects of seafaring (area E). In addition to these, however, maritime archaeology involves those sites which are not submerged and which contain evidence either about ancient shipping alone, e.g. beached craft

Fig. 1.1 A diagram illustrating the scope of maritime archaeology and its relationship to the allied topics of nautical archaeology and archaeology under water.

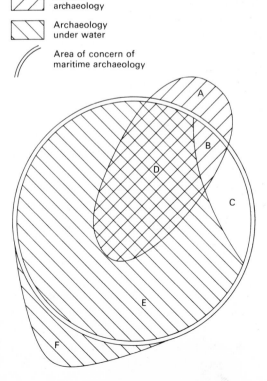

Nautical archaeology

Archaeology under water

Area of concern of maritime archaeology

(area B), or about the whole range of past maritime activities, e.g. drained sites (areas B and C). But since these last were originally under water, it remains true to say that nearly all the evidence must come from submerged sites, so that the constraints of the underwater environment can reasonably be said to be one of the main characteristics of this sub-discipline.

Another outstanding feature, as things stand in the late 1970s, is a remarkable lack of development or systematisation, when compared with most other archaeological sub-disciplines. This arises directly from the fact that it is a relatively new study, and is only now reaching the position where the data-base is sufficiently extensive to allow some tentative steps in defining the discipline. In order to understand this academic immaturity, it is necessary to have a brief look at the history of the subject, an exercise which will also place in context the specific examples of research problems which are described later in this book.

1.2 The development of maritime archaeology

Ever since ships first voyaged on the sea, there have been shipwrecks, and these in turn have always attracted the attentions of potential salvors; only wrecks in deep water or off totally uninhabited coasts will have completely escaped salvage. On many of the more accessible or valuable sites, this work has continued intermittently through the centuries until the present, in some instances accompanied by increasing antiquarian curiosity, and sometimes merging in the recent past with genuine archaeological investigations. For many thousands of years, the only tools available for such work were nets, grabs, or grappling hooks, aided in warmer, clearer waters by the services of free divers. In recent centuries, these operations have been made more efficient by the development of means of getting men onto the sea-floor: first in bells (seventeenth century), then in enclosed barrels (eighteenth century), later with 'hard-hat' standard diving gear (nineteenth century), and finally in the past thirty years with self-contained breathing apparatus (Davis 1955). Over the same period, archaeology has emerged from the unrestrained speculations of antiquarians into a systematic and disciplined study, with the aims and objectives indicated above. However, in relation to many other sciences, archaeology was a late developer, and can be recognised in its modern form only in the later nineteenth century, with the work of such pioneers at C. J. Thomson (1788–1865), O. Montelius (1843–1921), and General Pitt-Rivers (1827–1900) (Daniel 1967; Clarke 1968, 4–11). It is thus not surprising that little in the way of maritime archaeology can be detected before the opening years of the present century.

Glancing at these earlier times, one can see some enquiring minds which were fascinated by the possibilities of such remains. An early

reference to such interest comes from the eleventh century A.D., when
Abbot Ealdred of St Albans sent his men to the ruins of Roman
Verulamium to collect stones for his new abbey, during which operations they found 'oak timbers with nails sticking inside and smeared
with naval pitch', an event deemed worthy of note in his *Life* (Ellmers
1973). A few centuries later, as a result of the interest of Cardinal
Colonna in the tradition of large Roman ships said to lie within Lake
Nemi in Italy, an attempt was made to salvage one by the architect Leon
Battista Alberti (1446). Continued interest in this site led, a century
later, to one of the earliest recorded examples of diving, when a crude
suit was used in a reconnaissance by a certain Franchesco Demarchi
(1535). Moving on several centuries, and into colder waters, it was still
antiquarian curiosity which inspired the fine watercolours made for the
Deane Brothers of finds recovered by them from various historic wreck-
sites around Britain. At about the same time, the first really scientific
consideration of the potential for the preservation of human artefacts
within marine sediments was published, although by one of the pioneers
of geology, Charles Lyell, in his *Principles of geology* (1st edition, 1832).
Chapter 16 of volume 2 is headed 'On the imbedding of the remains of
man and his works in subaqueous strata', and includes a summary of
recent shipping losses to show the extent of the material being deposited,
as well as accounts of contemporary submarine finds which exhibit high
degrees of preservation. He concluded that 'it is probable that a greater
number of monuments of the skill and industry of man will in the course
of ages be collected together in the bed of the ocean, than will exist at
any one time on the surface of the Continents' (*ibid.*, 258). However,
more general nineteenth-century attitudes to such antiquities are nicely
illustrated by the case of an old boat found at Rye (Sussex) in 1822,
which was put on display in London for a time, but broken up when
public interest flagged (Rice 1824).

Naturally, the earliest archaeological studies in this subject resulted
from boat finds on land, beginning with the great series of early medieval
craft found in Scandinavia, the first systematic excavation being that in
1863 by Conrad Engelhardt of the fourth-century A.D. boat from
Nydam (Denmark). However, while modern archaeology was developing on land, there seemed to be no archaeologists adventurous enough
to go under water in the standard diving equipment of the day. Even in
1907, when the Society of Antiquaries of London wished to investigate
a site from which much Roman pottery had been dredged up north of
Herne Bay in Kent, they employed a 'Certificated Diver', Mr Hugh
Pollard, to go and have a look (Smith 1909). However, a year later an
amateur archaeologist took the plunge, in the unlikely person of a
Benedictine priest, the Reverend Odo Blundell, of Fort Augustus in
Scotland. He was interested in the history and construction of a crannog

(lake dwelling) in Loch Ness a couple of kilometres from his abbey, and he soon concluded that the only way to find out how it was built was to have a close look at the bottom of it. He persuaded a diving crew from the Caledonian Canal Company to provide him with a suit and assistance, and went down without any major problems on 7 August 1908 (Blundell 1909). A sketch of this artificial island done after this dive is shown in fig. 1.2. In the following summer this remarkable character dived on a number of other crannog sites (Blundell 1910) – work which initiated a British Association research project on Scottish man-made islands.

During this same decade, the attention of all those interested in classical antiquity was being drawn by a series of spectacular finds of ancient works of art from the Mediterranean. The first of these was off the island of Antikythera, midway between Crete and the Greek mainland, where, in 1900, Greek sponge divers discovered a pile of marble and bronze statues in 60 metres of water. On learning of this find, the Greek Government organised recovery operations, using Naval craft, with operations being directed from the surface by the Director of Antiquities, Professor George Byzantinos. Over the next year, an impressive collection of statuary and other objects was recovered, including the famous Antikythera youth and an early mechanical calculator; the find apparently represented the remains of a Roman vessel carrying Greek treasures to Rome after the victories of Sulla in 86 B.C. (Weinberg *et al.* 1965). Seven years later, an almost identical sequence of events occurred off the Tunisian coast at Mahdia, where a similar cargo of loot was also found by sponge divers. In this case, the Tunisian Department of Antiquities continued to support salvage operations until 1913 (Frondeville 1965). The value of these chance finds, in both artistic and archaeological terms, was such that the great potential of underwater sites was widely appreciated among classical archaeologists from the early years of this century, a fact which had great consequences when the invention of the aqualung finally allowed that potential to be exploited. Salomon Reinach summarised this realisation when he wrote that 'the

Fig. 1.2 A drawing of Cherry Island crannog in Loch Ness made after the first dive on the site by the Reverend Odo Blundell in 1908.

richest museum of antiquities in the whole world is still inaccessible. I mean the sea-bed of the Mediterranean . . .'

But the exploitation had to wait until after the Second World War. The decades between the wars saw advances only in a few limited areas, along with a few spectacular chance finds, such as that at Cape Artemision. Undoubtedly the most publicised operation in this period was the draining, on Mussolini's orders, of Lake Nemi in order to reveal and raise the famous Roman craft known to lie there (Ucelli 1950). The project was a success, providing both a spectacular museum display, and much new and detailed information about the construction and sheathing of Roman ships (fig. 1.3). However, the extent to which they could be regarded as typical was in doubt, since, with their marble columns, heated baths, and decks paved with mosaics, they were evidently very special craft. Much less widely known was the fundamental work done by the Jesuit, Father André Poidebard, on the harbour remains of the Palestine coast, beginning at Tyre in 1934. Himself a pioneer of both aerial and underwater photography for archaeological purposes, he brought both skills to bear, with the assistance of French naval personnel and local sponge divers, on the problems of identifying and mapping these extensive remains. His criteria for recognising, and to some extent dating, these huge structures have remained valid into the aqualung age (Poidebard 1939; Frost 1963a, 65–114).

Fig. 1.3 A view of the second Roman ship in Lake Nemi after initial cleaning, 1930.

Although various attempts at producing a self-regulating underwater

breathing apparatus had been made previously, it was the work of a French Navy officer, Jacques-Yves Cousteau, and an engineer, Emile Gagnan, in 1942, which finally achieved an aqualung which could be used by ordinary people. The cost of the old standard 'hard-hat' gear, the considerable strength and endurance required to use it, the amount of training and experience necessary to work effectively within the suits, the large number of surface assistants required, and above all the cumbersomeness of the diver on the bottom, had all ruled out the possibility of genuine archaeological work in the old equipment: on all these scores the appearance of the aqualung represented a revolution. Of course, it also represented an advance for those interested in wreck-sites as a source of souvenirs or profitable antiquities, so that the early years after the War saw considerable depredation of undersea sites, a loss which still continues, despite the strict laws regarding sea-bed antiquities enacted by most coastal states.

One of the first serious attempts to investigate a classical wreck-site systematically was undertaken by Captain Cousteau himself, when he led his Undersea Research Group in an excavation of a large amphora mound off the island of Grand Congloué, near Marseilles. Although a number of techniques and tools were first developed on this site, the archaeological standards appear, in retrospect, to have been unacceptably low – for example, no plan of the wreck-site was ever produced – and there is still considerable controversy as to whether there were one or two wrecks on this site (Benoit 1961). Nevertheless, the practicability of disciplined excavation under water using aqualung divers had been demonstrated, although it was several years before any further progress was made. In the meantime, it was left to concerned individuals, such as Frederic Dumas, one of Cousteau's associates, to record what they could between the looting. Another activist was Commander Philippe Taillez, who, while chief of the French Navy's Diving School, organised the excavation of a first-century B.C. wreck on the Titan reef off the French coast, and who was particularly conscious of the inadequacies in the archaeological control of his work. As he wrote in the conclusion to his report: 'We have tried sincerely, to the best of our ability, but I know how many mistakes were made . . . If we had been assisted in the beginning by an archaeologist, he would surely have noted with much greater accuracy the position of each object; by personal inspection he would have drawn more information from the slightest indications, (Taillez 1965, 91).

Unfortunately, in France no diving archaeologist appeared until a great deal had been lost. It was an American team from the Museum of the University of Pennsylvania, working off the Turkish coast, who first demonstrated that it was possible for archaeologists to work on the sea-bed, even in 30 metres of water. In 1960, George Bass led a team including Peter Throckmorton, Joan du Plat Taylor, and Frederic Dumas in excavating a site, off Cape Gelidonya, of a ship which sank around 1200 B.C. (fig. 1.4). The result was a major archaeological triumph, both in terms of techniques, which allowed few if any concessions to the fact of being under water, and in terms of a substantial contribution to studies on late Bronze Age trade in the eastern Mediterranean (Bass 1967). This project initiated a great series of American-sponsored underwater excavations in Turkish waters, notably on the fourth- and seventh-century A.D. wrecks off Yassi Ada. Members of these teams were also responsible for the extensive excavations undertaken on a fourth-century B.C. wreck near Kyrenia in Cyprus directed

Fig. 1.4 An archaeologist at work on the remains of a Bronze Age wreck at Cape Gelidonya in 1961. *1960?*

by Michael Katzev. This project concluded with the raising and conserving of the surviving ship's structure, which is now on display in Kyrenia Castle (Swiny & Katzev 1973; Katzev 1974).

In touching on only the more outstanding milestones in the development of maritime archaeology in the Mediterranean, a great deal of important work has been overlooked, especially in countries other than France or Turkey. The last decade has seen a general increase in positive government support for such work; for example, considerable progress has been made in Yugoslavian waters since 1969, when a well-regulated system was established based on 'working teams' in every major coastal town by the Office for the Protection of Monuments (Zagreb) (Vrsalović 1974). Another hopeful sign for the future has been the success of French archaeologists in excavating sites from which many of the surface finds (notably amphorae) have been looted, but on which extensive buried remains have been found, sometimes including areas of ship's structure: examples include the sites of Dramont D (Joncheray 1975), Grand Ribaud A (Carrazé 1975), La Roche Fouras (Joncheray 1976b), and La Tradelière (Fiori & Joncheray 1975). At the same time, the standards, ideas, and procedures laid down by George Bass and his

Fig. 1.5 The Swedish warship *Wasa* being towed across Stockholm harbour on a concrete pontoon after having been lifted in 1961.

team over fifteen years ago remain the model which present-day workers seek to emulate.

However, over the past couple of decades maritime archaeology has not been limited to Mediterranean waters. Possibly the most spectacular project of all has been carried out in Sweden, where the warship *Wasa* has been raised from Stockholm harbour and conserved intact. Built in 1628, this ship appears to have possessed a fundamental design fault, for she capsized on her maiden voyage. Her remains were relocated in 1956, and after several years of preparatory work under water, she finally resurfaced in May 1961 (fig. 1.5) (Franzen 1966). From a technical point of view, this underwater work, which involved tunnelling under the wreck in order to pass cables around her, was a major feat in itself. Similarly, the excavation of the sea-bed around the wreck-site after the vessel had been lifted, in order to recover elements of the ship's decorations and other items which had fallen from her, was itself one of the most intensive undersea excavations undertaken up until that time. But Swedish maritime archaeology has not stopped with the *Wasa*, and fieldwork has continued on many other spectacular wrecks preserved within the worm-free waters of the Baltic (see, for example, Cederlund & Ingelman-Sundberg 1973; Cederlund 1977).

Elsewhere in Northern Europe, probably the most extensive work has been that undertaken by Dutch archaeologists, notably G. R. van der Heide, on the drained lands of the polders, which, with their moving shoals and sudden violent storms, had been a graveyard of ships since seafaring commenced in that area (van der Heide 1976). Unfortunately, the sheer volume of this material, along with other unfavourable circumstances, has meant that little detailed information has yet emerged from these sites. However, the evidence to be gleaned from this material, concerning North Sea vessels between the twelfth and nineteenth centuries A.D., will undoubtedly prompt a considerable revision of established ideas. Elsewhere in the Netherlands, the discovery and excavation of occasional finds of river boats, such as those at Zwammerdam (de Weerd & Haalebos 1973), has contributed to knowledge of such craft in the early centuries A.D.

Across the Channel in Britain, similar chance finds have complemented those in the Low Countries, and revealed new aspects of Romano-British shipbuilding; a notable example was the discovery and excavation of the Blackfriar's Roman ship (Marsden 1966). Other vessels of later dates have since been found in the same vicinity (Marsden 1971). For specialists interested in the early medieval period the focus of attention has remained the dramatic discoveries made at Sutton Hoo (Suffolk) in the summer of 1939, where a royal ship-burial preserved, along with outstanding treasures, the impression of a sixth-century A.D. English ship. Between 1965 and 1967 this site was re-excavated at the instance of the British Museum. Another important medieval boat find occurred in 1970 when a ninth-century vessel was discovered at Graveney in Kent (fig. 1.6). The rescue excavation of this craft by the National Maritime Museum, Greenwich, initiated a major research programme into the archaeology of boats in north-west Europe (Greenhill 1976, 221–33), which is still continuing.

Archaeological research in British waters developed slowly, and has been concentrated almost exclusively on remains of the post-1500 period. The first historic wreck-site to be positively identified was a Dutch East Indiaman, *De Liefde* (1711), off the Out Skerries (Shetland Isles) (fig. 1.7) (Bax & Martin 1974). That was in 1965. The events

Fig. 1.6 The late Saxon boat from the Graveney marshes, Kent, after initial excavation, 1970.

which followed were initially more related to commercial salvage than archaeology, but the activities of bodies such as the Council for Nautical Archaeology (founded 1964) and others, began to improve standards and a few archaeologists have taken up diving. The vessels of the Dutch East India Company, several of which were lost off British shores, have continued to attract attention, perhaps the most spectacular site being that of the *Amsterdam* where the ship herself has sunk into beach sands near Hastings (Marsden 1972; 1974). Another subject of continuing interest has been the wrecks of the Spanish Armada of 1588, beginning with the location in 1968 of the remains of the *Santa Maria de la Rosa* (Martin 1975) and the *Girona* (Stenuit 1972). The growing number of club

Fig. 1.7 The rocky shores of the Out Skerries, Shetland, where the remains of the Dutch East Indiaman *De Liefde* (1711) were located and identified in 1965.

divers since the mid-1960s has also increased the range of historic wreck-sites being discovered, sometimes by chance, and sometimes as the result of a methodical search; the positive identification of the site of the remains of the *Mary Rose* (1545) in the Solent between 1967 and 1971 is perhaps the most outstanding example of the latter (McKee 1973). The new field of research has achieved limited success in gaining acceptance in academic circles, and it was as late as 1973 that Britain's first Institute of Maritime Archaeology was established at St Andrews University. The same year also saw the first steps in legal recognition of the special problems posed by these developments, with the Protection of Wrecks Act, 1973.

Outside Europe, the most active area for underwater work on historic wrecks has undoubtedly been Northern and Central America, where the great treasures in gold and silver contained in the wrecks of the Spanish plate fleets has put a special edge on their exploitation. Undoubtedly much of this has been guided by commercial rather than archaeological considerations, but recent years have seen various attempts to control the situation. Many maritime states of the U.S.A. have imposed legal controls on underwater sites, and some have also established state underwater archaeological units to supervise operations: some of the systematic surveys and excavations undertaken by these teams in recent years have been of a very high calibre. Less spectacular, but equally informative, finds of wrecks of the War of Independence have been made along the eastern coasts of the U.S.A., as at Yorktown (Bass 1966, 123) or in the Penobscot River with the site of the *Defense* (Mayhew 1974). Similar sites have also received attention off the coasts of Canada, some at the instigation of the National Historic Sites Service, as with the excavations on the wreck of the French warship *Machault* (1760) (Zacharchuk 1972), and some from groups of amateur enthusiasts, as with the *Sapphire* (1695) (see fig. 3.28, p. 117) (Barber 1977). Also of note have been the studies undertaken on the remains at porterage sites along rivers in the mid-west, revealing a fascinating cross-section of the trade goods sent into the interior in the eighteenth and nineteenth centuries from east coast settlements (Wheeler & van Gemert 1972).

So far as the rest of the world is concerned, systematic work is only just beginning, and there is less to report. Israeli workers have studied wrecks in the Red Sea as well as the Mediterranean, notably in the Sharm-el-Sheikh area (Linder & Raban 1975, 44–7). An interesting wreck of a seventeenth-century Portuguese vessel has been known off Mombasa, Kenya, for many years (Kirkman 1972; Wheeler *et al.* 1975), and a major investigation of this site by an international team began early in 1977. Recently, work has started on an investigation of a fourteenth- or fifteenth-century A.D. wreck near Sattahip in Thailand (Weier 1974), and other important sites are reported to lie in this area.

The few reports available concerning fieldwork in Japan show an awareness of the subject there which may yield important results in the future (Osaki 1973). A notable hive of activity in maritime archaeology since 1971 has been Western Australia, where, under the aegis of an excellent series of legal provisions, the State Museum has established a specialist unit, directed by Mr Jeremy Green, and staffed by a full range of appropriate specialists (Pearson 1976; Green & Henderson 1977). Their principal concern has been with the sites of some of the Dutch East Indiamen wrecked on their shores, notably the *Batavia* of 1629 (fig. 1.8) (Green 1975), the *Vergulde Draeck* of 1656 (Green 1973*a*), and the *Zeewijk* of 1727 (Ingelman-Sundberg 1977). Equally noteworthy has been their application of similar techniques and standards to the wrecks of the colonial period, i.e. the early nineteenth century (Henderson 1976).

This brief history of the subject has obviously been far from exhaustive, and many important research projects have been omitted; some will appear in the appropriate sections of chapter 3. However, in the course of this survey, certain important attributes of this sub-discipline have emerged. Above all, its extreme youth is apparent; its modern

Fig. 1.8 The remains of the stern of the Dutch East Indiaman *Batavia* as excavated by the Western Australian Museum, 1973–5.

development was dependent on the invention of the aqualung, which occurred only just over thirty years ago. Furthermore, the whole business of separating archaeology from pure salvage or treasure hunting, and building up a new profession of diving archaeologists, meant that the first twenty years of this period saw only faltering steps, and that in most parts of the world genuine archaeological excavations have only been attempted within the past decade. A related feature is the wide variety of backgrounds from which the practitioners of this subject have been drawn, including naval diving (e.g. Captain Cousteau and his team), commercial salvage operations (e.g. much of the work in the U.S.A.), as well as conventional archaeology (a succession with Professor Bass at its head). That this was inevitable, in view of the nature of the new technology and the other skills required in such work, must be accepted, but it has given the whole subject a flavour which has set it apart from more conventional archaeology. These considerations have also influenced the types of problems which have been tackled in recent years; the early threat to amphorae wrecks in the Mediterranean has focussed attention there on merchantmen of the classical period, while the lure of treasure and the prominence of cannon elsewhere has concentrated work outside that sea on the centuries after A.D. 1500. This short summary of the chequered development of the subject should at least explain, if not excuse, the uneven range of topics discussed later. Finally, it should be apparent why maritime archaeology has lacked a general statement of its theories and concerns to date, and why such a synthesis should now be attempted.

1.3 Summary and prospectus

The framework within which this general theory of maritime archaeology is to be articulated should by now be fairly clear. The scope of the discipline has been established by the definition stated at the beginning of this chapter (p. 4), and some of the general implications contained within this statement have been discussed. Above all, it is the contention of this book that maritime archaeology is essentially a sub-discipline of archaeology, and that its principles, theories and methods should be firmly based on those already established for conventional archaeological research. However, in the following chapters, no detailed knowledge of archaeological theory on the part of the reader will be assumed; if a greater insight into the basis of some of these ideas and principles is required, reference should be made to the following: Clark 1939; Wheeler 1954a; Clarke, 1968.

As indicated above, an archaeological sub-discipline can be described by considering, first, the kind of evidence examined and the manner in which it is investigated, and, secondly, the range of problems which this body of research seeks to tackle. Chapter 2 is concerned with describing

the first of these defining characteristics, and in particular deals with the
various special features of the marine environment, since, as explained
above, almost all the material evidence lies under water and, as a result,
nearly all the necessary fieldwork has to be undertaken there. As is made
apparent in the course of that chapter, this situation presents both
advantages and disadvantages, neither of which are overwhelming, but
both of which have a considerable impact on the basic theory of maritime archaeology. Chapters 3 and 4, which make up the bulk of Part One,
are concerned with outlining some of the problems towards which
research in this subject has already made a noteworthy contribution
(chapter 3) or might reasonably be expected to so contribute in the foreseeable future (chapter 4). With a relatively new field of research such
as this, the tally of achievements to date is inevitably small, so it is
reasonable to include anticipated contributions in any assessment of the
scope of the subject.

Having thus defined the sub-discipline, Part Two of the book
attempts to set out a general theory of maritime archaeology. The first
elements, presented in chapter 5, consist of certain modes of data
analysis which are particularly applicable to this material, and which are
closely related to the phenomenon of the shipwreck. The next chapter
is concerned with various aspects of the basic unit of study, the ship,
which constitutes the immediate object of enquiry on any particular site.
Chapter 7, on the other hand, is concerned with the ultimate objectives
of this research, the understanding of past maritime cultures. Chapter 8
is a short postscript to the whole presentation, dealing with some of the
implications of these ideas for the organisation of research in maritime
archaeology.

2

The constraints of work under water

If one of the principal defining characteristics of maritime archaeology lies in its reliance on fieldwork under water, it follows that many of its special features, both strengths and weaknesses, will be determined by the constraints of that environment. However, before discussing, first, the problems posed by work under water (section 2.2), and then its operational advantages (section 2.3), a brief description is attempted of what is involved in such work, although for comprehensive treatments of this topic, the reader is referred to one of the following: Bass 1966; Wilkes 1971.

2.1 The organisation of work under water

It is almost impossible to describe to someone who has never dived what it is like to work under water; for various technical reasons, even the most realistic of underwater films gives a partially false impression. Much of the peculiarity of the experience can be traced to the fact that the diver is effectively weightless under water, his natural situation being in midwater, rather than walking (in a terrestrial sense) on the sea-bed. Among other effects, this means that heavy work is difficult, since every powerful action by a diver provokes a reaction which may send him floating away from his task; it also makes even the weakest of currents an appreciable problem. Visually, the underwater world is perceived by a diver in a distorted way, for two main reasons. First, he is looking through a face-mask, which means that he is viewing his surroundings through air, a glass port, and water; together these produce by refraction an apparent increase in the size of everything by one third. Secondly, sea-water filters out certain areas of the light spectrum, so that at depth the whole seascape appears in a green-blue monochrome. Overall visibility is also more restricted under water; in many areas it is effectively nonexistent, and in most seas a range in excess of 20 metres is considered good, and anything in excess of 50 metres phenomenal. Other senses, such as hearing or smell, are effectively useless under water. All these factors, taken together, mean that a diver has to concentrate to orientate himself under water, since the relative dependence placed on various senses is different from that pertaining on land; the psychological consequences of this on his ability to do useful work is a subject of continuing research (see, for example, Baume & Godden 1975).

In addition to these general considerations, there are various specific factors which afflict anyone under water, and which affect perceptive powers and levels of performance. The most universal and insidious of these is undoubtedly cold, which can become a debilitating factor even in tropical waters. Another effect which can steal up on a diver unawares is nitrogen narcosis, which arises from taking in nitrogen at pressures of more than 3 or 4 atmospheres (achieved by diving to depths greater than about 25 metres). Known to the French as 'ivresse des profondeurs' (literally 'intoxication of the depths'), its effects are excellently summarised by the 'Martini Rule' (i.e. every extra 10 metres of depth equals one more glass!). In addition to these, there is the ever-present possibility of accident involving an attack of the bends, an air embolism, or a burst lung. In view of this, it is not surprising to learn that one of the greatest debilitating factors among divers is, in fact, anxiety! At the same time, it must be emphasised that these difficulties can be rendered at least tolerable by thorough training, and that a great deal of effective work can be performed under water. The specific limitations imposed by these factors on archaeological work on the sea-bed is one of the topics covered in the next section.

Turning now to the equipment used by a diver to enable him to go under water, obviously the most important is that which supplies him with air. For reasons of mobility and other factors mentioned in the last chapter, all archaeological work involves divers using modern self-regulating breathing apparatus, rather than the old and cumbersome 'hard-hat' gear. The most common variant of this equipment is that in which the air is supplied by a cylinder of compressed air carried on the diver's back, giving him complete freedom of movement. An alternative system is to have air pumped down to the diver at medium pressure; this surface-demand, or 'hookah' system is cheaper to operate and easier to maintain; it thus presents advantages in situations where the divers are only working within a restricted area of the sea-bed, as is often the case in archaeology (fig. 2.1). A diver will usually wear some sort of rubber or Neoprene suit against the cold; this can be either a 'dry-suit' in which the water is excluded entirely (in theory, at least!) or a 'wet-suit', in which a thin layer of water is allowed next to the diver's skin, which should quickly warm up to body temperature and act as an extra layer of insulation. For propulsion, a diver will usually have a pair of fins on his feet, and, in order to counteract his natural buoyancy and that of his suit, he will be carrying a certain number of lead weights on a belt. Finally, as already mentioned, he must have a face-mask over his nose and eyes. Beyond this basic list, there are a wide range of items which may be necessary in any particular situation, such as a knife or a buoyancy jacket, and any number of instruments and gauges; some of these can be seen on the divers in figs. 2.1 and 2.3. This brief description of some of the equipment involved should make it clear that diving is itself an activity which demands a certain level of expertise and concentration, and this in turn reduces still further the mental powers available for the job in hand.

The use of all this gear obviously demands a certain amount of training; certainly no-one should ever attempt to dive without having first attended a course with a recognised sub-aqua club or diving school. It also goes without saying that considerations of diving safety should always take absolute priority over all other demands, including those of archaeology. For the control of diving procedures on archaeological projects neither the naval, commercial nor amateur diving codes are entirely satisfactory; probably the most appropriate manual to follow is the *Code of practice for scientific diving*, issued by the Underwater Association (Flemming & Miles 1974).

Before proceeding to a discussion of the various stages of fieldwork in archaeology, and their application under water, an attempt must be made to describe the differences between sea-bed sediments and terrestrial deposits. As on land, there are extreme situations where

Fig. 2.1 A diver preparing lead ingots for raising from the foot of an underwater cliff at a depth of 20 metres on the *Kennemerland* (1664) site, Out Skerries, Shetland.

there is no overburden at all, but simply bare rock; this is quite common on very exposed coasts, but much rarer in deep water, just as most rocky areas on land are in higher parts. At the other end of the spectrum are those sea-beds which are totally composed of silts and muds; the ocean floor is generally so composed, as is the sea-bed in shallower waters around more sheltered shores. However, the technology for locating remains within such sea-beds is still very primitive and expensive, so the undoubted archaeological potential of such areas has yet to be effectively exploited. The majority of wrecks discussed in this book have been found on sea-beds intermediate between these two extremes, such as the ones illustrated in figs. 2.1, 2.3, 2.5, 2.9 or 2.10. On such sites, the sea-bed consists of coarser deposits, such as sands and gravels, in some instances interspersed with areas of boulders or even of exposed bedrock. Frequently it is these areas of bare rock which have allowed the wreck to be found initially, by holding some wreckage proud of the sea-bed, although the quality of the surviving remains will be determined principally by the nature and extent of the sedimentary deposits

Fig. 2.2 A diver using an underwater metal detector within a shingle-filled gully.

(Muckelroy 1977*b*). Finally, there is a misconception common among people who have never been under water that undersea sediments are in perpetual motion, an impression gained by watching beach sand at the sea's margins; excepting the top few centimetres of any sea-bed, which are as liable to disturbance as similar levels on land, this is simply not true, long-term stability being the rule on most sites, including those in quite exposed situations.

In archaeological fieldwork anywhere, the first requirement is to find one's site. In practice, many sites above and below water are found by accident, but there is still a role in both environments for deliberate searches. On land, the principal use of fieldwalking nowadays is in attempts to reconstruct the totality of the prehistoric landscape, in so far as the surviving remains will allow, while the objectives of an underwater search might be to locate a documentarily recorded wreck of specific importance, or to gain an overall impression of the archaeological potential of a stretch of coastline. The basic procedures are similar in both situations, the principal requirement being for observers who can pick out and recognise the often slight surface indications of a buried archaeological deposit, a skill which can only be acquired by experience. So far as technique is concerned, the principal difference under water is that, with restricted visibility, search paths have to be closer together than on land, and there are far greater problems in controlling and recording the progress of a line of searchers (see Martin 1975, 57–97). In both environments, the visual approach is now widely supplemented by the use of electronic gadgets of all types; fig. 2.2 shows a diver-controlled underwater metal detector in use. Because of the expense and other limitations of teams of divers, such remote-sensing devices are increasingly being employed in underwater searches, especially those which can be operated entirely from a boat; among these, the magnetometer, detecting local aberrations in the magnetic field caused by concentrations of metal debris, has proved the most useful (Hall 1972; Clausen & Arnold 1976). However, the positive description, identification, and assessment of any features located electronically will always have to be undertaken by experienced diving archaeologists.

Once a site has been located, and excavation has been determined on, then the procedures become more specialised. Obviously, sea-bed sediments are very different from terrestrial deposits, having been laid down by distinctive processes, and tending to be less consolidated. Frequently they are not susceptible to standard techniques such as trowelling; in such cases, a gentle fanning action with the hand is most appropriate for significant areas (fig. 2.3). The removal of spoil is as big a problem on the sea-bed as anywhere else. Where the volume produced is small, then a bucket and shovel is as effective as it is on land (fig. 2.4).

Where the volume of material is slightly greater, a low-powered dredge can be used to transfer waste material a few metres across the site (fig. 2.5). In certain circumstances, analogous to those in which a pick might be used on land, such a dredge can itself be used as a digging tool. If even greater quantities of spoil have to be removed, in the type of situation in which a mechanical digger might be used on land, a larger bore air-lift can be employed, carrying the spoil several metres up, and allowing it

Fig. 2.3 Excavating a relatively unconsolidated deposit by a gentle fanning action with the hand.

Fig. 2.4 Using a bucket
and shovel in the
excavation of a shingle-
filled gully.

Fig. 2.5 Using a water-
powered dredge to remove
spoil from the excavation
face; the dissection of the
deposit itself is being done
by fanning.

to be carried away down current. An air-lift, suitably moored, can also be used to remove smaller quantities of spoil from a controlled excavation and for generally keeping the water around a working area free of silt. Of course, all these tools are only relevant where the deposit is relatively fine; larger stones have to be moved individually, as on land, although such tasks can be made considerably easier by using air-filled lifting bags, or other such devices.

So far as excavation strategies are concerned, all the procedures followed on land are theoretically possible under water: trenches, boxes, quadrants, or open areas have all been used on maritime sites. On many, however, vertical sections cannot easily be created because of loosely packed sediments, a restriction which is considered less serious nowadays, in view of the general preference for open-area excavations (Barker 1977). Nevertheless, this can still be a major drawback on sites where the size of the team, limited funds, or other operational constraints, allow only a small area to be opened at any one time. In defining suitable strategies, a fundamental distinction must be drawn between those sites on which a complete ship and its contents are being investigated and those on which the remains are not contained within any structure. In the former case, the procedures should be analogous to those used on an excavation of a deposit-filled building on land, while in the latter, they should be modelled on the techniques applied on terrestrial open sites, such as flint scatters or middens.

In surveying underwater sites, restricted visibility is responsible for the major modifications (Throckmorton *et al.* 1969). Long-range optical instruments such as theodolites or alidades can only be used in special circumstances under water, and the only satisfactory replacements for them to emerge to date have all been very expensive. The most promising of these involve either sensitively measured tension wires (Lundin 1973), or the employment of sonic rangemeters of various types (Kelland 1976). Over short distances, chains or tapes can be used as on land (fig. 2.6), although currents can introduce far greater distortions than even strong winds. Detailed drawings of features, horizons, or sections can similarly be drawn, and to exactly the same standards of accuracy, using ordinary lead pencils and plastic drawing film (fig. 2.7). Only minor modifications should be required in standard recording systems, although a larger amount of transcription may be demanded, since finds cards or record sheets cannot usually be taken under water themselves. It must also be admitted that the legibility of most people's handwriting deteriorates markedly as soon as they go under water!

A photographic record of a site during excavation should always be made, using either a standard camera placed in a waterproof housing, or a purpose-built underwater camera. Again, the main difficulties result from restricted visibility; it is generally impossible to get the whole of a

Fig. 2.6 Surveying under water; the diver is holding one end of a tape while his colleague takes a reading at the other

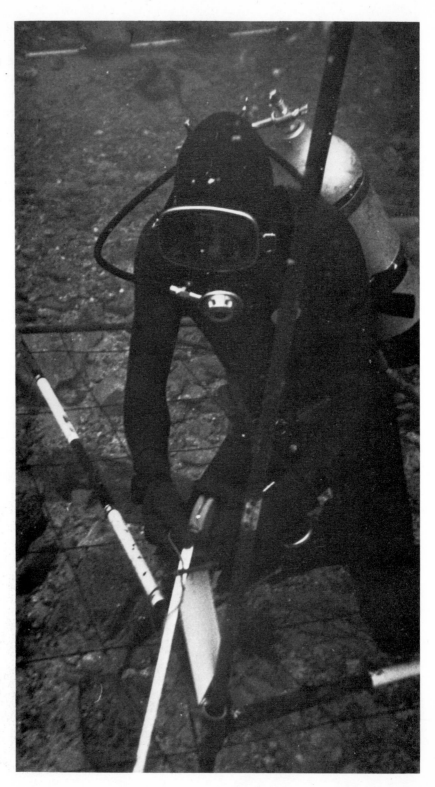

site in one photograph, and recourse has to be made to photomosaics for illustrative purposes (see fig. 3.19, p. 96). Monochrome prints also frequently suffer from a lack of contrast and fine detail, as a result of low light levels and the filtering out of the red end of the spectrum. The effects of this can be seen in many of the underwater photographs used in this book. Photogrammetric planning techniques can be used on underwater sites and are almost obligatory on deep wrecks, where the consequent saving in diving time is crucial (Bass 1966, 118). In situations of very low natural light or visibility, the only answer is the use of expensive image-intensifying television systems.

When it comes to lifting objects from the sea-bed for transport to the laboratory or museum, special precautions may be necessary. As on land, very fragile items may have to be bandaged up or strapped to rigid supports. However, an object being retrieved from a marine site has to be carried through the air–water interface, which is often turbulent, and may also have to endure a boat journey. The most effective solution in such situations is frequently to embed the artefact in a box of silt or sand on the sea-bed, and keep it so encased until arrival at the laboratory (fig. 2.8); obviously, the box has to be packed to the brim and kept lidded in order to avoid the contents slopping around during carriage. Where heavier objects are concerned, such as ship's timbers, cannons, or

Fig. 2.7 A diver making a drawing of details on the exposed hull of the *Mary Rose* (1545) in the Solent; because of the very restricted visibility and light levels on this site, only a small section can be studied at any one time.

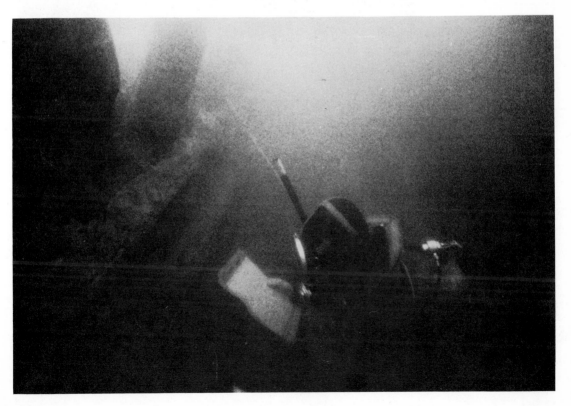

anchors, the lifting power of air-filled containers in water can be harnessed, at least to get the object to within a metre or so of the surface; very often, the greatest problem is presented by getting it from there on to dry land.

There is no direct parallel on land for marine iron concretion. The degeneration of iron in sea-water creates compounds which serve to bind together everything in the neighbourhood – sand, stones, epifauna, other artefacts – into a hard matrix (fig. 2.9; see also fig. 3.26, p. 113) by processes which vary according to region, and whether the iron object is lying on or within the sea-bed (North 1976; Hamilton 1976). Faced with such a concretion, the excavator has no means of knowing what is contained within it before breaking it up, while at the same time the hardness of these substances necessitates fairly violent treatment. Further complications arise in those instances where the degradation of the iron has proceeded to total dissolution, and only a cast of the original object remains. In practice, there is no totally satisfactory way of dealing with these formations. Probably the best solution is to raise the concretion in as large sections as possible, and dissect them in the laboratory under controlled conditions, in the light of a series of X-ray

Fig. 2.8 Hank of rope packed in a sand-filled box preparatory to lifting.

photographs taken previously of the piece (Hamilton 1976). Where only casts survive, one can recover the shapes of the artefacts by injecting the hollows with latex, plaster, or even lead (Katzev & van Doorninck 1966; Fiori & Joncheray 1973), but this is a delicate and time-consuming operation for which the facilities and personnel are often not available. Furthermore, detaching such formations from the bedrock or neighbouring objects in the first place is often not easy; using a hammer and chisel can be very destructive, so that experiments on using other techniques, notably small explosive charges, have recently been undertaken (Green 1975, 57–63; Martin & Long 1975). At present, the great variation in the characteristics of these formations between sites means that *ad hoc* solutions have to be developed for each new situation.

After removing material from a site, the next stage is its conservation and stabilisation, a subject which constitutes a complete and separate science in itself. The details of the processes involved are thus beyond the scope of this book, having little direct bearing on the nature of maritime archaeology as a discipline. However, the considerable expense and expertise demanded by such work must be noted, since it can tie up a significant proportion of a project's budget, and restrict the types of

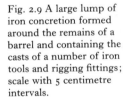

Fig. 2.9 A large lump of iron concretion formed around the remains of a barrel and containing the casts of a number of iron tools and rigging fittings; scale with 5 centimetre intervals.

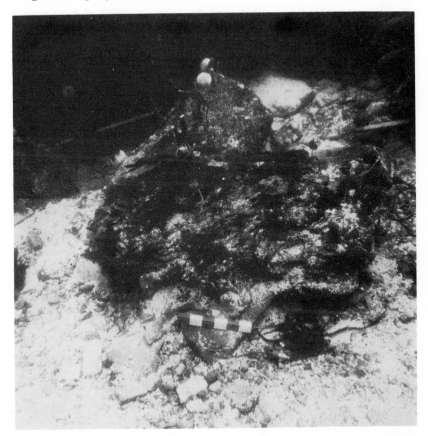

material which can be recovered. To take an extreme example, the discovery and raising of the *Wasa* took just five years, while the preservation of its woodwork has so far taken over fifteen. But the difficulties involved in such work are not relevant to the process of extracting information from artefactual evidence, and so constrain the research under discussion here only indirectly, a point ignored by those commentators who have presented them as the central problem of maritime archaeology, thus overlooking more fundamental considerations. At the same time, there must on any particular project be the closest possible liaison between archaeologist and conservator, since either may incidentally note evidence of interest to the other (Hamilton 1976, 86–96).

2.2 Some problems in work under water

From the last section, it is clear that the diver himself is the biggest problem under water; his ability to perform effectively, and to make reliable observations, can be severely restricted. These limitations need not be totally debilitating, but they impose certain constraints on the scope and potential of any work under water. Some of the factors behind this impairment of faculties have already been discussed; the concern here is with their consequences, as demonstrated by some recent studies in underwater psychology. Perhaps the most dramatic demonstration of reduced performance appeared in the dexterity test, which took an average of 28% longer in 3 metres of water, and 49% longer in 30 metres (Baddeley 1966). Other tests have shown that tasks such as sentence comprehension or time estimation deteriorate similarly with depth. A particularly worrying discovery has been that a number of divers respond very poorly to peripheral stimuli while performing a given task, which means that, if they are concentrating on staying alive under water, they will perform badly at the job in hand, or, if they are concentrating on their work, they may miss any danger signals. In these studies, reduced performance under water in terms of both speed and quality of work has been demonstrated, but the processes involved have not been analysed.

One attempt to achieve greater understanding has involved a programme of research suggesting that memory is to some extent 'context dependent'. In other words, an idea or a skill is recalled best in a situation similar to that in which it was learned, a fact which is exploited whenever the police take a witness back to the scene of a crime. Initial work demonstrating this effect showed that, while a list of words was best memorised when both learned and recalled on the surface, if it had been learned under water, it was better recalled there than back on the surface (Godden & Baddeley 1975). However, recent work has shown an even more serious effect; experiments with a manual task under water have shown that workers learning it from scratch in that context consistently performed better than those who had already learned it on the surface. It appears that a task learned on the surface has to be unlearned under water before it can be reassimilated, presumably because of different sensory inputs to a diver under water (Godden 1977). There are several possible consequences for maritime archaeology arising out of this work. First, there is a chance that instructions given to a site worker on the surface will not be remembered correctly once he is on the bottom. Secondly, observations which he has made on the bottom may not be recalled once he has returned to the surface, and experiments have shown that even the most thorough and searching debriefing will not eliminate this effect. It is for this reason that all site notes must be made under water, and nothing left to memory. Finally, there is the worrying possibility that excavation or other archaeological techniques learned on land may not be accurately applied once the worker has gone under water, and that information may thereby be lost. To introduce a personal note here, devoid of any scientific justification, I find that it is easier to slip into the mental attitude of a land excavator when under water if I am using the tools one uses on land, such as the finds tray, site plan, and, above all, the trowel.

While these general principles are being studied, their particular impact on the type of work demanded by archaeology remains uncertain, although it has been recognised that special considerations may apply, since more delicacy and careful thought are required than in most other underwater activities (Godden 1975). It is to be hoped that an underwater psychologist will one day undertake some experimental work on the archaeological situation. Incidentally, the recognition of these problems does not in any way support the view, at one time widely canvassed, that there can never be such a person as a 'diving archaeologist', and that all underwater work should be entrusted to a special kind of heroic superman, known as a 'professional diver', who will bring up the artefacts for expert examination, and report on the details of the site to surface-bound archaeologists. The weaknesses in such a system must be apparent from what has been said above about recalling information, even after setting aside the most important objection that there are a number of archaeological skills which must be exercised directly on the sea-bed by trained persons.

One of the most important points to emerge from these investigations into diver performance has been that almost any task takes longer to perform under water than on land. This mental retardation effect is reinforced where simple physical tasks are concerned by the fact that water resistance makes all heavy work slower and more tiring than it would otherwise be. It is particularly unfortunate, therefore, that while almost everything takes longer under water, the period of time which anyone can spend there per day or per week is strictly limited. The first restriction is air supply. If high-pressure air from a bottle is being used, then a diver must surface whenever his cylinder becomes empty, and either collect a new, full one, or finish his work there and then. In 10 metres of water, a standard-sized bottle will last for about 60 minutes with most divers, while at 30 metres it will only last about 20 minutes. Of course, it is not uncommon for divers to take down two, or even three, bottles on their backs, and increase their endurance proportionately. It is one of the great advantages of a surface demand system that, so long as the surface compressor is kept supplied with fuel, the air supply to the divers is continuous. Thus, the time limitation imposed by the air supply is one which is not insuperable, although supplying very large volumes of compressed air, by whatever means, can be costly.

A problem which cannot be overcome is the requirements of decompression tables. The need for such tables arises out of the fact that, as a diver breathes compressed air, he absorbs quantities of inert gasses into his bloodstream, notably nitrogen, which, if the pressure is reduced too rapidly, may coagulate into bubbles in the bloodstream, blocking it and possibly cutting off the blood supply from a vital organ, such as the brain or the spine. The consequences can range from a minor skin irritation to paralysis or death. Although the precise mechanisms of these processes are not understood, experience has shown that there are times at every depth within which the chances of a decompression accident are minimal, and the sum of this experience has been tabulated by various navies. In addition to these 'no-stop' times, the tables also show how long to spend ascending for various bottom times exceeding the limit. The 'no-stop' times decrease rapidly with depth; thus, while the time allowed at 10 metres is nearly 4 hours, the 'no-stop' time for 20 metres is only 45 minutes, that for 30 metres is 20 minutes, and for 50 metres is only 7 minutes (figures taken from the Royal Navy Physiological Laboratory 1972 tables). While these times can be increased by undertaking decompression stops in shallow water, the increase in bottom time is often remarkably small compared with the extra time spent ascending; for example, an extra 15 minutes spent at 30 metres will involve an extra 23 minutes in ascent time. Such decompression stops can be extremely tedious and chilling, and on certain sites involve unacceptable risks. The only safe way to circumvent these difficulties is to undertake decompression in a special chamber on the surface, as is done with all commercial deep diving (i.e. diving below 25 metres), but such facilities are extremely expensive.

The third, and ultimately the most important, of all the factors restricting underwater time is the matter of cold and exhaustion in the diver. These two concerns are linked because one leads to another; water is a good conductor of heat, tending to lower a diver's body temperature to its own level, and thus sapping his reserves of energy. This is an important consideration even in tropical seas, because really high water temperatures are only found for the first few metres below the surface. This fundamental restriction is thus pretty generally applicable, and is dominant on shallow-water sites, where the other considerations listed above have less impact. It is also vital that all divers are positively aware of the problem, since the effects of cold can creep up insidiously, impairing effectiveness, and increasing the danger of an accident through carelessness. As a guide, it is fair to say that, in British waters at the height of summer with an efficient wet-suit, few people can achieve a long-term average of more than 4 hours a day immersion; the use of an effective dry-suit might increase this figure by an hour or two. Of course, there are many cold archaeological sites, and tiring jobs, to be found on land, but more can usually be done to make life bearable there, and the effects of cold are not usually potentially dangerous.

The archaeological consequences of these restrictions in the amount of time a diver can spend on the sea-bed are legion. As usual the prime one is to increase the expense of work under water; either the team has to be retained for longer to achieve a given task, or it has to be made larger than would otherwise be necessary. Another result is that it is often impossible to achieve continuity of personnel on any particular task: a job started by one worker cannot be left with him, but must be passed to other workers, each of whom has to pick up the strands from his predecessor at the start of each shift. Similarly, it may not be possible for any particular diver to go down at just the required moment to deal with a new situation which has arisen; this can be exceedingly frustrating if the presence of the site director or supervisor is required, or if some task has to be done by a specialist, such as a photographer or draughtsman, who has already used up his diving time quota for that day. In general, this means that reliance cannot be put entirely on any particular individual, and the range of expertise possessed by all members of the team should ideally be much greater than is strictly necessary on a land site. Otherwise, there is the fact that one's time always seems to run out just as a particularly interesting or challenging deposit is emerging, and that diving safety sometimes requires that a job be left half-completed which, from an archaeological viewpoint, should not be so left. On some sites, tasks which take too long have to be avoided, or split up into manageable lengths in some way which may be less than totally satisfactory.

The net result of all these factors in practice has been admirably described in the final paragraph of Miss Honor Frost's personal account of the early years of archaeology under water, *Under the Mediterranean*:
'It is my personal belief that archaeological discipline can
be practised undersea, but this only if scientists and divers
are aware of what is involved. It must always be

remembered that human beings are contending with a strange element. The mental effort required from a man working in deep water increases in proportion to the physical effort he makes. It is amusing to hear professional divers harping on the big "holes" they have dug. In a discussion on technique it sounds, from the archaeological point of view, comic and faintly naughty, yet their insistence on exertion illustrates a basic fact. A diver pits himself against a force of nature; work is concentrated into a few brief minutes, during which he undergoes an emotional test. In the early days he had to suck for every breath of air; now demand-valves have been improved; but he is still limited by a small bottle and knows that he dare not get out of breath. Digging his "big hole" with an air-lift, he has to hold this powerful machine, then set himself an objective, such as freeing a certain amphora in one dive. He sucks and he pulls, until his objective becomes an obsession; judgment, already impaired by depth, hardly governs his actions. If he is experienced he will realise what is happening to him; if not, being alone on the bottom, he may wrench the amphora and break it. Land archaeologists have tests and tribulations of a different order; they do not "take it out" on their trench. The diver becomes emotionally part of his big hole.'
(1963*a*, 258–9)
While to the non-diver this may sound unscientifically frantic, to anyone who has worked under water it rings all too true.

A further problem faced in supervising an underwater excavation is the inability of divers to talk to each other on site without the use of expensive and rarely available equipment. For more frequently used ideas, divers have developed a range of hand signals which can be made to serve in many situations; furthermore, most teams soon evolve supplementary signals for specific messages needed during the work in hand. However, a really complicated message can only be transmitted by writing it on a slate for the other diver, a lengthy and often inaccurate process. Further problems arise when two divers are trying to co-operate on a complex task, when their hands may not be free for signalling. In order to even begin to overcome such problems, a rigidly enforced command hierarchy must always be operated under water, so that everyone knows whose orders are to be obeyed. Furthermore, most divers find that there are some people they can work with more easily than others – it seems to be a matter of having similar thought patterns – and a project director must be guided by the personal preferences of his workers in such matters. But, having allowed for all this, the fact remains that there are often messages which one worker may wish to convey to another, or orders which a supervisor may try to issue, which are never transmitted, because the person concerned cannot face the effort of trying to make himself understood. As a consequence, the work may continue in an unsatisfactory or inefficient way, or an important record or photograph be omitted entirely.

The other aspect to this communication problem is the fact that the diver cannot speak readily with those on the surface; if he wishes to consult with a particular expert, or to receive new instructions, he has to swim up to the surface himself. Once again, the result is that a site worker will, quite naturally, be tempted to take the responsibility of

Fig. 2.10 An 'underwater telephone booth' on the wreck-site at Yassi Ada, Turkey.

how to proceed with a given problem onto his own shoulders, in a situation where, on land, he would have called for assistance. On the other side, those on the surface cannot easily tell the site workers on the bottom of any changes in plan, but must wait until the end of a shift before enforcing a change, which may mean several hours wasted. In order to avoid this situation, some directors will not let a new shift enter the water until the reports of the previous shift have been thoroughly understood and considered, and any procedural changes decided on, with a resulting loss of time between every shift. The waste and inefficiency introduced by this communication difficulty has been eliminated for some Mediterranean teams by Michael Katzev's invention of an 'underwater telephone booth', an air-filled plexiglass dome within which divers can communicate with each other, or with the surface (fig. 2.10). This device also has a considerable safety value (Bass & Katzev 1968). The only other way around this difficulty is to ensure that every team member has the expertise and training to enable him to exercise his own initiative in dealing with most eventualities, a happy situation which will seldom be realised.

In British waters, and in many other parts of the world, one of the principal bugbears for any project director is undoubtedly the weather. A stormy period at the critical moment can ruin a work schedule, and mean that nothing can be achieved despite the continuing financial outlay. Equally infuriating can be the occasional rough day which disrupts the programme and breaks the continuity of the work. It is the very unpredictability of this factor which is so taxing; at the very least it can be frustrating, and at the worst it can completely destroy a team's morale. In planning a season's work in such regions, therefore, allowance for days lost through bad weather must be made in the light of the available meteorological records, although it is rare for the pattern in any particular year to follow closely the statistical average. Of course, there is always a chance that one will be lucky and lose fewer days than anticipated, thus gaining a useful bonus in working time. Unfortunately, however, since shipwrecks have a tendency to occur in exposed situations, the general rule is usually for the conditions actually experienced on site to be worse than the norm for the area. Once again, the net result of all this is to increase the costs of maritime investigations yet further.

In the previous section, a brief description of techniques in archaeology under water was essayed, the general approach being that standard land archaeological procedures could be applied with only the minimum of adaptation. While this is essentially true, there remain some restrictions which will always affect the quality and quantity of information gleaned from underwater sites. The discussion began with search techniques, where the most outstanding problem is quite simply that underwater prospecting takes so much longer than its terrestrial counterpart. From an archaeological viewpoint, however, the more important constraint lies in our limited ability, at present, to search those areas where historic remains are likely to be buried under several metres of sediments, leaving no surface indications. Sub-bottom profilers have recently been developed which can observe features below the sea-bed, but their depth of penetration is generally limited, and the interpretation of their print-outs is an art which few have mastered (Frey 1972). As with all such devices, total proof of identification can usually only be gained by actually digging down to the feature and having experienced observers look at it – a procedure which can become cumulatively very expensive if the machine operator reports several dozen possible targets of equal probability in a given area. Since the best preserved ship-remains are likely to be found in such sediments, this limitation in techniques is a serious one.

For the excavator, sea-bed deposits can present their own peculiar problems, some of which were touched on above. The marine equivalents of terrestrial burrowing animals are crabs, which can alter the appearance of a section before your eyes, and which have presumably been so disturbing surface levels for centuries. An additional difficulty under water lies in the propensity for a sea-bed to smooth itself out, especially during rough weather. On some sites, such as that of the *Mary Rose* (fig. 2.7), any trench will fill up overnight with seaweed and loose silt, so that the first half-hour of any day's work is wasted on cleaning it out. However, the deposits on this site are convenient to the extent that they will hold a nearly vertical section. Other sediments, such as silts, sands, or gravels, may not be so obliging, and compromises have accordingly to be made. Even then, trench walls may only be stable in the short term, and during calm weather. The effects of one day of storms were dramatically demonstrated during one season on the *Trinidad Valencera* site, which has a basically sand substrate: all excavation faces had been rounded off to slopes of less than 45°, and most of the trenches were nearly half refilled. Gales and wet weather can disturb a site on land to some extent, but not usually to such a degree as this. Of course, the severity of such processes is reduced the deeper the site lies, but never entirely eliminated.

It is in surveying and recording under water, more than any other activity, perhaps, that the fundamental restrictions of that environment become most serious. Even when measuring across relatively short distances of a metre or two, problems can arise if the water is not still; even a weak current will cause a tape to bow out. This tendency will be reinforced if the current bears with it quantities of seaweed and other debris, which can catch in a tape and make it sag as well. The fact that the diver is himself virtually weightless can nullify any attempts to eliminate such errors by pulling hard on the tape. Furthermore, if its whole length is not visible from one end, the surveyor may not even be aware of the error. Establishing a true horizontal can also be tricky; in theory, a plumbline works under water, but it becomes unreliable in any current, and the same applies to any attempt to use a float for the same purpose. However, levels can be made to work satisfactorily.

All instinctive impressions are to be distrusted under water, and absolutely everything must be measured or otherwise recorded totally objectively. The matter of visual size distortion has already been mentioned; it has been found that it usually takes many years of regular underwater work before a diver's powers of estimation can automatically compensate for this effect. There is no natural horizon under water, and it is not uncommon for divers to be mistaken as to which way is up; there is thus no instinctive way of knowing whether a plane is even approximately horizontal. Furthermore, a surveyor or draughtsman likes to be able to look at his finished result and know that it 'looks right', and to make checks if it does not, but often under water one

Fig. 2.11 The surviving portion of the port side of the English carrack *Mary Rose* near the bows. In drawing the elevation (*below*), the complexities of the ship's lines were compounded by localised springing of the planking, and the whole vessel's 60° heel to starboard (see fig. 3.17). The section across the hull at frame 279b (*right*) shows its concave profile as well as the stacking of collapsed timbers in the outboard trench; the recording of all this was additionally hampered by generally very low light levels and limited visibility. It is this structure which is being drawn by the diver in fig. 2.7.

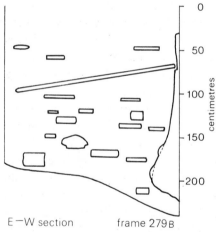

E−W section   frame 279B

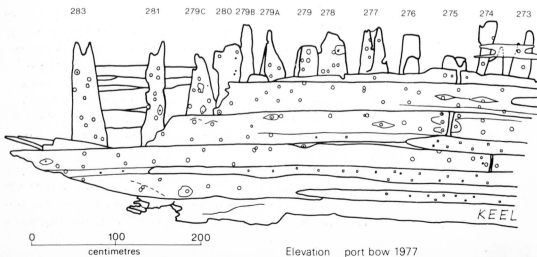

283   281   279C   280 279B 279A   279 278   277   276   275   274   273

KEEL

0   100   200
centimetres   Elevation   port bow 1977

cannot see the whole of a site or an object in one glance, making it difficult to judge the finished product. In such circumstances of low visibility, and especially when a drawing has had to be worked up on the surface, the first attempt is often patently not correct, the cause usually being the debilitating factors mentioned above, which can have particularly severe effects on people's abilities to handle figures. Further problems arise when trying to record the shape of a ship, when her precise orientation, etc., is not known; a ship consists of an amazing series of planes and curved surfaces which are very difficult to comprehend outside the frame of reference of the vessel herself (fig. 2.11). The result of trying to draw in such a circumstance may be more objective, but it takes two or three times as long as it would otherwise.

Further difficulties emerge when one tries to survey across long distances, defined as lengths greater than twice the usual visibility range for any particular site. The simplest solution is to force the short range surveying techniques described above to extend across much greater distances than would usually be deemed acceptable on land; in these cases, therefore, all the difficulties just described are magnified. The results can sometimes be satisfactory, however, on sites such as that of the *Trinidad Valencera*, which consists of a flat sandy bottom in shallow water with minimal currents, with visibility usually in the range of 10–15 metres. Here, tapes have to be run up to 70 metres away from permanent site datum points at the beginning of each season, and generally the cumulative error seems to be little more than 30–50 centimetres or so, when referred to other fixed points on the sea-bed (fig. 5.16; Martin 1975, fig. 14). While such an error is not excessive, it is a type which would not even be possible on a land site, where optical instruments could be used. As mentioned above, the way round these long-range surveying problems is to make use of modern sophisticated devices such as a tension wire or a sonic rangemeter. The tremendous value of the latter has been clearly demonstrated recently on the site of the *Mary Rose* in the Solent, where underwater visibility rarely exceeds 3 metres. The requirement was to survey a run of timbers, over 35 metres long, representing this ship's side, and the results are estimated to be accurate to a level of $\pm 2\%$. They differ significantly from a previous survey undertaken by experienced and conscientious workers using only conventional methods with tapes (Rule 1972, fig. 2). Unfortunately, there are not very many such rangemeters around, and their use can be expensive in both equipment and trained personnel (Kelland 1976).

If one wishes to survey across even greater distances, then the only widely available technique is to buoy the points concerned, and survey them from shore stations in the conventional way. Obviously an appreciable error will be introduced by the impossibility of checking that a buoy is directly above the designated point; furthermore, the technique is of little assistance on sites well away from land. The force of this restriction can be illustrated by considering the problem of relating precisely a number of wrecks from a battle which took place on the high seas, a task which would be well beyond the capabilities of any of these techniques, although the information itself might be critical to the interpretation of the course of that battle. Similar considerations arise when an undersea site is being related to various land features, and where an inaccurate measurement may lead to a totally false interpretation of, say, the way in which a vessel came to be wrecked. Once again, this is an area of difficulty for which there is no real parallel on a land site.

As indicated above, the technical problems of conservation are outside the scope of this book; however, their archaeological consequences are not. Above all, the treatment of artefacts from marine contexts is expensive, involving both a great deal of attention from trained persons, and the use of costly equipment. Furthermore, many materials, once removed from the sea, begin to disintegrate, so that it is sheer irresponsibility to raise objects for which conservation facilities have not already been organised. There are thus circumstances where, while the archaeological investigation of a site is desirable, the actual raising of material has to be restricted. In particular, this often means that a ship's hull has to be reburied after it has been surveyed *in situ*. Since this process will involve studying only the top side of the remains, the information contained on the underside, which will often be better preserved than the possibly eroded and damaged upper parts, will have to go unrecorded. While careful recording and intelligent interpretation can minimise the errors, the fact remains that the archaeological investigation will have been incomplete in such circumstances. Examples of such situations can be found in all areas, including the Mediterranean, with wrecks such as La Roche Fouras (Joncheray 1976*b*) or the fourth-century one at Yassi Ada (van Doorninck 1967; 1976), and in the Baltic, as at Jutholmen (Cederlund & Ingelman-Sundberg 1973). An alternative procedure, which has been followed to some extent on some of these projects, is to lift a few timbers for study on the surface, and then to rebury them in a specified area; of course, this involves a certain amount of damage to both the pieces themselves, and the structure from which they have been taken. The degree to which a purely sea-bed investigation could be inadequate and misleading was demonstrated on the site of the *Dartmouth* (1690) in the Sound of Mull, where it was thought initially that raising and conserving the hull remains would be out of the question, and so a comprehensive record was made of the upper surface of the structural remains, and certain deductions reached. Later, it became possible to lift and treat a large part of the surviving hull remains, in the course of which a great deal of additional data came to light, especially concerning the way in which the various sections were fitted together, and regarding the lines of the vessel as indicated by the underside of the section raised (see Martin 1978, and section 3.5).

Similar expense can be involved in the conservation of iron taken from the sea, and the equipment required is likewise not widely available. In archaeological terms, this can mean, first, that, as with wooden structures, iron conglomerates may have to be left on the sea-bed on an otherwise totally excavated site. This can be even more serious than it appears at first sight, since other artefacts may be contained within the surrounding concretion, and will thus remain totally unrecorded. And, secondly, a general lack of suitable laboratory facilities and expertise has meant that the information content of the hollow casts left in such concretion by totally disintegrated objects has frequently been overlooked in the search for other objects surviving within it. The tally of iron objects from such sites is thus heavily biassed away from items which have not survived in any solid form.

A final point is that conservation procedures can involve considerable alterations to the chemical and physical nature of objects, thus vitiating many investigations conducted on such material after conservation. For some very fragile materials, such as cloth or leather, it may be impractical to conduct any studies before stabilisation, so that extensive and definitive study may never be possible. While a conscientious reporter should always indicate when such restrictions have applied, this has not been the case with all reports published to date. A particularly extreme example of this substantial change after conservation arises when the 'hydrogen reduction' process is used for the preservation of iron objects – a process which otherwise has a lot to recommend it – since this technique involves changing completely the metallographic structure of the object.

With most of the difficulties described above, the principal consequence is that, to overcome or ameliorate their effects, extra expense is involved. Ultimately, this is the biggest problem of all – the relatively high cost of maritime archaeology. For each man-day spent on a land site, the director can expect to receive 8 hours work, while on an underwater site he is lucky if he gets half that amount, and in many situations he can count on less than an hour a day. In addition to this, it has been suggested that most divers are between 20 and 50 % less effective under water, and that the work can be regularly disrupted by a lack of continuity in personnel on site, as well as by spells of adverse weather. Furthermore, the greater cost of actually getting people onto the site must be remembered; the personal equipment worn by each diver is likely to be worth in excess of a hundred pounds, and the project equipment supporting the workers (air-lifts, dredges, air-compressors, boats, etc.) is likely to be worth several thousands. And nowadays the cost of the fuel needed to operate all this gear is substantial. Finally, while insurance is an expense incurred on all excavations, the premium is likely to be three or four times as high where a maritime site is concerned.

It is difficult to be specific in trying to establish relative costs, if only because circumstances vary so widely, both on land and under water, but the figures must run something like the following. The basic cost of an underwater project will be between two and four times as much as the cost of a land excavation of comparable length and size of team. However, the land director will be getting between two and four times as much 'time on site' out of his workers as his maritime colleague will be, depending on the nature of the latter's site. Once they are on the bottom, the divers are likely to be achieving only half as much as their land counterparts, once the unproductive site clearance, laying out, and tidying up has been allowed for. Thus, *in toto*, for every 'bit of archaeological work' done, a maritime site is likely to be between eight and thirty-two times more expensive than a comparable land site. However, as will be explained in the next section, there are some compensations for this depressing statistic, which together explain why work in maritime archaeology can be very worthwhile.

Before leaving this matter of expense, the point should be made that underwater work is not only expensive in terms of money; it is also prodigal of human resources. At the very least, this is because it may involve a highly trained archaeologist, be he a site worker or the director, hanging around for a whole day in order to do an hour's work. But it is even worse than that: on several occasions above, as when discussing the problems of communication under water, it was suggested that the only way forward was to ensure that the whole of the team were trained to a higher level than would generally be considered necessary on land. While this happy situation will rarely prevail in practice, the point must be borne in mind; a properly conducted major maritime archaeological project in an area could place a severe strain on the available resources of trained personnel.

In the last analysis, the matter of expense is not an archaeological problem, but a social one; is the community willing to devote resources to these studies or is it not? For present purposes, the more important considerations are those which cannot be solved by money alone, but which are either inherent in the nature of this sub-discipline or beyond our current technical expertise. And these difficulties are in addition to those presented by all archaeological investigations: problems of trying to study a whole society from its material remains, the uneven survival of those remains, and the arbitrariness of our recording of them, to name only a few (Clarke 1968, 14–20). Together, these help to determine the scope and character of this field of research.

2.3   The advantages of excavation under water

In the last section, nearly all the problems raised involved operational difficulties rather than any inherent limitations in the sites themselves. In fact, the reverse is the case, and many of the strengths of this type of work arise from the numerous favourable characteristics of underwater sites. However, before discussing these, note must be taken of a limited number of operational advantages which arise incidentally during underwater investigations.

When outlining excavation techniques under water, a range of tools for removing spoil was described – from the bucket to the air-lift. The humble bucket is similarly used on land, but for shifting larger amounts of material recourse is made to machines such as the wheelbarrow and the mechanical digger. From the archaeological viewpoint, these implements have the great disadvantage that they can disturb a site with their wheel tracks, and must be used only on the uppermost, sterile levels, or run on duck-boards or metal sheeting. A dredge or air-lift under water has none of these undesirable characteristics, and can carry spoil across archaeologically significant areas with a minimum of damage (fig. 2.5). Even a bucket is less cumbersome under water, since the diver can swim across delicate structures with it, while his counterpart on land has to walk along gangplanks. As a result, it is feasible under water to consider excavating in the centre of a deposit, as for example in the middle of a ship, without undue concern for the preservation of the surrounding structure or other remains.

The other great gain in the use of these tools for the removal of spoil is that they involve singularly little effort on the part of the excavator himself, when compared with his colleagues on land, who have to carry heavy buckets and push wheelbarrows. Apart from the fact that this makes life more pleasant for the underwater worker, it can also represent an appreciable saving in time and energy. There is probably an archaeological gain as well, in that the automatic removal of spoil allows a continuity of observation, and thus a greater concentration on the dissection of the deposit concerned leading, hopefully, to a more accurate observation of its salient features.

That the existence of relatively unconsolidated deposits acts as a restraint on the creation of vertical-sided trenches under water was listed above as one of the problems of this work. However, this phenomenon also has its positive aspect in that it facilitates the extraction of artefacts and other items from the sediments. Disturbing a deposit under water, for example with a fanning action of the hand, will put its constituents into suspension, at least for a moment, and allow them to sort themselves according to the varying specific gravities of the material involved. So long as the archaeologically significant objects are either lighter or heavier than the deposit within which they are lying, then they will be sorted out from their matrix. Of course, in controlled excavation under water, this effect is operated on very small quantities of material at a time, and very often the artefacts, being more dense than the sediments, stay *in situ* while the latter are removed. An analogy can be drawn between this process and the wet sieving or flotation of terrestrial deposits (see, for example, Jarman *et al.* 1972), and there is some reason to suspect that it can result in a comparable improvement in the rate of recovery of objects from a deposit. There is a need for more tests to be done on this; the only figures available to the author concern a short test undertaken on the spoil produced during the excavations on the *Kennemerland* site in 1973, where the excavators were mostly students with little previous archaeological experience. The result of a close inspection of a sample of the spoil on land was to increase the number of finds by about 20%, but this increment consisted almost entirely of small pieces of a mottled brown stoneware, well camouflaged within a sand and gravel deposit. The other reason for stressing the importance of this effect is that, when excavating under water, one is less conscious of the difficulties of separating out every element of the sea-bed than in most land situations.

There is a further consequence of this automatic sorting of material under water which, while not being strictly a matter of excavation procedure, can serve a useful cross-checking purpose. When spoil is ejected from the end of a dredge or an air-lift, it too is sorted according to the various specific gravities involved, so that the heaviest items will fall nearest the exhaust. It is thus an easy matter for a supervisor or director to check whether any heavy artefacts have been overlooked by recent excavators, simply by inspecting one end of the spoil mound. Of course, this check will not reveal any light or fragile materials accidentally sent up the tube, but in these cases it is unlikely that anything will have survived at all. Incidentally, this fact can also be very useful on those occasions when one accidentally lets a tool, such as a trowel, be sucked up the air-lift, since one can predict quite accurately where it will have fallen.

The other main operational advantage of work under water is a more nebulous idea, and concerns the kind of excavation strategy which the various constraints mentioned above allow the director of an underwater project. There are two elements here. First, the greater expense of any task under water means that there is a considerable incentive for him to be as economical as possible in his programme, and for him to undertake only those operations which he is convinced are necessary for the solution of his research questions. Of course, this should be true of all excavations, wherever they are conducted, but on land there is certainly, in practice, a temptation to investigate a feature 'just to make sure' that previous interpretations hold good. It is this sort of luxury which an underwater director has to do without; he has to arrange his strategy so that he is as sure as he is ever likely to be after a minimum of fieldwork.

Secondly in any 24 hour period, with less than 25 % of the equivalent work on land being possible under water, and with the director himself being unable to spend more than a specified length of time each day under water, he has much more leisure than is usual between each stage in the excavation process. Thus many more hours for mulling over a problem will be available and this may lead, on some occasions, to more economical and effective solutions being devised. This may be another point at which there are compensations for the time restrictions discussed in the last section, and by which their consequences may be, to some extent, alleviated. The net result of these considerations should be that, all other things being equal, the excavation strategy on an underwater site as it finally emerges should be more elegant and effective than a comparable one evolved for a land site. It is, however, difficult to give precise examples which may illustrate such a situation, partly because the questions asked of sites on land and in the sea vary so widely, and partly because the full potential of this effect has probably not yet been realised, since few directors have had enough experience of underwater work to allow them to identify the most appropriate procedures at every stage of a project.

As indicated above, most of the advantages of archaeology under

Fig. 2.12 A section of the organic deposit lying about 30 cm below sea-bed level on the *Trinidad Valencera* (1588) wreck-site, including a musket stock, and other wooden items. Scale in inches.

water involve the sites themselves. The most well known of these is that, in suitable circumstances, marine sites can contain a wide range of fragile organic remains in an excellent state of preservation. Although such items can lead to considerable expense and inconvenience for the conservator, to the archaeologist they indicate that assemblages from underwater sites can include a more complete range of materials than their land counterparts. Briefly stated, the reason for this preservation lies in the oxygen-free environment which can exist within the sea-bed, inhibiting those biological and chemical processes which can hasten the degradation of organic materials. A dramatic demonstration of this can be found on the site of the Spanish Armada ship *La Trinidad Valencera* (1588) in Ireland, where the scatter of wooden, leather, and rope items illustrated in fig. 2.12 was found only about 30 centimetres below the surface of the sand (Martin 1975, 223–4). The enclosing grey-black sands suggested a reducing environment, occurring either naturally or as a result of neighbouring iron concretions. While such favourable conditions for preservation are more common in fine sediments, such as silts, clays, and sands, they can also exist in coarser deposits; fig. 2.13 shows a boot emerging from a gravel matrix on the wreck-site of the Dutch East Indiaman *Kennemerland* (1664) (Price & Muckelroy 1977, 197). Iron concretion itself can also be suitable, in some circumstances, for the preservation of such remains. These considerations apply not only to artefacts of an organic nature, but also to plant and animal remains which may themselves be of considerable archaeological significance; fig. 2.14 shows a pile of peppercorns recovered from a horizon formed of splinters and other organic remains, also from the wreck of the *Kennemerland*.

Fig. 2.13 The remains of a leather boot partly exposed within a gravel deposit on the *Kennemerland* (1664) site. Scale in 5 centimetre divisions.

Of course, the other important element often preserved as a result of such favourable conditions under water is the ship's hull itself, or at least a part of it. Since survival is usually dependent on total burial, there is a tendency for it to be the lower parts of hulls which are preserved, with certain consequences for the scope and potential of maritime archaeology (see chapter 6). If wood is left exposed to open sea-water, it will usually succumb to the voracious appetites of various wood-eating marine animals, notably the gribble, *Limnoria lignorum*, and the ship-worm, *Teredo navalis*, which is in fact an elongated clam (Love 1961). Since these creatures do not exist in fresh or brackish water, wooden vessels lying in such conditions are more likely to have survived intact proud of the sea-bed. The exceptional conditions of the Baltic are already well known in this respect, having produced the spectacular find of the warship *Wasa* (see fig. 1.5, p. 16) (Naish 1968): hundreds of other similarly complete vessels from medieval and later times have now been recorded within its waters (Cederlund 1977, 87). Among the other localities which have produced equally spectacular remains are the Great Lakes of North America (fig. 2.15). Similarly, these particular creatures do not inhabit deep waters, with consequences for the state of preservation of archaeological materials deposited there (see section 4.7). However, the bulk of finds to date have not been in these exceptional situations, and so have tended to include only parts of ships' structures, as with the French wreck-site known as Planier III (fig. 2.16) (Pomey 1973). As with most such sites in the Mediterranean, this area of structure was buried under a mound of amphorae, and preserved within a deposit of sand and silt. However, hull remains can also be found in much less promising situations; structural elements from the *Dartmouth* (1690) had been pinned down by the vessel's iron ballast, and buried only slightly below the surface of a gravel sea-bed. In fact, the

Fig. 2.14 A pile of peppercorns recovered from an organic deposit on the *Kennemerland* (1664) site.

Fig. 2.15 Photograph of a
wreck from the war of 1812
(either the *Hamilton* or the
Scourge), now lying at a
depth of about 90 metres
in Lake Ontario; it was
taken with a Klein
Associates Hydroscan
Side-scan Sonar.

Fig. 2.16 Overview of the
Planier III wreck-site off
the Mediterranean coast of
France.

remains had been planed off at this level, so that their upper surface was practically flat, and bore the marks of both gribble and teredo activity (fig. 2.17) (Martin 1978).

The uniqueness of underwater sites in this respect should not be overstated, since there are many terrestrial sites which have produced a wide range of organic remains. Obviously, sites on marshland can present favourable conditions for preservation, as have been shown by the spectacular finds of human remains in Danish bogs (Glob 1969), or of neolithic trackways found in the Somerset Levels (Coles *et al.* 1975). Similar conditions have been found in many long-established towns, which are frequently situated close to waterways for economic reasons, and which are thus often water-logged only a few metres below modern ground level; in Britain, this situation has recently been encountered at York, London, Dublin, and many other important medieval centres. Similar survival characteristics have been observed during excavations at Trondheim in Norway (Long 1975), and perhaps most spectacularly of all in the Russian medieval city of Novgorod, with its timber-made streets (Thompson 1967). But such conditions are still the exception rather than the rule on land, while under water the reverse is the case.

Fig. 2.17 A section of the upper surface of the structural remains on the *Dartmouth* (1690) site, after clearing, showing its state of preservation.

The second main claim usually made on behalf of wreck-sites under water is that they represent 'time capsules'. More than is ever the case on land, except perhaps with sites buried suddenly and without warning by a volcanic eruption (e.g. Pompeii or Herculaneum), a shipwreck is the product of an instantaneous and unpremeditated catastrophe. Everything which was on board the vessel is suddenly pitched onto the sea-bed and, if conditions are favourable, preserved for posterity. It can thus be said that all the artefacts found on the site are contemporary, and in this context the word 'contemporary' has a much more precise meaning than is usual in archaeology. In most situations where two or more artefacts are so described, it means that they were in general circulation within the same period, an interval whose length can extend up to a matter of millenia, according to the precision in dating achievable for that epoch. Even with very recent centuries, it is unusual for archaeologists to consider periods shorter than a decade, and many items from post-medieval periods can still only be dated to the nearest century. In a shipwreck, however, the term 'contemporary' means that the objects were in use at precisely the same time, to the nearest day, and were considered necessary by a group of persons occupied in certain well-defined activities. The range of studies, and other implications of this situation will constitute one of the main themes of Part Two.

So far so good; but this concept of the 'time capsule' must be used with caution on any particular wreck, since underwater sites are as liable to contamination by later activities as any site on land. One important source of such extraneous material will be other shipwrecks occurring on the same spot as a result of events similar to those which caused the initial disaster. Thus wreckage from the *Advena* (1912) spreads over part of the remains of the *Kennemerland* (1664) in the Out Skerries (Shetland Isles), and three other wreck-sites are close by (Forster & Higgs 1973, 294). Similar situations have been found all around the Mediterranean; for example, at Grand Congloué, many experts believe that two ships were wrecked on precisely the same spot within a century of each other. The reef at Yassi Ada on the Turkish coast has been described by Peter Throckmorton as a veritable graveyard of ships, bearing as it does the remains of over a dozen vessels (Bass 1966, 50), while at least as many ships were apparently lost within the Bay of Marzememi in Sicily, where their cargoes often overlap (A. J. Parker, personal communication). As on the roads, there are accident black-spots at sea, and the basic factors which caused wrecks in the past are likely to have continued operating throughout history, at least where sailing vessels are concerned. Of course, in most of these cases, the various wrecks concerned are sufficiently far apart in date for archaeologists to distinguish between the elements derived from each of them, although at Marzememi this has called for a very specialised knowledge of the dates and origins of the various pottery types involved. At the same time, there are frequently objects, such as amorphous lumps of ironwork or broken woodwork, which really could have come from any of the wrecks known to have occurred in that area, at which point the concept of the 'time capsule' has indeed been upset.

There is one further consideration which may, in some instances, further erode this basic idea. As indicated in the last chapter, a ship-wreck very often inspires a good deal of activity around the site immedi-ately after it has occurred, as various types of salvage are attempted. It is quite possible that those involved in such work may themselves drop objects onto the site, and this material, being very nearly contemporary with the wreck herself, will be very difficult to distinguish. It may also result in some seriously erroneous conclusions; for example, should one or two English clay pipes be discovered on a Dutch wreck lying in British waters, the excavator might be very tempted to construct a whole theory concerning the export of English clay pipes to the Low Countries, with many important implications, in view of the thriving Dutch clay pipe industry. However, the more prosaic explanation would actually be the more reasonable, that they had been dropped by con-temporary salvors. This possibility of immediate contamination is further reinforced in circumstances where the ship's structure may have remained proud of the sea-bed for some time, creating scour-pits around itself, and attracting any rubbish which happened to be scudding around at that time. In certain circumstances such extraneous debris might get inside the ship herself, in which case it would be almost impossible to distinguish it on the criterion of location alone. Obviously, such explanations can only be invoked for a small proportion of any wreck collection, but they may cast doubts on some particular finds, and pose a serious problem, since it is often the unusual and the unexpected which give the archaeologist his most striking insights.

While these two substantial grounds for caution must not be over-looked, the fact remains that wreck-sites do represent total communities of a special type frozen in time, and as such, can present information of a quality not generally paralleled on land. Together with the unusually good preservation characteristics of marine sites, this constitutes the greatest strength of archaeology under water.

A final point to be mentioned in establishing the positive aspects of such sites is that they alone contain the full range of material evidence relating to ancient seafaring, which is the raw material for maritime archaeology itself, as defined above in section 1.1, p. 4. It is here that the basic identification of maritime archaeology with fieldwork under water is asserted, which has been the justification for considering various aspects of underwater activities in the present chapter. The exposition began with a discussion of the organisation of fieldwork under water, leading to an investigation of its principal weaknesses and strengths. Setting aside for the moment the matter of expense, which is essentially an economic, social, and political problem rather than an archaeological one, it should be reasonably clear that there is a fair balance of advantage and disadvantage in this work. Of greater relevance to the present thesis, however, has been the demonstration that there are several points at which work under water differs considerably from that on land. It is just these points which constitute an important element in defining the sub-discipline of maritime archaeology. But they are by no means the whole of the story; a more fundamental role in this definition is played by the types of research problem towards which this study seeks to make a contribution, and it is to this subject that the next two chapters are devoted.

3

The contribution of current work under water

Maritime archaeology must stand or fall on the basis of the new information it can provide regarding past societies and their seafaring: a discussion of some of the important advances made in the first quarter century of its existence will therefore both help to define more closely the area of research embraced by the subject and serve to demonstrate its significance. The nine topics presented below are by no means the only ones which could have been chosen, but they are intended to give a balanced view of the whole picture, while emphasising some of the highlights. In many cases, the projects and sites discussed are not those which have hit the headlines with spectacular finds of gold, silver, or works of art; the selection has simply been on the basis of substantial contributions to knowledge.

3.1 Mediterranean shipbuilding in classical times

Ever since the Renaissance, the ships of the Greeks and Romans have been a favourite subject for antiquarian enquiry, in which speculation has been able to range unfettered on account of the paucity of the evidence, limited as it was to literary sources and representations on monuments, mosaics, and frescoes (see Basch 1972, 2–11). The principal difficulty with written reports was that they tended to assume a certain level of basic knowledge on the part of the reader, even when consciously attempting a technical description. Furthermore, such passages generally concerned exceptional and noteworthy craft, rather than common vessels, as with the description of the gigantic merchantman of about 1900 tons (Casson 1971, 184–6) built for Hiero II of Syracuse in c. 240 B.C., given by Athenaeus (5.206d–209b). Pictorial representations of all types suffered from the difficulty that they generally only showed the part of the ship above the waterline, that they were two dimensional, and that they could always be discounted in any detail by the objection of 'artistic licence'. The net results of many centuries of such studies were exceedingly disappointing, as many twentieth-century scholars recognised, and the high hopes placed in maritime archaeology as the solution to this impasse were vividly expressed by G. D. Toudouze: 'Texts and figures, archaeologists and sailors are in themselves insufficient. To solve the question one necessary object, so far lacking, is needed: a wreck' (1934, 45).

The first wrecks to become available to scholars were those on the floor of Lake Nemi (Ucelli 1950), although any general deductions derived from them could be, and were, challenged on the grounds that these were exceptional craft. However, no-one could have such doubts about the scores of classical merchantmen discovered along the south coast of France after the Second World War. The first to be systematically investigated was that at Grand Congloué, near Marseilles, the publication of which after ten years of study also served as a summary of the findings from several other French wreck-sites discovered during the 1950s (Benoit 1961). The most notable of these were the sites at Cap Dramont (Site A, Santamaria *et al.* 1965), the Titan reef (Taillez 1965), and Monaco harbour (Benoit 1961, 145–6). Over the same period, a series of important sites was investigated off the Italian coast, including those at Albenga (Lamboglia 1961; 1965), Spargi (Roghi 1965), and Torre Sgaratta (Throckmorton 1969), along with some ship finds on land, such as those in the Roman 'Portus' at Fiumicino (Testaguzza 1964), and the sixth-century A.D. vessel at Pantano Longarini in Sicily (Throckmorton 1973*b*). During the 1960s, further significant contributions were made by Professor George Bass and his colleagues working off the Turkish coast, notably from the excavation of two wrecks at Yassi Ada, one of the fourth century A.D. (Bass & van Doorninck 1971;

Fig. 3.1 Schematic drawings comparing the techniques of edge-joining in shell planking as between the typical procedure used during the Roman republican period (*above*), and that discovered on the seventh-century Yassi Ada hull (*below*).

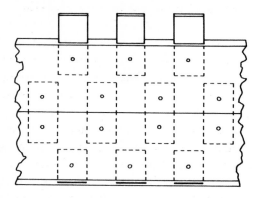

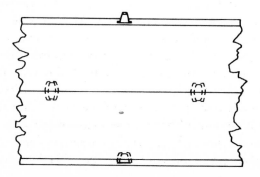

van Doorninck 1976) and one of the seventh century A.D. (van Doorninck 1967). In Cyprus a fourth-century B.C. merchantman discovered in 1967 near Kyrenia has been excavated and raised (Swiny & Katzev 1973; Katzev 1974). The 1970s have similarly seen many major projects, although it is too early to assess their relative significance; certainly the results of some recent investigations off the south coast of France have been of great importance, as with the work at Planier III (Pomey 1973) or Madrague de Giens (Tchernia & Pomey 1978).

This brief survey of recent projects highlights some important points. First, the geographical spread of activity is very uneven, with a bias towards the north-western shores of the Mediterranean, and with large areas of the Sea, especially in the east, not represented at all. Secondly, the date range of these sites is unsatisfactory, since over half of those in the western basin belong to the last two centuries B.C., while those in the east date from either the beginning or the end of the period. Finally, the level of investigation has varied widely: only one hull has been lifted entirely and permanently conserved, that at Kyrenia, while on many of the early French projects structural elements were lifted for study without their sea-bed contexts being thoroughly understood. Generally, most of the recording has been done under water, in some cases with nothing at all being lifted to the surface. Nevertheless, a picture has emerged of shipbuilding at this period which differs significantly from that previously assumed, and which owes everything to these pioneering efforts.

The most distinctive feature of classical naval architecture was the practice of marrying together the planks of a ship's hull with frequent mortices and tenons along their edges, producing a strong, self-supporting hull looking more like a product of the carpenter's art than the shipbuilders' (fig. 3.1). This technique allowed the hull to be set up on the keel before any of the internal frames had been fitted, the ship's lines being dictated by the shaping of the planks alone. Contrary to modern practices in wooden shipbuilding, the internal frames were relatively slender, being inserted into the hull only after the planking was fully assembled. This method of almost sculpting the lines of the ship with the planking meant that it often varied quite considerably in thickness, as a consequence of planing areas down after erection to fair off the lines more precisely. On the hull of the Kyrenia ship, J. R. Steffy has been able to demonstrate that both faces of the planking had been substantially trimmed down after fitting (van Doorninck 1976, 127), and a variation of over a centimetre in the thickness of the planking has been reported on the wreck at Chrétienne A. A variant on this technique has been discovered on a second-century B.C. wreck at Binisafuller, Minorca, where round dowels were used instead of the usual tenons (Parker 1976). Similar edge-joined planking has been found on the world's oldest surviving vessel, the Cheops boat from Egypt (Land-ström 1970), and this technique seems to have been standard from early times in the Nile valley; however, whether this can be said to prove that the idea spread from there across the whole Mediterranean world is another matter.

Another previously unsuspected feature of classical naval architecture has been the discovery that some vessels possessed a V-shaped hull of a sophisticated design usually associated with nineteenth-century developments. This point is illustrated by the two keel sections shown in fig. 3.2. The upper one, from the Titan wreck, shows a flat-bottomed ship of the type one would expect of a merchantman in which there was a premium on cargo space. The lower one, from the Grand Congloué vessel, shows a more pointed hull, which would cut through the water more cleanly than the other and give relatively more speed, although at the expense of room in the holds. Similarly fine midships sections have been observed on the wrecks at Chrétienne A and Mahdia (Frondeville 1965); a possible explanation for this feature might be that the endemic

Fig. 3.2 Sections across the keel and adjoining structures on the wrecks of Titan (*above*) and Grand Congloué (*below*) showing the different hull profiles resulting.

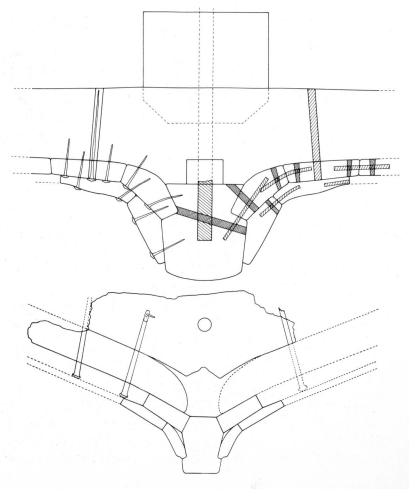

piracy of the period before Pompey the Great placed a premium on speed. A possible relationship between these structural differences and the variety of words applied to merchant ships has been suggested (Casson 1971, 157–70), although evidence to substantiate this is unlikely to be forthcoming. Similarly, in the present state of knowledge, any attempt to identify separate national shipbuilding traditions is likely to be highly suspect; certainly, the distinction between Greek and Roman practices proposed by Ferdinand Benoit (1961) was not warranted by

Fig. 3.3 An overview of the hull and working grids on the site of the large Roman wreck discovered at the Madrague de Giens near Hyères (Var, France).

the evidence available to him, and has not been supported by subsequent excavations. The same caveat of lack of evidence must also be applied to any attempt to identify evolutionary trends over the classical period; Nevertheless, some recurrent features do suggest certain long-term developments.

While the technique of hull construction described above represents a summary of the evidence from most wreck-sites of the classical period, there are a small number of hulls in which the internal frames have evidently played a more active part in determining the ships' lines. Most of these come from late Roman times, but the earliest example of this is the wreck of the first century B.C. at Madrague de Giens (fig. 3.3). Here, the manner of fitting the trenails pinning the mortices and tenons of the ship's planking shows that at least some of the frames had been installed after the third strake had been fitted. On the fourth-century A.D. vessel at Yassi Ada it is fairly clear that the midships half-frames had been erected early on in construction, possibly after only five strakes had been fitted (van Doorninck 1976, 126–7). In these cases, the few frames inserted early on represented only guides and supports for what was still essentially a shell construction technique, but in the sixth-century Pantano Longarini vessel, and the seventh-century one at Yassi Ada, the hull above the waterline was constructed by a purely skeleton-first process, with no mortices and tenons between the planks. And even below the waterline, where the hull was constructed by a shell-first process, it was evidently not expected to contribute much to the strength of the vessel, since the mortices and tenons were tiny and very irregularly placed (see fig. 3.1) (Throckmorton 1973*b*; van Doorninck 1967). It is thus unwise to stress the absolute dominance of shell-first technique in classical times, although whether these deviations represent an evolutionary trend, local isolated experiments, or a continuing and parallel tradition of frame-first shipbuilding, only further excavations and research will reveal. It should be noted that the possibility of a long-standing skeleton-first tradition has been suspected by some historians on the basis on the linguistic evidence (see Morrison 1976, 165–6).

Another sign of greater reliance being placed on frames for hull strength is the bolting of floor timbers directly onto the keel, giving the internal skeleton greater rigidity. This had been done on all the ships mentioned in the last paragraph, although not on every single floor timber; in the case of the Madrague de Giens wreck, between four and six of them had been so attached (P. Pomey, personal communication). This feature has also been noted on the late Imperial wreck at Monaco (Basch 1972, 47–9), and is hinted at by a 71 centimetre bronze bolt on a second-century A.D. wreck at Cape Taormina (van Doorninck 1967; 1972). The corollory of this situation is a tendency to create less strength in a ship's planking, and one of the clearest signs of this is the abandonment of double planking as a regular feature. All early vessels investigated have shown signs of being double-planked (e.g. the Kyrenia ship), but the latest vessel on which it has been found is that wrecked on the Titan reef in the first century B.C. A century later, even the massively built Nemi ships were only single-planked (Ucelli 1950). Another early feature designed to strengthen and preserve the shell of a ship was sheathing it in lead, in order to repel the wood-eating ship-worm. This practice appears to have continued somewhat later than double planking, as is shown by the lead cladding on the Nemi ships, a demonstration made even more impressive by the fact that, in the absence of the ship-worm in the lake's fresh water, this provision was entirely superfluous. However, to date no later vessels have been found with this sheathing. Finally, this tendency towards less strength in the shell, and correspondingly more in the vessel's frames, is accompanied by other signs of cheaper construction techniques, such as the increased use of iron bolts, rather than copper ones or wooden dowels. Although cheaper and easier to fit, iron fittings deteriorate more rapidly in sea-water than the other types do.

The totality of this evidence strongly suggests a tendency, over the period of the Empire, towards less concern with durability, in favour of ease and cheapness in construction. While considerably more research, both archaeological and historical, is required into this matter, it seems at least possible that the stimulus behind this trend was a long-term rise in labour costs relative to material costs over these centuries, especially where skilled labour was concerned. By cutting out one skin of planking, and the lead sheathing, and substituting iron fastenings, the construction costs of a vessel could be drastically reduced, although at the price of heavier framing and a reduced working life. This could be contemplated if the supply of materials, and especially timber, for new boats was relatively cheap. The Mediterranean world has always been poorly endowed with large timbers, but the expansion of the Empire north-wards into Europe may have eased this supply situation.

Since amphorae and other heavy items of cargo have generally pinned down only the lower parts of ships' hulls, much less has been learned from such sites about the upperworks of classical vessels. However, the pictorial evidence concerning these elements is correspondingly more extensive, and can be more surely interpreted in the light of the new understanding of ships' hulls. In addition, a few sites have produced remains of direct relevance. Several representations show vessels with a small forward-raking mast in the bows, carrying an *artemon* or steering sail. Material evidence for such a facility has come from the second-century A.D. wreck at Torre Sgarrata, where the appropriate mast step was found (Throckmorton 1969). Another wreck excavated by Peter

Throckmorton produced the only remains found to date of the upper parts of a transom stern. All classical ships appear to have had hulls pointed at both ends, but several Roman vessels apparently possessed a squared-off gallery projecting over the stern, as shown in a third-century A.D. mosaic from Mostra Augustea (fig. 3.4) (Casson 1971, pl. 154). The sixth-century A.D. Pantano Longarini ship, of which only the upper part of the stern survived (fig. 3.5) undoubtedly had such a gallery (Throckmorton 1973b). Another feature of this wreck can similarly be related to pictorial representations; several deck beams ran through the hull planking and projected externally, a practice also noted on the seventh-century ship at Yassi Ada (Bass 1971, 25).

So far, attention has been concentrated on the wrecks of moderate sized merchantmen of about 100 or 200 tons, between 15 and 25 metres long, with a few larger vessels of up to 40 metres also being mentioned (e.g. Albenga or Pantano Longarini), because it is these types which have been most frequently betrayed by their amphora cargoes. Of larger craft, which figure so prominently in surviving literary descriptions, little has been found except for the cast in concrete of Caligula's famous obelisk carrier, discovered in the foundations of the Portus lighthouse at Fiumicino; this revealed that it was a massive 95 metres long and 21 metres wide (Basch 1972, 13–14). The Fiumicino excavations also uncovered a large collection of classical-period small boats, ranging

Fig. 3.4 A section of a mosaic from Mostra Augustea, showing the transom stern gallery of a ship.

from 5 to 19 metres in length, and dating from the second century A.D. or later (Testaguzza 1964).

But the most outstanding omission from this discussion so far is of fighting vessels. Classical-period warships were specialist craft, built for speed under oars, and carrying few stores (Casson 1971, 90); the chances of any such vessels sinking intact and being pinned onto the sea-bed would thus seem to be remote, and many early writers on archaeology under water were pessimistic about the possibility of it ever making a substantial contribution to studies in this field (e.g. Basch 1972, 52). Fortunately, their worst fears have been proved groundless by the discovery of at least two second-century B.C. warships near Marsala in Sicily, and their excavation since 1971 by Miss Honor Frost (Frost 1972*a*; 1973*a*; Frost *et al.* 1974; Basch & Frost 1975). Work on this material is still continuing, but the supreme importance of the results can be gauged by what has already emerged. The ships showed signs of having been forced into the sea-bed, perhaps by being rammed during a battle; the first wreck excavated lay stern down at an angle of 27°, while the so-called 'sister ship' seemed to have been broken in two amidships. They were dated to the early second century B.C. on the basis of associated pottery. On both hulls a number of inscriptions in the Phoenician script were discovered, many being indications of how the structural elements were to be assembled. These, together with the

Fig. 3.5 The sixth-century A.D. wreck at Pantano Longarini, Sicily, showing the remains of its transom stern gallery.

marks of paint-pots and the way the paint had run from them, showed clearly that the timbers had been prefabricated, recalling the mass-production techniques said to have been used by Rome to create a fleet in the First Punic War. However, the inscriptions showed clearly the Punic affiliations of the shipbuilders, and incidentally cast new light on the meaning of several Punic nautical terms. The first ship, of which the midships and stern remained, also exhibited several gaps between planks in its hull, presumably as a consequence of prefabrication, which had been filled with a white putty-like caulking material, unparalleled elsewhere. Even the finding of ballast stones over the hull has been of importance, since some writers had stated that classical warships would not have carried any ballast at all; the idea that this may have been installed only temporarily, as proposed by Professor Morrison (1976, 169), is at present without any substantial foundation.

While the identification of the first vessel as a warship was largely conjectural, being based on its unusual location and angle of rest, and the absence of any sign of a cargo, there can be little doubt about the 'sister ship' lying nearby. Although this site has so far only been surveyed, a ram had already been identified and investigated at the bow end of its keel (fig. 3.6). It was of a type occasionally illustrated in contemporary pictures, for which Lucien Basch has suggested an Illyrian origin (Basch & Frost 1975, 201–19), although the finding of this example has revealed more than any number of illustrations. The ramhead itself was missing, but the cheek pieces which held it in place at the foot of the stem-post had survived, and showed by the way they had been cut across the grain of the wood that they had been designed to allow the ram to break off under strain, lest the attacking vessel be permanently locked onto its sinking victim (*ibid.*, 224–6). The full potential of these finds will take many years to assimilate, although their overall importance has already been fully established. At the same time, researchers must guard against imposing the details from these examples

Fig. 3.6 The fore-foot and seating for a ram on one of the Punic wrecks found near Marsala in Sicily. Scale in 10 centimetre units.

onto all classical-period warships without qualification; as Miss Frost
has written: 'some scholars would lead us to suppose that in antiquity
each period sported a single pattern of ship!' (1975, 222). This is a
danger common to all aspects of this topic, and can ultimately only be
cured by the accumulation of a large number of securely dated and
thoroughly investigated wreck-sites. However, the first quarter century
of research in this field has amply justified its promise, and should
pressage further advances in the next few decades.

3.2   Mediterranean trade in pre-classical and classical times

In archaeology, there has recently been an increased interest in the
economic aspects of past societies, which has affected even classical
archaeology, with its long-standing preoccupation with works of art and
architectural studies. Trade networks within the Mediterranean world
have thus attracted some interest, and in such research there has been a
substantial contribution from maritime archaeology. Since the evidence
does not come exclusively from this field, this chapter can only outline
that contribution by discussing a few specific topics, and by consciously
overlooking the information available from other sources. Of these, the
limited amount of documentary material available is obviously of prime
importance, and authoritative consideration of it can be found in the
works of Rostovtsev (1926) and Tenny Frank (1933–40). The other
main source of evidence lies in the distribution of artefacts found on
ancient sites on land; at present, this source is cumulatively more

Fig. 3.7 A plan of the
Cape Gelidonya wreck-
site.

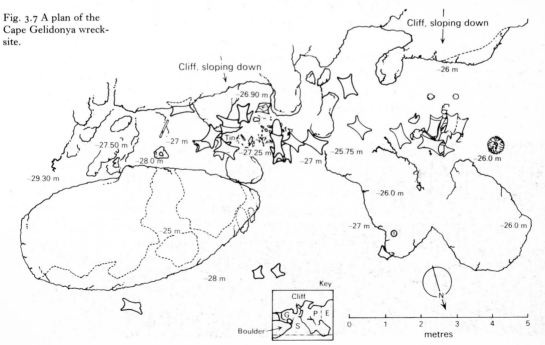

extensive than that arising from maritime studies, as has been demonstrated by Dr A. J. Parker (1973, fig. 1) in a discussion of the exports of southern Spain. However, there are some aspects of trade for which only wreck-sites can provide adequate data, and some of these will be indicated below.

Obviously, one such area is trade in prehistoric times, where the historical records are either non-existent or very difficult to interpret. Thus the information derived from the excavation and study of the Late Bronze Age shipwreck at Cape Gelidonya, dated to around 1200 B.C., has been of great significance (Bass 1967). The site (fig. 3.7) consisted of a rocky bottom on which none of the hull had survived in any coherent form. The most prominent remains were a couple of piles of copper ox-hide ingots (fig. 3.8), and the rest of the cargo comprised copper bun and slab ingots, wicker baskets containing bronze scrap, a lead disc, pieces of unworked crystal, and jars filled with coloured beads and (perhaps) spices (Muhly *et al.* 1977). Although the main part of this cargo, the copper, had probably been picked up in Cyprus not

Fig. 3.8 A pile of copper ox-hide ingots from the Cape Gelidonya wreck; they have been rearranged after lifting in the same pattern as they were lying on the sea-bed. Scale in 10 centimetre units.

long before the disaster, other items showed that the ship had traded all over the eastern Mediterranean. Balance-pan weights, stone anvils, stone rubbers, and tools indicated that the merchant on board was in fact a travelling smith, prepared to trade his wares and manufacture implements wherever there was good custom. Objects belonging to the crew from the apparent 'cabin-area' of the wreck, and especially the one cylinder seal found, which was probably the official mark of the merchant himself, all suggested that he was a Syrian, and that the ship was based in a Syro-Palestinian port. Although, as Basch (1972, 51–2) has pointed out, this identification is only deduction, it is very difficult to see how any other interpretation is possible.

'The conclusion that the ship at Gelidonya was a thirteenth- or very early twelfth-century Phoenician merchantman, however, applies to but one ship', Professor Bass has written, and he continues:
'This alone has little historical significance, for a single
ship, found by chance, does not necessarily represent a
merchant fleet. More significant, the excavation at
Gelidonya has led to a careful restudy of the types of
objects carried on board, and this restudy of parallel
material from other sites, even *without* the finds at
Gelidonya, would have led to the conclusion that a great
deal of commerce was in the hands of Phoenician seamen
and merchants during the late Bronze Age' (1967, 165).
The previous consensus had been that trade at this time was predominantly in the hands of Mycenaean traders, a view founded on the distribution of Mycenaean pottery along coasts and up navigable rivers around the eastern Mediterranean. In his study of the parallels to the Cape Gelidonya material, Professor Bass has demonstrated that all the objects which might actually reflect the traders, rather than just their sources of supply, point to Phoenician involvement. After all, it had always been supposed that Cyprus provided the bulk of the copper at this period, yet no one had proposed that therefore trade was exclusively in Cypriot bottoms. Of course, it is also unrealistic to suppose that any one group would have held a complete monopoly of trade and seafaring, as Bass himself pointed out (1967, 166); the question is rather a matter of who held the dominant position. While the Cape Gelidonya wreck is at present pre-eminent in such studies, a wider range of such sites is promised by several recent discoveries as at Kos in the Aegean.

The sixth-century B.C. wreck in the Straits of Messina (Owen 1970; 1971) and the fourth-century B.C. one at Kyrenia (Swiny & Katzev 1973; Katzev 1974) together reflect a similar coasting trade, being general merchantmen with a variety of cargoes acquired from a number of different ports. The amphorae on the Kyrenia ship indicated visits to Samos and Rhodes, while the volcanic rock used for a collection of grinding stones was either from Kos or another Cycladic island. The large cargo of almonds was, however, almost certainly from Cyprus itself, and may suggest that disaster struck as the ship was leaving the island for an undiscoverable destination. The Messina wreck contained an even greater diversity of objects, including a dozen different amphora types of both Greek and Punic origins, lead ingots, scrap bronze, etc. The one qualification to be made to the assertion of Dr Owen that 'the remains of a cargo, therefore, are nearly as good as a written itinerary of a ship's route' (1970, 28) is the possibility of transhipment.

The majority of wrecks investigated in recent years have been from the period between the second century B.C. and the first century A.D., and it is therefore the trade systems of these centuries on which most study has been concentrated. As indicated by Parker (1973, fig. 1), it is only for the trade in metals that underwater sites alone provide the archaeological evidence. Many Spanish wreck-sites have produced ingots of locally produced lead, while Spanish copper has come from the Planier IV wreck and from Agde (Benoit 1962, 150). Tin pieces have been found on the Port Vendres II wreck and elsewhere, as well as mineral colourants, although the sources of supply of the latter are not known (Parker 1973, 361–3).

However, although they are by no means unique to underwater sites, it is the amphorae from wrecks which have yielded the greatest store of information, and which hold the greatest promise for the future. Amphorae were the universal liquid containers of the classical world, the oil-drums of their time, and their shapes, marks, fabrics, and other features can be used to identify their dates and places of origin. At the lowest level, wreck deposits, being strictly contemporary assemblages, assist in typological studies. A clear example of this is given by Parker (1973, 372–5) in a demonstration that a certain type of amphora with a collar-lip (known as Dressel 15), bearing many superficial resemblances to a class of Catalonian wine amphora, must in fact be an Italian form because of its consistent associations on several wrecks. But more direct economic information can also be gleaned from underwater sites, as demonstrated by Dr Parker's studies on Spanish exports in the last two centuries B.C. (1973, 365–71). Spanish amphorae have been found on several sites off the French coast, including Grand Congloué B and Titan, besides numerous wrecks in Spanish waters, a distribution which illustrates the extent of the export at this period of fish sauce (*garum*), and possibly wine and oil as well, from southern Spain and Portugal. A trade in reverse is suggested by a group of early spheroid amphorae from Spain (developing into Dressel 20), which can be shown to be derived from types exported from Italy to Spain in the second century B.C. (Parker 1973; 375–6); once again, all the relevant examples have come from underwater sites.

One restriction on the economic interpretation of these objects arises from the fact that it is often impossible to identify their contents. In a few cases they bear painted labels, but these are rare. Some specific shapes have been shown to have been designed for certain commodities; thus the Dressel 20 seems to have been intended for oil in the first two centuries A.D. (Callender 1965). More generally, the fact that workshops are known to have produced several varieties at the same period has led to the suggestion (e.g. in Parker 1973, 366) that different forms were usually intended for different commodities, although a convincing equation of shape and contents has yet to be achieved for most varieties. Many amphorae were lined with a resinous compound, and it has been proposed that these may have been used in the carriage of wine; while this may frequently have been so, any automatic identification is contradicted by the lined amphora from the Gandolfo wreck, which carries a fish sauce label. One promising recent development has been the use of gas chromatography in investigating the walls of amphorae for traces of certain fatty acids which would betray the former presence of oil in the container (Condamin *et al.* 1976). More certainty in these matters may be achieved after more examples have been studied, although the excessive looting of amphorae in past decades has probably severely reduced the scope.

The potential information content of stamps and other marks on amphorae has only recently been considered extensively. The generally excellent state of preservation of most amphorae from underwater sites results in a relatively high proportion of stamped ones compared with land contexts. The meaning of these marks is still not totally clear, although the general concensus is that the name on the stopper indicated the grower, while that on the jar itself referred to the shipper (Benoit 1961). It has further been suggested that less formal incisions sometimes noted on the bodies of these containers indicate the production of individual potters for purposes of piece-work payments (Carrazé 1972). Among shippers, the most famous and widespread is undoubtedly the firm of Sestius, whose products have been found on at least three underwater sites and thirteen land sites, and most dramatically on the first wreck at Grand Congloué, where over a thousand amphorae bearing this name were recovered (fig. 3.9). The firm, which was based in southern Italy, probably in the region of the Bay of Naples, seems to have continued in business for upwards of a hundred years in the second and first centuries B.C. (Benoit 1965, 28–9). It is occasionally possible to suggest that a name on a vessel can be related to a known businessman, as with the spheroidal amphora from the Planier III wreck bearing the name of M. Tuccius Galeo, who may be identified with the friend of Cicero of that name (*Ad Atticum* 11.12.4; Tchernia 1969).

Moving on from amphorae, note should be taken of the contribution being made from wreck deposits to the study of the trade in bricks, tiles, and mortaria from central Italy to North Africa, southern Gaul, and other parts of the western Empire (Hartley 1973). Being stamped, the products of particular brickyards can be traced across these areas, and the picture which emerges is of a major commerce in bulky, low-cost items, presumably being carried as a sort of paying ballast. This point leads on to the question of the organisation of shipping at these periods. The general impression is of a greater specialisation of cargoes than is apparent at earlier periods, although the uneven spread of evidence may be misleading. It appears that there was a trade boom following the Second Punic War, founded on the export of wine and foodstuffs from southern Spain and Italy, which may in turn have called into being a fleet of specialised carriers, many of whose remains have been betrayed by their amphora cargoes. This specialisation may have been further encouraged by the need to supply the Roman armies in Southern Gaul and Spain; indeed, it has been suggested that the Titan ship was carrying supplies for Caesar's army at the siege of Marseilles (51–49 B.C.) (Taillez 1965, 90). Some sites have also raised interesting questions

Fig. 3.9 Examples of the amphorae from the Grand Congloué wreck bearing the Sestius stamp.

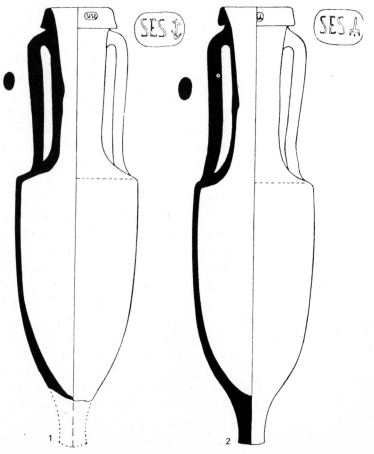

about the relationship between principal and supplementary cargoes; the latter may involve the transport of extremely low-cost items over long distances, as with the coarse pottery on the Madrague de Giens wreck (Tchernia & Pomey 1978). Finally, most of these sites have involved vessels of between 100 and 200 tons, while there is much evidence suggesting that ships of up to 500 tons were reasonably common (Casson 1971, 172). The only wrecks in this league excavated to date are those at Albenga (*c.* 600 tons) and Madrague de Giens (*c.* 400 tons).

The paucity of underwater excavations in the eastern Mediterranean, especially relating to the late Hellenistic and Roman periods, means that little has been deduced regarding maritime trade patterns in that area. For example, no remains have been found that reflect the regular traffic in grain and other commodities between Alexandria and Rome, which was conducted in huge freighters of up to 1500 tons (Casson 1971, 173).

One worthwhile topic for future research has been proposed by Professor Moses Finley, a historian with a lively appreciation of the potential of archaeology. He has pointed to the many questions posed by the position of Rhodes as an entrepot in Hellenistic times, and in particular the volume and character of its transit trade, and he has suggested that much light could be shed on such matters by a systematic cataloguing and study of Rhodian amphorae and their stamps (Finley 1971, 179–80). Such a study would, of course, benefit greatly if a larger number of wreck-sites were to be investigated in the eastern Mediterranean. In the meantime, the potential for such studies has been shown by past work in the western basin; the next few decades should see considerable advances in our understanding of these matters.

3.3   Early Mediterranean harbours

In the definition of maritime archaeology given above in chapter 1.1 (p. 4), it was emphasised that the subject was not exclusively concerned with ships, but also encompassed related coastal features. Anchorages, harbours, wharves, and such installations are as much a part of maritime activities as the ships themselves, since without them few vessels could be launched, cargoes could not be loaded or unloaded, and there would be no refuges in times of foul weather. For a number of geographical reasons, connected with the lack of substantial tides, coastal geology, etc., harbours and other similar remains have survived in an observable form in many parts of the Mediterranean, to a degree unparalleled in any other region, including Britain (Fryer 1973). Survival has also been assisted along some coasts, especially that of North Africa, by the relative decline in economic activity over the intervening two millenia.

For many early workers, the problem of whether any pre-Roman harbours could be identified, and if so where, never even arose, since it was widely accepted that at those periods voyaging only took place by day, and that at night ships were usually beached. Such an attitude can even slip out unawares from modern pens, although it has been thoroughly discredited. Even in late Bronze Age times there appear to have been many large ships around, far too big for beaching, even infrequently, as Egyptian and Syrian inscriptions testify (Frost 1972*b*, 95–6). Having accepted this evidence, then the problem of identifying Bronze Age harbours, at least in the eastern Mediterranean, is a real one. The northern shores of the Sea are generally rocky, with plenty of promontories and islands, in the lee of which shelter could, and still can, be found. However, the eastern and southern shores are generally flat and featureless, with few natural anchorages; it therefore seems likely that some artificial construction would have been necessary from an early date.

It was the logic of this situation, applied in particular to the famous ancient cities of Tyre and Sidon, that led Father A. Poidebard to undertake surveys in the 1930s which demonstrated that both cities had possessed extensive anchorages, protected by adapted offshore reefs (Poidebard 1939; Poidebard & Lauffrey 1951). Relying heavily on aerial photography and the reports from 'hard-hat' divers, he mapped remains spreading for several kilometres along the coast, and established the basic principle behind the constructions. Taking Sidon as an example, it can be seen from fig. 3.10 that the system involved both an inner and an outer harbour. Many details of the inner one, up against the settlement, have been obscured by later works, but the constructions on the offshore reef have survived, albeit heavily eroded. The engineers of this period were unable to undertake large-scale building in any depth of water, so that the lines of their constructions were dictated by the presence of natural reefs; hence the large size and unusual shape of these harbours. The reefs were artificially built up on their offshore faces, where necessary, in order to give greater protection from the sea, and cut down on the inner side in order to create wharves. Remains of such

Fig. 3.10 A map of Sidon and the remains of its ancient harbours.

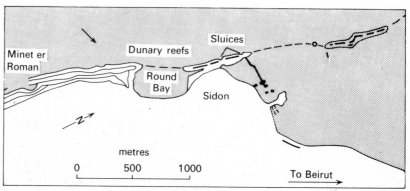

massive sea-walls can be seen at the similar harbour system of Arwad, further north along the coast (fig. 3.11). At one place on the reef off Sidon there are beam sockets in the rock, relating presumably to warehouses. The jetty projecting from the south-east corner of the reef is probably of Roman date, and shows that these installations had a useful life of many centuries. The gap left between this jetty and the reef itself illustrates another concern of these builders, to allow sufficient currents to flow to arrest the silting up of such sheltered stretches of water. The enclosed inner harbour, being more completely calm, was in even greater danger of silting up, so that its entrances were placed cunningly to avoid trapping any silt-bearing currents, and the outer wall was provided with wave-traps and sluices which could be opened periodically to flush out the harbour.

The great weakness of Poidebard's work, as he left it, was the lack of dating evidence; he could only offer it as a probability that these remains, and those at Tyre as well, were Bronze Age in origin. Recently, however, a possible dating method has been proposed, based on the evidence of small sea-level changes in historic times afforded by rims of *Vermutus*, a genus of vermiform gastropod which can only live at precisely sea-level. Rims now lying at other levels thus bear witness to previous levels in that locality, and can be dated by associated artefacts or radiocarbon (Sanlaville 1972). From this evidence, Miss Honor Frost has shown that at least some of the reef constructions must be pre second century B.C., and that, while many of them probably date from the Persian period, other elements must be older, and may have originated in the early Bronze Age (1973*b*). At the same time, underwater surveys using aqualungs, notably by Miss Frost herself, have added considerably to the details of Poidebard's surveys, especially in the waters around the reef at Sidon (Frost 1973*b*, 76–86). Additionally, she has produced the first records of the similar works at Arwad (Frost 1972*b*, 101–2). At Tyre, inspection under water has shown that some of the man-made moles identified by Poidebard as protecting the southern harbour are in fact natural, and doubt has also been cast on the identification of the

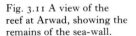

Fig. 3.11 A view of the reef at Arwad, showing the remains of the sea-wall.

small, closed, southern harbour, which now appears to have been dry land, at least in Roman times (Frost 1972*b*, 107–11).

The problems presented by these 'proto-harbours' along the Syrian and Lebanese coast, while constituting one of the most important elements in recent harbour research, are different from those encountered on most sites, where extensive artificial constructions may be found. Harbour surveys have been undertaken in many parts of the Mediterranean, often as part of a systematic search along a length of coastline, as with the surveys of Messrs Yorke and Davidson along the North African coast (Yorke & Davidson 1969). Other more intensive surveys have been carried out on several specific sites, including

Fig. 3.12 A map of the offshore remains at Carthage.

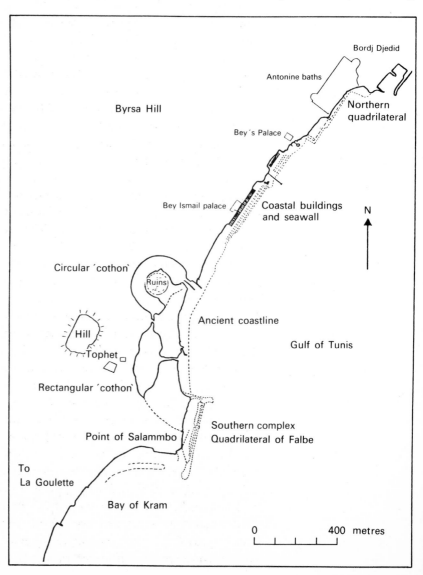

Apollonia in Libya (Flemming 1965; 1972), Athlit in Israel (Linder 1967), Cosa in Italy (Lewis 1973), Phaselis in Turkey (Blackman 1973*b*) and Kenchreai (Scranton & Ramage 1967) and Porto Cheli in Greece (Jameson 1973) among many others. Obviously much important data concerning the design of the totally man-made 'Portus' at the mouth of the Tiber emerged from the excavations at Fiumicino cited above (Testaguzza 1964). Dr N. C. Flemming has assembled the available evidence from around the Mediterranean, in most cases on the basis of personal inspection in an attempt to quantify sea-level changes during historic times by reference to archaeological evidence, with important results (Flemming 1969; Flemming *et al.* 1973). Finally, much of the surviving pictorial evidence has recently been reviewed with the intention of relating it to recent archaeological discoveries, and identifying further research problems (Williams 1976).

Before trying to assess the significance of such work over the past quarter century, it is worth looking in more detail at one particular site, in order to highlight some of the problems and potential of this area of research. The site in question is that of the harbours of ancient Carthage, the Phoenician colony near present-day Tunis which rose to be a Mediterranean power and engaged in an unsuccessful fight to the death with Rome, being finally razed to the ground in 146 B.C. A Roman colony was later founded on the site, and it maintained a prosperous existence into Byzantine times. The layout of the maritime remains is shown in fig. 3.12, as surveyed by a British team led by Messrs Yorke and Little in 1973, as part of the UNESCO 'Save Carthage' programme. The most prominent features are the two lakes lying behind the shoreline, which are now stagnant ponds, but which appear to be the remains of two enclosed harbours, known as 'cothons'. Along the coast itself there are, working up from the south, an apparent mound in the Bay of Kram, a large complex of masonry covering about 25 000 square metres known as the 'Quadrilateral of Falbe', some buildings extending into the sea (fig. 3.13) north of the lakes, and finally another area of offshore masonry lying in front of the Roman town baths of the Antonine period (Yorke & Little 1975; Yorke *et al.* 1976).

The first difficulty apparent on this site, as on many others, is the extent of the destruction of remains wrought by recent building. Here, a map drawn by the French traveller Falbe in 1833 is of some assistance (Yorke & Little 1975, fig. 2), and shows that the biggest changes have been effected on the lakes, and that the coastal features are still remarkably intact. The continued development of Carthage as a seaside suburb of Tunis makes the continuance of this immunity doubtful; it is this modern building which has inspired the current international research project. However, the remains at Carthage have not been totally obliterated by continued use of the site as a port, as is the case with so many other important ancient harbours, such as Marseilles or the Piraeus.

The next question which arises here, as on most Mediterranean harbour sites, is whether there has been any change in sea-level since classical times. The general conclusion reached by Dr N. C. Flemming for the whole of the western Mediterranean was that there had been no net eustatic change of sea-level to within an accuracy of ± 0.5 metres (1969, 85). However, on this site, in particular within the buildings which projected into the sea to the north of the lakes (fig. 3.13), there were floors and pavements lying 0.25–0.4 metres below current sea-level. Following present-day practice, it would be safe to assume that, on this particular stretch of coast, such floors would have been at least 1 metre above sea-level, so that the evidence suggests a subsidence of the land by about 1.25–1.50 metres. Such a movement is acceptable within current geological interpretations of this area (C. Vita-Finzi in Yorke & Little 1975, 98–9). Recent experience has shown that it is generally prudent to investigate for such a movement on all Mediterranean harbour sites before trying to interpret them.

Fig. 3.13 A view of the submerged foundations of coastal buildings of the Roman Imperial period at Carthage. Scale in 10 centimetre units.

The next hazard, which this site also shares with many others, lies in relating the observed remains to surviving documentary sources. In this case, the fundamental text is by Appian (*Libyca*, 96ff.) which is in turn derived from a lost account by Polybius of the siege and destruction of

Carthage in 146 B.C. This tells us that the round 'cothon' was for military use, and the rectangular one was for commercial vessels. He states that Scipio blocked the entrance to these 'cothons' with a mole, which reached out to a 'choma' or broad quay outside the city wall, which became the focal point of the struggle, and from which the final assault on the city was launched, with a force of over 4000 men and several siege engines. His description of the 'cothons' fits the two lakes too closely for coincidence, and this identification makes more sense when it is noted that they were apparently larger in the nineteenth century. It is naturally tempting to push the identification further and assume that the entrance to the 'cothons' ran to the south, that Scipio's mole is represented by the mound in the Bay of Kram, and that the 'choma' is now marked by the Quadrilateral of Falbe. However, this is pure supposition. The suggested entrance to the 'cothons' to the south is the only feature of this which is reasonably certain, although the argument is based on nautical commonsense, in view of the prevailing north-easterly winds, rather than archaeological evidence. On the other hand, the mounds detected in the Bay of Kram (fig. 3.12) have been shown to be natural sand waves (Yorke *et al.* 1976).

Ultimately, the interpretation of these remains depends on the archaeological evidence, and this wails at just the same point as most other harbour surveys, in the matter of dating. Some features are definitely from the Roman period, as with the northern complex which is evidently an extension of the second-century A.D. Roman baths. Other items can be shown to be probably Roman on the basis of their masonry styles; this includes nearly all the constructions within the Quadrilateral of Falbe itself. These, together with the known changes in sea-level, suggest that this whole area was probably dry in Roman times. However, most of the other elements cannot be securely dated, including the outer moles of the Quadrilateral, which may thus be either Roman or Punic. This is probably as far as one can go, at least until the current land excavations in the areas around the harbours have established a more detailed chronology for the site, and more is known about Punic harbour technology (Hurst 1975; 1976). However, the theory can be put forward for consideration that at least the southern end of this area must have been conceived as cover for the entrance to the 'cothons', and so may be Punic in origin (Yorke *et al.* 1976, 176). A final suggestion arises from the similarity in size and shape which this Quadrilateral bears to the southern closed port at Tyre (Frost 1972*b*, 110–11), and from the fact that both have recently been shown to have been seaside terraces in Roman times: is it not inconceivable that they both started life similarly as harbour installations?

Setting aside these difficulties of interpretation, what has been learned from these investigations? Several details of a Roman marine terrace of the second century A.D. have been noted which can possibly be related to a representation of waterfront buildings on a mosaic found in Carthage and now in the Bardo Museum (Yorke & Little 1975, fig. 6). A number of insights have been gained into harbour constructions of possibly Punic origins which, as has already been hinted, may make more sense if similar works at other sites are identified and surveyed. It must also be noted that, as the archetype for all Punic settlements, any information about Carthage is of great value, especially any relating to its maritime activities, since the Carthaginian hegemony was founded on a command of the sea. But, while these wider maritime aspects are of importance, perhaps the project's greatest significance lies in the way these features relate to and shed more light on the layout of the whole city and its evolution. In this case, as with so many Mediterranean centres, the harbour and other coastal installations determined the location and orientation of the whole town plan. It is thus extremely unsatisfactory when a land-based archaeologist simply notes in a report on such settlements that 'remains of harbour works can be distinguished under water', without making any attempt to survey or otherwise investigate them.

The idea of small, totally land-locked harbours, known as 'cothons', has been identified as a peculiarly Punic idea, although only two are known outside Carthage. One is on the North Africa coast at Mahdia, where the rectangular basin measures only 125 by 62.5 metres, while the other is on the margins of the Punic sphere of influence, at Motya in Sicily. In this latter case the entrance channel is only 5.38 metres wide in one place, and was probably only about 50 centimetres deep, so it could only have been used by very small boats (Isserlin 1971). The uses to which these structures could have been put are thus rather varied, and reduce considerably the points of similarity between them. In fact, it could be that the cultural relationship between them was tenuous, and that they rather represent the same type of solution to similar problems, namely the need to build a sheltered anchorage on a featureless, sandy shoreline. This was certainly the impetus behind the only other totally excavated harbour in the classical world, the hexagonal basin built by Trajan after A.D. 100 as an extension to the Claudian 'Portus' serving Rome; no-one would suggest Punic influence in this case.

As mentioned previously, the northern shores of the Mediterranean are generally more rocky than the southern, and so there are many more sheltered bays which served as anchorages from earliest times. The Greek and Roman cities which grew up alongside such bays continued to make use of them, although they generally liked to have in addition an enclosed inner port, within the circuit of the city walls, which could be closed off entirely, with a chain, in times of emergency. The analogy with a 'cothon' is obvious. A good example of this arrangement can be seen at Phaselis in Southern Turkey, where the city itself is on a peninsula with a small enclosed bay at one end of it, while on either side there are large bays which are naturally sheltered by the promontory, although the northern one has been improved with a mole (Blackman 1973*b*). One of the best endowed of this type of port was that at Piraeus, the harbour for Athens, with which it was linked from the fifth century B.C. by the linear fortifications known as the 'Long Walls'. Once again the town itself stood on a promontory, around which there were three enclosed bays – Zea, Munychia, and Kantharos – along with an outer anchorage in the Bay of Phaleron (Shaw 1972, 90–3). Another type of harbour plan is represented by that at Apollonia in Cyrenaica (modern Libya), as surveyed by Dr N. C. Flemming. Here, a land subsidence of 2–2.5 metres means that all the harbour works and wharves are now totally under water, and a lack of subsequent occupation has preserved them from disturbance; thus many details of quays and slipways can be seen, for which there are very few parallels elsewhere in the Mediterranean.

To the technology of harbour-works, the Romans brought two major innovations: experience in large-scale construction, and hydraulic concrete (i.e. concrete which will set under water). With these, they could construct satisfactory harbours almost wherever they liked. One of their largest and most impressive totally artificial ports is that of Caesarea in Israel: built for King Herod, it covers an area in excess of 10 ha (Linder & Raban 1975, 58–62). Another spectacular piece of Roman engineering was discovered by Bob Yorke and his colleagues on the Tunisian coast at Thapsus, where there is a mole over 1000 metres long, curving out from the shore, apparently totally man-made, whose construction would have involved the deposition of about 200,000 cubic metres of rubble (Flemming 1972, 162–3). And in Italy itself, along with the major works at 'Portus', there are several impressive Roman marine constructions, especially around the Bay of Naples, which have also attracted underwater investigators in recent years (Taylor 1965, 178–85).

A site which perhaps serves to summarise the whole subject of harbour research in the Mediterranean is that of the port of Alexandria, the Greek city planted on the Egyptian coast, later the terminus of the annual grain fleets supplying Rome. In fact, this site attracted what was probably the first survey of an ancient harbour, by a French engineer, Gaston Jondet (1916). The peninsula on which part of the later city was to stand, and the offshore reefs on either side of it, ensured that it was known as a major anchorage from Bronze Age times, being referred to in Book IV of the *Odyssey*. When the city was founded, work began on improving the harbour facilities, the most famous amenity undoubtedly being the 'Pharos' or lighthouse, massive fragments of which can still be found under water around the island it stood on (Frost 1975). Although the distinction between Hellenistic and Roman work is difficult to make, it is probable that a good deal of the remains mapped over the past century are in fact of Roman origin, and show the continued adaptation of this superb natural site for man's purposes (Taylor 1965, 160–2). Ultimately, the details of any harbour-works depend on the natural configuration of the site in question; in harbour studies there can be no standard patterns. Thus every additional piece of survey work or excavation on a classical port contributes something to the overall picture.

3.4 Ships of the early medieval period in north-west Europe

Maritime archaeology can be said to have started with the study of Viking ships, and the topic has been under constant review since the mid-nineteenth century, so that it is with much justification that Basil Greenhill has written: 'We know today more about the evolution of the ship within two hundred and fifty miles of the Skaw between A.D. 800–1200 than about the development of almost any other kind of ships and boats until modern times' (1976, 202). Of course, this situation has not arisen simply as a result of scholarly interest; little progress could have been made without numerous finds. These we owe to two customs prevalent in pagan times in these regions, the idea of sacrificing weapons and tools to the gods in pools and bogs, and the tradition of boat burial. The former is principally associated with the pre-Viking Age, while the latter practice, which has produced a total of over 400 recorded boats in graves in northern Europe, endured from the early Roman Iron Age until the end of the Viking period (Müller-Wille, 1974).

The ships of the Viking period (c. A.D. 800–1100), which made possible the phenomenal outpouring of Scandinavian raiding, colonisation, and trading of those centuries, represented the culmination of a boat-building tradition which can be traced back to the start of the northern Iron Age. Like the Mediterranean tradition described in section 3.1 it involved a 'shell-first' technique, the ship's lines being created with the strakes before any internal frames were inserted, although unlike the southern tradition the shell was formed with overlapping planks, caulked together. This clinker technique produced a more flexible hull, ideally suited for a small rowing boat, which has meant that the tradition has continued in northern Europe for the building of such craft into the present century. However, it was also capable of development for larger craft, including sailing vessels, and it is this evolution which can be traced through the first millennium A.D. As in other chapters, it is not proposed here to enter the shoals of the debate on whether this tradition drew its roots from the techniques of building skin boats, dug-outs, or whatever.

Possibly the earliest indisputable representative of this tradition is the Halsnoy boat of *c.* 350 B.C., a light rowing boat, fitted with rowlocks, and made up of a few light clinker planks sewn together (Brøgger & Shetelig 1951, 34). The light internal frames had been tied to cleats standing proud of the surface of the strakes, a technique which was extremely wasteful of wood, since each piece had to be fashioned from an initial timber of over twice the final thickness. Despite this disadvantage, this method remained in use until well into the Viking Age. Certain advances on the Halsnoy craft were evident in the Björke boat, found on an island near Stockholm and dating from *c.* A.D. 100. Only 7.16 metres long, it consisted of just three planks, the bottom one being shaped in a manner reminiscent of a dug-out, but these were attached to each other with iron rivets. A development on this 'extended dug-out' approach was represented by the fourth-century A.D. Nydam oak boat, which had five strakes on each side, attached to a 'keel-plank', a slightly heavier timber than the others, specially shaped to take the garboard strakes. In the same bog deposit as this vessel were several elements from another boat, built of fir, displaying several more 'advanced' characteristics, including a true keel of 'T-shaped' cross-section, and side formed of numerous narrow planks. Because of the wood used in it, Norway has been suggested as a place of manufacture, so that its features may represent a tradition parallel to that of the keel-plank boats described above, rather than an advance from them (Greenhill 1976, 182).

Dating from a couple of centuries later, the Gredstedbro boat from Denmark represents the first example of one on which the planks are fixed to the frames with dowels, rather than via protruding cleaks. While considerably more economical in both timber and labour, this method may have met with some suspicion initially, since it involved piercing the ship's hull; this may explain why the older technique remained in use for some craft until the tenth century. Of broadly similar construction was the Sutton Hoo ship, whose imprint in the sand was found in Suffolk in 1939: over 27 metres long, this example showed how large a vessel could be built within such a tradition. However, its form was still that of a large rowing boat; the question of whether it might have carried a sail remains open (Bruce-Mitford 1975, 420–3). It was apparently equipped with a permanent side-rudder, a new development in this period, and an essential prerequisite if one was to maintain control of a vessel under sail. This feature was also present on the larger Kvalsund boat from western Norway, which can be dated to around A.D. 700 (Brøgger & Shetelig 1951, 36–8).

Thus, on the eve of the Viking Age, around A.D. 750, the most complex type of craft in Scandinavian waters was a large open rowing boat, with a flexible, clinker-built hull, and light internal framing, of the Kvalsund type; such craft of the eighth century have been found in other Norwegian bogs, as at Bårset or Fjørtoft, as well as in the rich Swedish graves of Vendel and Valsgårde (Christensen 1972, 165). However, over the next century, certain technical developments took place which transformed these craft from rowing boats (with possible auxiliary sail in a following wind) to full sailing vessels with long-range capabilities. This transformation, which seems to have occurred quite rapidly in the later eighth century, involved deepening the keel, increasing the ship's freeboard, and strengthening the internal structure of the vessel by inserting cross-beams between the rib-heads. With these improvements, a ship could hold a course across the wind more surely, afford to heel more sharply with the wind, and harness the full power of a large square sail. The process of strengthening the ship to take the greater and more concentrated pressure of a sail also involved massive and complex frameworks for stepping the mast, and a thickened water-line strake (the *meginhufr*) linking the ends of the cross-beams and bracing the vessel longitudinally (Christensen 1972, 166–7).

The earliest of these Viking ships, and one of the most richly ornamented, was the Oseberg ship (fig. 3.14) found in 1903 in a Norwegian grave-mound along with a wide range of other goods and the bodies of two women. It has been dated by the style of the carvings on its stem and stern to *c*. A.D. 800. That the problems of harnessing wind power had not been satisfactorily solved in this instance is suggested by the way in

Fig. 3.14 The Oseberg Viking ship in its burial mound immediately after excavation.

which the mast-partner had cracked, and been repaired with two iron bands. The ship was 21.44 metres long and 5.10 metres in the beam, and generally of a light construction. Its profile was also unusual in having a very sharp angle at the *meginhufr*, as if the top two strakes on each side were viewed as being some-how additional to the ship's basic form. All these features, along with the ornate decorations executed on its stem and stern, indicated that here was a special craft designed for use in sheltered waters by persons of high rank (Brøgger & Shetelig 1951, 108–15). While this might suggest that it should not necessarily be taken as typical of craft at this transitional period, the recently found contemporary ship at Klastad, in Norway, exhibits essentially the same form, but without the fine ornamentation, and with a cargo of whet-stones which strongly suggests a working vessel (Greenhill 1976, 211).

From the second half of the ninth century come the Tune and Gokstad ships, also found in Norwegian grave-mounds at the end of the nineteenth century. The Tune ship was the smaller and less well preserved, displaying a high standard of workmanship, although with surprisingly little freeboard for a sailing ship (Brøgger & Shetelig 1951, 104–7). The Gokstad ship, the largest and most impressive of this group of Norwegian grave-boats, obviously represents an eminently sea-worthy vessel; it is 23.33 metres in length and 6.25 metres in the beam. The structure was more strongly built than earlier grave-boats had been, with heavy cross-beams set low in the vessel in a manner anticipating later medieval practice (Brøgger & Shetelig 1951, 79–103). However, the context in which the boat was found, and the fact that the strakes are lashed to the frames via cleats, suggests that this may also have been a prestige craft constructed along traditional lines, and not necessarily representing common late ninth-century practice. Although such a vessel could have undertaken a long-distance voyage – a replica made a satisfactory passage to the U.S.A. in 1893 – it seems unlikely that it was used for more than local trips (Greenhill 1976, 212). The Ladby boat, on the contrary, represented with its speed and seaworthiness the type of vessel used in raids across the North Sea: found in 1935 in a burial mound on Funen (Denmark), it had a length of 20.6 metres and a beam of only 2.9 metres (Brøgger & Shetelig 1951, 47; Greenhill 1976, 214–16). The load-carrying capabilities of this type of vessel were graphically demonstrated by a group of Danish scouts in 1967, who satisfactorily loaded four horses onto a replica of the Ladby boat, sailed it around, and unloaded them again, without difficulty or mishap (Crumlin-Pedersen 1970, 9).

Thus far, the development of northern European shipbuilding until Viking times has been described purely in terms of finds from bog deposits (for earlier periods) and grave-ships (for later centuries). The weaknesses of such material were discussed in section 1.1, so the account thus far must be regarded as inherently suspect, especially the evolutionary sequence implicit in it, because none of the finds may be representative of its period. This explains the great importance attached to the recent discovery and excavation of five vessels from around A.D. 1000 lying in shallow water in Roskilde Fjord, Denmark. Local tradition had retained knowledge of 'Queen Margrethe's ships' at this particular spot, but it was not until 1956 that divers first located timbers. Underwater investigations then proceeded until 1959, when work was stopped until a coffer dam could be placed around the site, and the water removed to allow a conventional excavation; this eventually took place in the summer of 1962 (fig. 3.15). The find consisted of two warships, two trading vessels, and a small craft which might have been a fishing boat or ferry, all apparently sunk deliberatately to block a channel. It thus represented a cross-section of ship types in use at that date in Denmark, although unfortunately all stripped of their fittings. The surviving parts of each vessel were raised, conserved, and put on display in a purpose-built museum at Roskilde (Olsen & Crumlin-Pedersen 1967; Crumlin-Pedersen 1970; 1972).

Fig. 3.15 Aerial photograph of the excavation of the five vessels of *c*. A.D. 1000 discovered at Skuldelev in Roskilde Fjord, Denmark, showing their arrangement and the temporary coffer dam surrounding the workings.

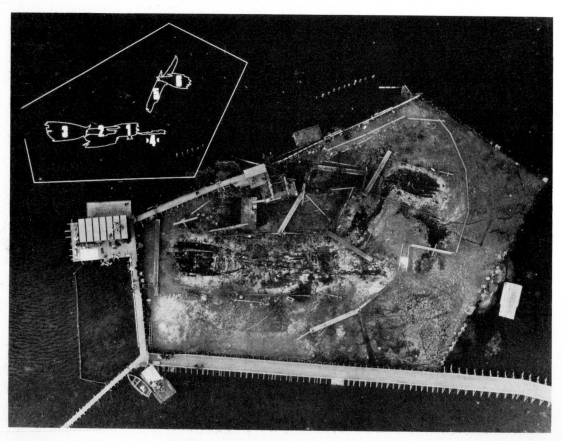

Of the two warships, one (Wreck 2) was a true longship about 28 metres long, of the type which might have taken part in the early eleventh-century Danish raids on England, carrying a force of fifty to sixty men. It was built entirely of oak, but little more can be said about its construction, since less than a quarter of its hull survived. The other warship (Wreck 5) was a smaller vessel, 18 metres long and 2.5 metres in breadth, possessing twelve oar holes on each side. While the main portion of the hull was similarly of oak, the three uppermost planks were of ash, which may indicate that this represents an example of the ship-type known to the English as *aesc* (i.e. ash), the class from which many devastating raids were made. This vessel was in many respects similar to the Ladby boat.

The two trading vessels were also of different types. The larger of the two (Wreck 1) was a sturdy craft (fig. 3.16) about 16.5 metres long and 4.6 metres in the beam. The planking was of pine, the keel and lower internal timbers were of oak, and the upper portions were of lime and pine. It is probable that this example represents a *knarr*, the type of vessel in which voyaging across the northern Atlantic was undertaken; it thus illuminates our understanding of the Viking colonisation of

Fig. 3.16 Skuldelev boat 1, the *knarr*, under reconstruction at the new Ship Museum at Roskilde, Denmark.

Iceland, Greenland, and (briefly) Vinland. The other merchant vessel (Wreck 3) was smaller, being only 13.5 metres long and 3.2 metres broad. It had a half-deck fore and aft, and an open hold amidships. There were three oar-holes on the port side forward, and two starboard, while at the stern there appears to have been only one on each side; presumably these were for manoeuvring rather than regular propulsion. The overall construction was light, perhaps so that the vessel could be dragged overland for short distances where necessary. This craft could have been used in the coasting trade around the Baltic and North Sea. Wreck 6 proved to be an enigma; it was only 12 metres long and 2.5 metres broad, had no deck, and its thwarts were set too low to be used by oarsmen. While it evidently lay in the mainstream of Viking nautical technology, it cannot be paralleled closely by any other remains, or by any literary descriptions; it might be a ferry, or just possibly a fishing boat.

While these five wrecks remain unique, it is difficult to discuss developmental sequences for each of the types; certainly it would be unwise to view them all as evolutions from the Gokstad ship, or any of the other grave finds. In terms of date and function, the two traders can be compared with the Graveney boat, found in the Kent marshes in 1970 and probably built around the mid tenth century A.D. (see fig. 1.6, (p. 18). About a third of the boat at the bows was missing, although it was possible to calculate that her overall length was a little over 14 metres and her beam about 3 metres. She was clinker built, but with a relatively flat bottom and only a keel-plank, to which the stern post was joined at an angle of about 30°, a design otherwise only evidenced in pictures. Relatively heavily built, this vessel was obviously intended for the carriage of bulk cargoes around the coasts of south-east England and the southern North Sea (Fenwick 1972; Greenhill 1976, 221–6). At the very least, she demonstrates that not all trading vessels in the North Sea at this period were of the pure Scandinavian type found at Roskilde.

In popular imagination, as in contemporary monastic annals, the Vikings are inextricably linked with raiding, piracy, and plunder, in which activities the superiority of their ships and seamanship played no small part. However, the Viking expansion overseas involved not only raiding, but also trading and settlement, giving rise to regular maritime trade-routes reaching from Scandinavia into the Mediterranean and across the North Atlantic to Greenland and North America. Of this activity there is little direct archaeological evidence, since even the trading vessels excavated to date have been stripped of their cargoes and fittings before abandonment. Thus, while the nautical archaeology of north-west Europe during the Viking period has made considerable progress, maritime studies in the wider sense have yet to make a start.

3.5 Post-medieval ship construction

With the cessation of the custom of boat burial in northern Europe after
A.D. 1000, the supply of archaeological material from ships and boats
dries up, and evidence relating to the following five centuries is extremely limited (see section 4.1). At the end of this period, European
naval technology had reached the stage when trans-oceanic voyages
were conceivable, and by the end of the sixteenth century European
seamen were in undisputed command of the oceans of the world.
Although other developments, such as the production of efficient fire-
arms, were partly responsible for this, the evolution of the three-masted
ship was a prerequisite, so that any knowledge concerning its origins is
correspondingly significant (Cipolla 1965). The crucial advances were
apparently made in the fifteenth century, since earlier vessels are
demonstrably related to types known in the first millennium A.D.; for
example, Henry V of England's great ship, the *Grace Dieu*, launched in
1416 and now lying in the Hamble River in Hampshire, has a clinker-
built hull derived from the Viking tradition (Prynne 1968). While
stability in nautical technology was not reasserted for several decades
after 1500, the conventional starting-date for the post-medieval period,
the archaeological evidence concerning even these final stages in the
transition is negligible, and the rest of this chapter will be concerned
predominantly with the study of ships that existed between about 1550
and 1800.

Alongside the archaeological evidence, documentary and representa-
tional sources are available for such research, and the relative importance of the three types of evidence varies according to topic and
period. In many respects, written evidence alone continues to be
inadequate until after 1800, since few writers set out consciously to
describe such a complex object as a ship and many of those who touched
on the subject were not themselves practising shipwrights or naval
architects. And even when the writer has an evident authority, as did the
compilers of the English Admiralty Establishments from the mid
seventeenth century onwards, who were setting specifications for shipbuilders to follow, there is still the question of the extent to which they
were obeyed. At the same time, students of the archaeological or pictorial
evidence must make considerable use of the more reliable written
sources in the interpretation of detail (e.g. Mainwaring 1644; Witsen
1671; Chapman 1768).

More revealing from a technical point of view are ship models and
plans, and as builders came increasingly to rely on such aids, particularly in the course of the eighteenth century, the significance of the
archaeological evidence is correspondingly reduced. The earliest
technical drawings of ships appeared towards the end of the sixteenth
century; in England, the work of Matthew Baker working in the 1580s

is particularly notable. During the seventeenth century, Admiralty boards and the governors of the great chartered companies were often provided with models of proposed vessels before authorising construction, but, while these are probably fairly accurate as regards lines, they reveal little in the way of constructional details. Plans become more widespread during the eighteenth century (Lyon 1974): the English Navy Board required detailed constructional drawings from 1716 onwards, and these became increasingly comprehensive as the century progressed. So far as the archaeological remains of such vessels are concerned, the importance of the evidence is thereby reduced to ascertaining the extent to which the established specifications were followed in practice, or modified in the course of the life of the vessel. But these considerations apply only to naval ships, and those of some of the more bureaucratic chartered trading companies; so far as the general run of merchant shipping was concerned, little was recorded until the end of the Age of Sail, so that the archaeological evidence remains paramount through to the early nineteenth century.

At the same time, it should be remembered that the basic premisses of naval architecture during these three centuries remained fairly constant, and that the principles and concepts involved are still fully understood, since similar vessels are still being built and sailed (e.g. sail training ships). The archaeological evidence is thus only relevant to a study of the details of ship construction, and their development over the centuries, and it is with such details that the rest of this chapter is concerned. This represents a level of investigation different from that described in sections 3.1 or 3.4.

Before the emergence of the basic three-masted galleon in the middle of the sixteenth century, the type which was to remain dominant for several centuries, the carrack was the standard vessel for oceanic voyaging, being used in the initial explorations of Asiatic and American waters. These great towering ships were probably first developed within the Mediterranean, but the form was soon adopted and modified by the seamen of Atlantic Europe. One variety is represented by the *Mary Rose*, an English naval carrack built in 1511, rebuilt in 1536, sunk off Portsmouth in 1545, and rediscovered in 1967–71 (Rule 1972; 1973; McKee 1973). While the extent to which her features are typical of those of other vessels in the English, or any other, fleets of that period must always remain in doubt, her remains are of prime importance in illuminating the general construction techniques of this type of ship, and the role she was designed to fulfil in naval warfare. Concerning the latter topic, she reflects an important moment of transition. On the one hand, she carried over 200 troops, along with an armament of 91 ship guns, 50 hand guns, 250 longbows, 150 Morris pikes, and 150 bills (McKee 1973, 50); the final objective of battle was evidently to board one's opponent, in the style of earlier medieval warfare. But the *Mary Rose*, when built in 1511, was also one of the first English ships to possess gun-ports. This invention, traditionally credited to a Brest shipbuilder working in 1501, allowed heavy artillery to be placed low down in the ship's hull, thus permitting a full battery to be carried without prejudicing the vessel's stability, and thereby inducing a revolution in tactics; the destruction of enemy ships from afar took over from closing and boarding. The details of these early gun-port lids have been elucidated by the two so far discovered on the site of the *Mary Rose* (Rule 1976). This ship was evidently equipped to undertake both types of warfare, and her final loss may be ascribed to the overloading which resulted.

So far as the details of her construction are concerned, only a limited amount has emerged so far, since the object of recent excavations has been to define the extent of the surviving remains. It is now clear that she is lying at an angle of 60° to starboard, with little of her port side surviving, but nearly all of the starboard side to above main-deck level being still there (fig. 3.17). It effectively represents a cut-away of a sixteenth-century English carrack which from an information view-point is almost as good as a complete ship, and in terms of public display and access is infinitely better. At the same time, a few points have emerged concerning the details of her construction: for example, it is now known that her hull was carvel built, while her upperworks were of clinker construction, and that nearly all her fastenings were of wood rather than metal.

The *Mary Rose* has often been compared to the Swedish warship *Wasa* (1628), since both ships were the pride of their respective navies, capsized on public occasions, and have recently been rediscovered and investigated. However, the comparison stops there, since the *Mary Rose* was an eminently successful warship with many years service behind her when she went down, while the *Wasa* capsized on her maiden voyage as a result of design faults. The *Wasa* was relocated in 1956 and finally raised in 1961, at that time the oldest surviving named ship in the world (see fig. 1.5, p. 16) (Ohrelius 1962; Franzen 1966). Her importance lay in the fact that she represented a ship as delivered by her builders, undamaged and unused, although the extent to which she was typical of her period must always be in some doubt, since she was undoubtedly

Fig. 3.17 The elevation of the stern of the *Mary Rose* (1545) in the Solent; the stern-post and transom planking as surveyed (*left*) and a reconstruction of how this can be related to the original form of the ship's stern (*right*).

Stern-post

Planking

a prestige ship, and, presumably, most contemporary vessels were more seaworthy. Her discovery has led to the confirmation of several constructional details which, although evidenced elsewhere, had been queried by many researchers. For example, the fact that her decks rise up towards the bow and stern (fig. 3.18) has settled one controversy, as has also the discovery that her mast is raked backwards by 8 or 9°. Other features which appear surprising in the light of later practice include the placing of the galley down in the hold amidships (rather than in the forecastle), and the huge whipstaff and tiller which control the rudder (Naish 1968). Considerable information has also emerged regarding the sails, and the way in which they had been stored (Bengtsson 1975).

A year after the *Wasa* capsized, the Dutch East Indiaman *Batavia* was wrecked on the Houtman Abrolhos, islands lying off the coast of Western Australia; its remains now lie in 2–6 metres of water, exposed to the full force of the Indian Ocean swell. Despite this, excavations by the Western Australian Museum, beginning in 1973, have revealed a substantial section of the ship's stern port quarter, buried under tons of dead coral heads (see fig. 1.8, p. 21) (Green 1975; Baker & Green 1976). Even though this represented only a small portion of the total vessel, and no part of the keel had survived, a great deal has been learned from

Fig. 3.18 The lower gun-deck of the *Wasa*, looking forward, after clearing.

it. Possibly most surprising was the discovery that, for reasons unknown, the ship had been double-planked throughout below the waterline. In addition, she had been sheathed with pine boards holding in a layer of pitch and animal hair, a standard protection against the ravages of the ship-worm, *Teredo navalis*, although in this instance it had been further reinforced by thousands of closely spaced large-headed nails, creating a further iron-rust layer on the outside of the hull. Another unusual feature of the planking was the way in which several strakes had been bent through 90° around the port quarter, forming a continuum between the side planking and the diagonal planking of the ship's square stern. Many details of the massive and complex lodging knees supporting this junction are also unparalleled elsewhere.

Much of the uniqueness of the features on these ships undoubtedly arises from the lack of comparable wrecks, although Dutch vessels are better represented than those of most other nationalities. A number of Dutch East Indiamen have been investigated in recent years (see section 3.7), and even the most broken up of these sites can yield interesting constructional details. For example, the wreck-site of the *Kennemerland* (1664), while containing no extensive structural remains, has nevertheless produced evidence of a particular type of trenail in use, apparently of a peculiarly Dutch pattern, as well as details on the varieties of timber used in its various components (Price & Muckelroy 1977). Among eighteenth-century East Indiamen, however, the most comprehensive information can be expected from the wreck of the *Amsterdam* (1749), now lying on the beach near Hastings in Sussex (Marsden 1972; 1974). The preliminary investigations of 1969–71 established the extent of the surviving hull, showing that she is complete to the level of the upper deck, along with other interesting features. For example, the presence of transverse partitions on the lower deck fore and aft of the main hatch was unexpected, and has been interpreted as the provision of additional stores for excess cargo (Marsden 1974, 142–3).

As an example of what can be learned from fragmentary hull remains of a ship for which some documentary evidence is available, the wreck site of the *Dartmouth* is instructive. This Fifth-Rate Naval vessel was built in 1655, and wrecked in 1690 on an island in the Sound of Mull, western Scotland, its remains being rediscovered in about 8 metres of water in 1973 (Adnams 1974). An area of the hull had been preserved, pinned down by mounds of iron ballast, including about 5.5 metres of the keel aft of midships, and a section of the starboard side 4 metres wide (fig. 3.19) (Martin 1978). The documentary material relating to this vessel is considerable, including papers in the Admiralty collection concerning her use and maintenance, a set of almost-contemporary drafts of naval vessels by William Keltridge (1684), and a sketch by

William van der Velde the Younger which is almost certainly of this particular ship (see fig. 6.1, p. 218) (Robinson 1958; Martin 1978, fig. 1). Nevertheless, the investigation of these remains has revealed several unsuspected features.

The keel itself was of interest for a complete scarph preserved in it; this had been cut vertically, which came as an initial surprise, since it had often been assumed that such a joint would have been cut horizontally to give greater vertical strength. Those on the *Wasa*'s keel are so cut (Naish 1968, 12–13), although those on the *Victory* (1763) are cut vertically like the *Dartmouth*'s (Longridge 1955, 7). Above the keel was a massive elm component, trapezoidal in section and over a metre wide, forming a rising deadwood beginning only a metre or so aft of midships, and reflecting the exceptionally fine lines of this ship. Furthermore, the frames were chocked into this piece or, further aft, simply butted against it in a manner very different from previously recorded practice. The intention seems to have been to strengthen the fine run aft of the vessel, as well as save on scarce-grown shaped timbers, which would otherwise have been required if the frames had run continuously across the keel.

Fig. 3.19 A photomosaic of the structural remains on the site of the *Dartmouth*; the keel and associated timbers can be seen along to top left-hand edge of the remains, with the starboard frames running down from them.

There may have been a similar desire for economy in the ribs themselves, in which the frame joints are chocked in a way previously thought to have been introduced by the Admiralty in 1714 (Longridge 1955, 19). Another implication of these chocks is that the ship's skeleton could not have been pre-erected, since it could only have kept its shape with the assistance of the strakes and ceiling planking.

The manner in which the strakes had been fixed to the frames was also of interest, since, in addition to the even spread of the original trenails, extra fastenings had been added to 'tighten' the aging hull in places of weakness, or to reinforce an old trenail which was working loose (Martin 1978, fig. 20). The pinning arrangements are even more irregular around the lowest three planks, which are known to have been replaced, along with the keel, in 1678; here the trenails fixing an unusually narrow strake actually cut through the join between it and its neighbours, while elsewhere care has apparently been taken to avoid old trenail holes in the underlying frames and deadwood. One strake had a rectangular patch let into it, presumably to stop up a crack which had developed.

Although only a portion of the bottom of the vessel had survived intact, there was considerable indirect evidence concerning the construction of her upperworks. For example, the spacing of the main-deck beams was reflected in the joints cut into a lodging knee recovered from the site. The thickness of the hull in these areas was evidenced by the length of the scupper liners found; these showed that, while at main-deck level the framing would have been within a couple of centimetres of the thickness lower down, higher up in the superstructure it was probably only half that thickness. Finally, a 15 centimetres thick elm timber discovered at one end of the site has been identified as a wale from above the waterline; this featured a 70 centimetres long recess, almost certainly indicating the size of the gun-ports.

This brief summary has only been able to touch on a few of the interesting constructional features which have emerged from this investigation; for a full discussion of the many technical and historical implications of these findings, reference must be made to the full report (Martin 1978). In structural details and building methods this example has clearly indicated the inadequacies of the written record; however, for the overall lines, appearance, and dimensions of the ship one is still beholden to that record. The fundamentals of post-medieval ship technology are not likely to be questioned by such archaeological research, but many important details can be understood in no other way.

3.6 The Spanish Armada, 1588

After two centuries of rapid development, naval architecture in Europe regained stability around the middle of the sixteenth century, after which basic techniques and concepts remained substantially unchanged for nearly three centuries. With English shipping the new era can be dated from Hawkins's reform and re-equipping of the Royal Navy in the 1570s, while in Spain it was associated with the appearance of galleons in the Americas' fleets, at the instigation of Don Alvaro de Bazan. The first major naval campaign involving the new generation of craft was thus the 'Enterprise of England' launched by Philip II of Spain in 1588, the dispatch of over 130 ships in *La Armada Felicissima* to establish control over the English Channel, and effect the transfer of the Army of Flanders into Kent (Mattingly 1959). But this fleet involved more than just a number of ships; it was equipped with a myriad of stores, armaments, and other *matériel*, drawn from many countries, and reflecting the whole range of sixteenth-century technology. It is this, along with the insight given into contemporary shipbuilding, that gives the study of the Spanish Armada from both archaeological and historical sources its wider significance.

That there is an archaeological aspect to the Spanish Armada results from another of its unique features. Around a third of the whole fleet was subsequently wrecked on the coasts of northern Britain and Ireland, on account of a number of factors, including an unusually stormy September, the inexperience of many of the crews in these waters, and, as described below, the damage sustained by many of the ships (Green 1906; Martin 1975). Furthermore, the locations of many of these wrecks are relatively well documented, since the whereabouts of any survivors were of great concern to the English authorities in Ireland. Wherever possible they were rounded up, closely questioned, and disposed of by the sword or, occasionally, by ransom; their verbatim statements furnish the prime evidence regarding these wreck-sites. The exceptional circumstances of these vessels also meant that many of them ran ashore in places where wrecks do not usually occur, with the result that some of them now lie in sheltered bays more than usually favourable to the survival of archaeological evidence (e.g. the *Trinidad Valencera*).

Thus the remains from the Spanish Armada reflect nautical activity at a particularly significant moment, and are themselves unusually well preserved. Furthermore, the constituents of this fleet had been assembled from the resources of all of Philip II's territories, including the Americas, Southern Italy, and the Low Countries, as well as the whole of the Iberian peninsula (Martin 1975, fig. 1). So far as the ships themselves are concerned, the ports of origin of those wrecks which have been investigated recently graphically illustrate the range of this material. The famous Tobermory galleon, which has been periodically salvaged since the seventeenth century and is almost certainly the *San Juan de Sicilia* (Hardie 1912), was an argosy from Ragusa (modern Dubrovnik) in the Adriatic. The *Trinidad Valencera*, now lying in Glenagivney Bay, County Donegal, was a Venetian merchantman, a grain carrier which had been requisitioned by Philip II in Sicily in 1587 (Martin 1975, 189–224). The *Girona*, whose remains were scattered around Lacada Point, County Antrim, was a royal galleass (a type of warship equipped with both a full compliment of rowers and a full three-masted galleon-rig) from Naples (Stenuit 1972). The only one of these vessels to have originated in Spain was the *Santa Maria de la Rosa*, which came to grief in Blasket Sound in south-west Ireland (Martin 1975, 23–135). And finally *El Gran Grifon*, which ended up on Fair Isle, was a hulk from Rostock in the Baltic (Martin 1972; 1975, 137–87). The Spanish Armada thus represents a veritable microcosm of late sixteenth-century European society, at least in its naval, technical, and economic aspects.

As mentioned above, one of the most interesting results of investigations to date has been the light they have shed on the construction of some of the vessels involved, and the evidence that has emerged to support the idea that the Spanish ships were, in many cases, not able to stand the rigours of the North Atlantic. It is perhaps significant that only one of the ships listed above came from a region bordering the

Atlantic, and that one, the *Santa Maria de la Rosa*, built at San Sebastian, gave several indications that it may have been constructed by someone versed in Mediterranean practice (Martin 1973, 448–50). The remains of this ship, located in 1968 after an exhaustive search of the stormy and treacherous Blasket Sound, were restricted to the ballast mound, under which lay a part of the bottom of the ship, apparently from the fore-part (fig. 3.20). Selective excavation uncovered the salient features of the hull remains underlying the ballast stones, including frames, the keelson, and a mast stepping box. The last showed signs of hasty workmanship, reflecting the fact that this vessel had a new mainmast installed at Corunna on 10 July 1588. The lower hull appeared to have been solid framed throughout, with every alternate timber being 20 centimetres wide and 30 deep, and the intermediate ones 15 centimetres wide and 25 deep. The ballast was partitioned with 'shifting boards', but no ceiling planking was found, except around the mast-step.

Although the basic distinction between Mediterranean and Atlantic traditions of shipbuilding can be overstated, the fact remains that this

Fig. 3.20 A view of some of the frames uncovered on the site of the *Santa Maria de la Rosa* (1588) in Blasket Sound, Eire. Scale in feet.

vessel was evidently different in certain fundamental respects from, say, the English warships opposing her. The keelson, frames, and strakes excavated in Blasket Sound were surprisingly slight for a vessel of 945 tons, and seemed to reflect a design philosophy relying on structural integrity for its strength, rather than on a massive internal skeleton, a concept usually associated with Mediterranean practice. Obviously, such a hull would be exceedingly vulnerable to even local shot-damage, and herein may lie one clue to the difficulties faced by many of these ships off Ireland. In the case of the *Santa Maria de la Rosa*, it is recorded that she had been hit 'between the wind and the water' (i.e. in her hull) (Martin 1975, 131); her excavated remains now make it clear how grave the consequences of such damage would have been. The Armada's supreme commander, the Duke of Medina Sidonia, appears to have been aware of the fragility of many of his vessels before he sailed, but the only response he got from his master, Philip II, was to the effect that 'it is still the fact that the Levant ships sail constantly to England' (Martin 1975, 134). True; but not usually under regular bombardment from the Royal Navy.

The wreck of the *Trinidad Valencera* has also yielded structural evidence, although only in the form of large unconnected timbers. In this instance, the site was more notable for the survival of much of the ship's cargo, part of a siege train to be used by the invading army once it had landed in England. The collection included the dismantled elements of gun-carriages and carts, especially wheels (fig. 3.21), axles and limbers, as well as smaller items such as scaling poles, small arms (fig. 2.12, p. 51), a barrel of gunpowder, and water flasks for the troops. But most spectacular of all were the five bronze cannon (fig. 3.22), including two of a set of 50-pounders which, while they had probably been mounted for shipboard use, were intended for a land siege train. This assemblage has highlighted an aspect of the Armada which is often overlooked, its role as a supply squadron. Although the Army of Flanders was to be the heart of the invasion force, the fleet itself was carrying a further 20 000 men and much-needed additional supplies.

The *Trinidad Valencera* site also illustrated the significance of these wrecks as a cross-section of late sixteenth-century society. Her Venetian origins were betrayed not only by the Venetian cannon found on board (fig. 3.22), but also by sherds of characteristic brightly painted Venetian earthenware. More surprisingly, a few pieces of Chinese porcelain were also found, reflecting the amenities enjoyed by the superior officers. The range of ordinary Spanish wares from this site was also of interest, since some items, notably the olive jars and plates from Seville, were apparently derived from the ship's first mustering at Cadiz, while other pottery types represented stores taken on at the final assembly point at Lisbon. These latter types were also present on the wreck of the *Santa*

Maria de la Rosa, along with a ware believed to have been made near San Sebastian, the ship's home port. The main importance of the excavations on the *Girona* site also lay in its contents, in particular with the jewellery and other personal possessions of the many noblemen among the hundreds who perished when she went down (Stenuit 1972). An interesting study has been made by Professor M. Dolley on the coinage from this site, reflecting as it does the types in circulation among these people in 1588 (Dolley 1974).

However, in historical studies the Spanish Armada is considered above all as a naval enterprise which failed, and the debate as to why this happened has gone on for many centuries, and is not over yet. Undoubtedly the most important archaeological contribution to these discussions so far has been in the demonstration that the old theory of inadequate, although massive, Spanish ships has some truth in it. However, there is another area of research in which the material evidence has some relevance, and that is in the question of the armament of the Spanish fleet. It has always been clear that the English artillery had proved more effective than the Spanish, both in the running battles up the Channel and at Gravelines. In the latter encounter several Spanish ships were disabled by gunfire, and one (the *Maria Juan*) sunk outright, while the English fleet reported no major structural damage. The modern debate was started by the late Professor M. A. Lewis in a

Fig. 3.21 A gun-carriage wheel as excavated from the sand on the site of the *Trinidad Valencera* (1588) in Kinnagoe Bay, County Donegal, Eire.

book (1961) which suggested, in essence, that the Spanish fleet had been equipped with a preponderance of heavy short-range cannon for fighting at close quarters, while the English had concentrated on lighter-shotted, long-range guns for stand-off battles in which they could use the greater manoeuvrability of their ships to advantage. However, this thesis remained less than totally convincing in view of the English fleet's evident superiority at short range (as at Gravelines) as well as long range. This qualification has now been eliminated as a consequence of researches in the Spanish archives by Dr I. A. A. Thompson (1975) showing that as compared to the English the Spanish were inferior in all types of armament.

The archaeological contribution to this debate can be considered under two heads. First, there is the question of whether material from the ships themselves actually matches the documentary evidence. A direct comparison is possible in the case of the shot recovered from the *Santa Maria de la Rosa* (Thompson 1975, 371); agreement is satisfactory if one assumes that the 50-pound shot found were only being carried as stores or ballast. Surprisingly, the full cannons from the *Trinidad Valencera* and the Tobermory galleon are in fact larger than had been predicted, although it is clear that only twenty to thirty such large land pieces were pressed into service on a few of the leading vessels, and that they remained exceptional, being very poorly supported by

Fig. 3.22 A drawing of some bronze ordnance from the wrecks of ships in the Spanish Armada; a 50-pounder cannon, a 6-pounder and a 4-pounder from the *Trinidad Valencera* (*upper*), and a 3-pounder demi-saker from *El Gran Grifon* (*bottom*).

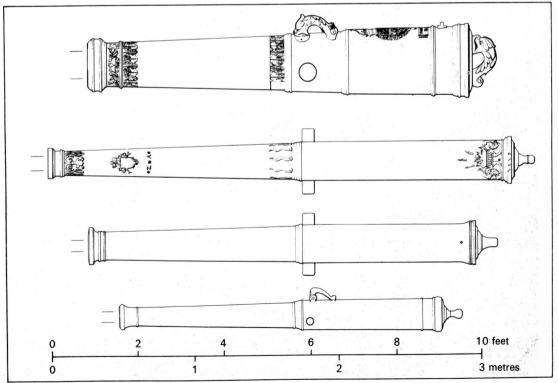

pieces firing shot in the 18- to 48-pound range. Little can be deduced from the cannon recovered from the *Girona* site, since most of the armament from this vessel had been jettisoned previously to allow her to take on more people. The *Gran Grifon*, twelve of whose pieces, out of a total of thirty-eight, have been identified on site, presents a somewhat different case, being the flagship of the supply squadron, and therefore not a leading fighting vessel. Her armament contained a fair number of obsolete items, including some wrought iron, stave-built guns, and appears totally defensive in character (Martin 1972). The aim was apparently to hold off any attackers with light-shotted, long-range guns, a strategy which patently failed in this particular case, since it is known that several English ships closed with her on 3 August, and inflicted considerable damage. Although the second-rate character of this armament remains clear, the contrast between it and that of the first-rate fighting vessels is now less striking in view of the recently revised assessment of the strength of the latter (Martin 1972, 69).

The other contribution from the archaeological evidence to this debate concerns the quality of the Spanish equipment. The inferiority of Spanish fire-power, even as now assessed, is not sufficiently marked to account alone for the discrepancy in effectiveness, so it has been suggested that another factor may have been that the Spanish pieces were frequently technically inadequate. There is some evidence from the shot recovered from the *Santa Maria* that it may have been excessively brittle, as a result of quenching immediately after casting (Wignall 1973). The bore of one of the *Gran Grifon* bronze cannon, which is markedly misaligned and had broken at some stage, also suggests technical inadequacies (Martin 1972, 63). The sample is, however, too small to make a firm assessment of its significance, and balance it against factors such as the inadequacies of the ships themselves, or the possible inexperience of the Spanish crews.

It also remains to be proved that this discrepancy in firepower was tactically decisive. Despite this handicap, the Spanish fleet managed to proceed up Channel in good order, thanks to commendable fleet discipline and seamanship. Once it had anchored off Calais, however, the fatal weakness in the whole plan became evident; there was no way of linking up with Parma's army without a secure deep-water port, and French neutrality forbade the use of any of the ones available on that coast. The English use of the old stratagem of fire-ships was thus only too obvious, and once the close order of the fleet had been broken, the enterprise was doomed. The inconclusive engagement off Gravelines only confirmed the outcome, although the damage inflicted during it undoubtedly weakened the ability of many ships to survive the voyage back to Spain. Much more could be written about the strategies pursued by each side, and the extent to which they achieved their objectives, or acquitted themselves honourably, but such considerations are beyond the scope of the present work.

In the last analysis, the archaeological contribution to these researches in naval history is limited, if only because to date all the evidence has concerned only one side in the confrontation, and, except in the case of investigations into ship's structure, has done little more than confirm the documentary evidence. It is significant, for example, that in Dr Thompson's paper on Armada guns (1975), the contribution from maritime archaeology is only mentioned in a footnote. It should also be remembered that the historical significance of the Spanish Armada itself has been questioned, especially by Continental historians; it settled nothing, and war between England and Spain continued for another two decades, punctuated by further armadas from both sides (Graham 1972). However, what remains undiminished from an archaeological point of view is the importance of the collections from these wrecks as representative of the products and technology of Europe at the end of the sixteenth century. In a very real sense, this material together represents one large and precisely dated closed group.

3.7 The expansion of Europe, sixteenth to nineteenth centuries

The rapid advance in nautical technology from about A.D. 1400 was associated with several other important developments besides the elaboration of naval warfare, probably the most important of which was the sudden enlargement of the sphere of influence of European nations to encompass the whole world. The story of this process, beginning with the Portuguese advance down the African coast in the mid-fifteenth century, is too well known to require repetition; it is sufficient to note that by the middle of the sixteenth century there were few areas of the globe, apart from Australia and the interior of Africa, which had not been visited by Europeans and, more importantly, brought within the European economic system. In this expansion of influence, the twin European technical achievements of effective fire-arms and reliable trans-oceanic shipping are among the prime causes (Cipolla 1965). Of course, there was a two-way operation of cause and effect in these matters; the demands of overseas trade in turn stimulated the development of more efficient vessels. Another important point to note regarding this first phase of European expansion is that, with the exception of the Americas, which were regarded in a somewhat different light, and will thus be dealt with separately in section 3.8, activity was restricted to the economic sphere, and most traders tried hard to avoid accepting any political responsibility for the lands in which they operated.

This dominance of the commercial factor was enshrined for most European nations by the great chartered trading companies which were established to control that nation's dealings with the east. Amongst these, the most successful in the seventeenth and early eighteenth centuries was undoubtedly the Dutch company, the *Verenigde Oost-Indische Compagnie* (VOC), established by the States General of the United Provinces in 1602 with a complete monopoly of Dutch trade with the East Indies, and plenary powers to represent Dutch interests in those parts, to the extent of waging war on the agents of other European nations who threatened their interests there (Boxer 1965). By dint of enterprise, hard dealing, and weight of numbers, the Dutch quickly supplanted the Portuguese who had controlled European trade with the east during the sixteenth century, and established a network of trade-routes and forts throughout the East Indies, extending as far as Japan, their principal entrepot being at Batavia (the modern Jakarta). For a number of reasons, principally associated with the survival of documentary evidence and the reputation of these vessels as treasure ships, the wreck sites of over fifteen Dutch East Indiamen have been investigated over the past decade or so, around the coasts of Europe, Southern Africa, and Western Australia (for a list, see Stenuit 1974, 253). As a group, they indicate graphically the commodities and products involved in this commerce.

The great majority of these wrecks involve ships outward bound from the Netherlands to Batavia, so that the bulk of the evidence concerns goods traded in that direction. Undoubtedly the principal export of Europe at this period was gold and, especially, silver, ultimately derived from the American mines. To traders out east, the value of specie lay simply in the weight of metal involved, so that it was dispatched both in ingot form and coined. The site of the East Indiaman *Slot ter Hooge* (1724) has yielded over 100 silver ingots (Stenuit 1975), but on most other sites the bullion has been in the form of coinage. An interesting feature of many of the assemblages has been the high proportion of issues from Spain or the Spanish Netherlands; the government of the United Provinces was never able to supplant this entirely by its own products (Marsden 1976*b*, 211–14). With all the early eighteenth-century wrecks investigated there is also a surprisingly regular pattern in the assemblages; they consist partly of mid seventeenth-century issues from both Spanish and Dutch sources, and partly of coins straight from the mint. The collection from *De Liefde* (1711) illustrates this pattern clearly; a chest of 3300 newly minted Utrecht ducatons was found together with some 1711 gold ducats and a selection of seventeenth-century ducatons and half-ducatons, dating from 1619 onwards (Bax & Martin 1974, 89–90). Whether the VOC was drawing these old issues out of reserve in the early eighteenth century, or pulling them in from general circulation, is unclear.

With so much of the value of these outward-bound cargoes being encompassed in the small space of the treasure chests, there was space

Fig. 3.23 A drawing of
four of the stamped lead
ingots recovered from the
Kennemerland (1664)
wreck-site.

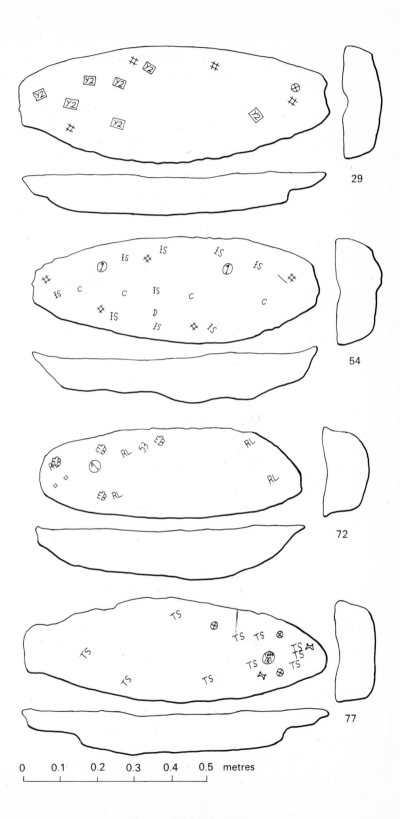

in the holds for bulk cargoes, in some instances of limited value or utility. One of these was lead, carried in ingot form for use on roofs, in ship-building, and in making shot. Over a hundred ingots have been re-covered from the site of the *Kennemerland* (1664) (fig. 3.23), represent-ing one of the largest assemblages of seventeenth-century lead to have survived, from which a great deal can be learned regarding the sources of supply drawn on by the VOC at this period. A larger collection has been found on the site of the *Hollandia* (1742) (Cowan *et al.* 1975), but its significance is reduced by the greater documentation available re-garding the eighteenth-century lead industry. Another substantial cargo apparently being carried regularly by outward-bound vessels, at least during the seventeenth century, was mercury, used in the extrac-tion of silver, and for medical purposes. Samples of this have been found on at least four East Indiamen, in some cases still contained within stoneware flagons (Stenuit 1974, 239–43; Cowan *et al.* 1975, 297–9).

A surprisingly high priority appears to have been placed, in allocating space on board outward-bound VOC ships, on the carriage of building materials from the Netherlands to Batavia. The objective was to create there a passable copy of a Dutch town, as described by Daniel Havant in 1693: 'The town itself is not unpleasing. There are many streets in which none but Hollanders live, including several with houses built in a special way after the Dutch fashion, with three rows of trees in front of them' (Boxer 1965, 207). Thus many sites have yielded many thousands of characteristic yellow Dutch bricks (measuring approximately 0.175 by 0.075 by 0.035 metres) being carried as a kind of paying ballast. Although apparently more common among seventeenth-century car-goes, they continued to be shipped on occasions in the eighteenth century, as on the *Adelaar* (1728). This same policy accounts for the 128 sandstone blocks discovered on the site of the *Batavia* (1629), together representing the complete prefabricated facade of a building (Green 1975, 49).

Apart from bullion and bulk cargoes, these vessels were loaded with the many European products considered essential to civilised life in the east, or which could be profitably traded around those coasts. In the former category can be included such items as the box of 250 clay pipes found on the site of the *Vergulde Draeck* (1656) (Green 1973a, 283). The large number of stoneware, earthenware, and glass vessels found on all sites are indirect testimony to the vast quantities of wine and brandy shipped out for the succour of the company's agents. Trading goods are obviously difficult to isolate in many cases, but some items have been found which, by their very uselessness, must have been intended for the native markets. Fine examples of this are the pocket sundials discovered on both the *Lastdrager* (1652) and the *Kennemerland* (1664) (fig. 3.24); they are of a type which will only work at the latitude for which they are designed (in these cases that of central Europe), so that they would have been highly inaccurate out east. Presumably their selling-point was snob appeal rather than utility (Stenuit 1974, 231). With such small trade-goods, there is uncertainty as to whether they were part of an official company consignment, or whether they represent a private venture by one of the individuals on board, an enterprise which, for most of this period, was illegal (Boxer 1965, 201–6). It is, however, highly probable that such a private stock is represented by one group of objects found together on the *Kennemerland* site, which consisted of between four and a dozen or so examples of thimbles, tobacco boxes, jewellery, and similar items, quantities which seem too great for personal use and too small for company purposes (Price & Muckelroy 1974, 262).

There are innumerable other points on which the archaeology of these wreck-sites illuminates this trade, but enough has been said to indicate its scope. Although there is considerable documentary evidence to set alongside these data, their importance lies in showing what was actually carried, as opposed to what occupied the attentions of the VOC bureaucrats. Regarding the return trade, less can be said from the archaeological evidence since so few of these vessels have been investigated. The earliest and most interesting of such wrecks was that of the *Witte Leeuw* (1613), found in 1976 off St Helena, which was carrying, along with the expected spices, a quantity of Ming porcelain, and what appeared to be a natural history collection. The fragmentary remains of

Fig. 3.24 A pocket sun-dial, complete with coloured compass card, from the wreck of the *Kennemerland* (1664).

the *Nieuw Rhoon* (1776) at Cape Town have also yielded Chinese porcelain, along with quantities of peppercorns trapped within the iron-shot ballast mound (Lightly 1976). Large quantities of peppercorns have also come from the outward-bound *Kennemerland*, presumably representing spillage from the cargo of her first return voyage (fig. 2.14, p. 53) (Price & Muckelroy 1977, 194). However, such evidence remains partial and fragmentary, and can only achieve its full significance when set alongside the available documentary sources (see, for example, Glamann 1958).

When looking at the trading activities of other European nations in this sphere, the archaeological evidence is negligible. Unfortunately, there have been no investigations to date on a wreck of one of the large Portuguese carracks which undertook this commerce during the sixteenth century. The only representative of Portuguese interest in the Indian Ocean excavated in recent years is from the end of the seventeenth century – a wreck off Mombasa which is probably to be identified as the frigate *Santo Antonio de Tanna* (Kirkman 1972; Piercy 1977). So far as the English East India Company is concerned, there is little archaeological material relating to the period before the mid eighteenth century, partly reflecting the fact that until that time its operations were very limited compared with those of the Dutch Company. However, the oldest wreck known in Australian waters is in fact of an English ship, the *Trial* of 1622; a wreck-site located in 1969 off the Monte Bello Islands has been tentatively identified with this vessel (Green 1977). The earliest English East India Company wreck-sites known in British waters are those of the *Valentine* (1776) off Alderney and the *Halsewell* (1786) off the Dorset coast. During the early eighteenth century, Dutch dominance was also challenged by a number of small companies based in other European states, the wrecks of whose ships have also been investigated recently. The Danish Asiatic Company's frigate *Wendela* (1737) has been located off Shetland, the most significant discoveries here being the coinage, which included a wide variety of non-Danish issues, reflecting the non-acceptance of their money out east. The wreck of a returning ship of the Swedish East India Company has also been found in the Orkneys, the *Suecia* (1740); her principal bulk cargo appears to have been die-wood (McBride 1977). The activities of these 'interlopers' reflects the diversifying of European contacts with the east during the eighteenth century, a process which led to greater political involvement in local affairs as, for example, in the British takeover in India. But this period is also marked by the greatly increased availability of documentary material, associated with a consequent decrease in the significance of the archaeological evidence. It is thus with reference to the first two centuries of the expansion of Europe that the information gleaned from these wreck-sites is of most importance.

3.8   The annexation of the New World

While the lands of the east were regarded primarily as targets for commercial exploitation, whose rulers, so long as they remained compliant
to European economic interests, were left in control of their domains,
the Americas were, from the very beginning, treated very differently.
The economic, political, and religious motives behind this were complex, but the consequence was that the whole of the West Indies,
Central America, and northern South America was annexed by the
Spanish Crown, and made subject to a rigid political and economic
administration. One of the principal objectives of this system was to
ensure that Spain herself derived the maximum financial benefit from
these lands, and that the fleets returning to Seville were well laden with
gold, silver, and other valuables. The wreck-sites of such of these
vessels as came to grief are thus prime sources for gaining insight into
the detailed workings of this exploitation. They can reveal what was
actually carried to Europe in these ships, the quantities and the qualities
of the goods involved, and thus supplement and illuminate the evidence
of the mountainous documentation surviving from the *Casa de la
Contratación* at Seville. However, the haul from many of these sites has
also proved to be exceedingly valuable, so that there have been many
considerations apart from the archaeological, leading on occasions to an
unfortunate loss of information, and less than adequate publication.

Although shipwrecks have occurred in the Caribbean and surrounding seas for all the usual reasons, the official treasure fleets faced several
additional hazards which have ensured the survival of a large number of
these wreck-sites. First, they were always heavily laden, often excessively so, and badly prepared to face rough conditions. Secondly, this
whole region is notorious for violent changes of weather, and especially
for its hurricanes; some of the most spectacular fleet losses were caused
by such storms. The convoys were probably most vulnerable at the
beginning of their voyages, when, having assembled at Havana in Cuba,
they sailed up the relatively narrow Florida Straits and past the Bahamas
before striking out across the Atlantic, hoping for a last fix on Bermuda
before making the long hop (see fig. 3.25). While the intention in taking
this passage was to take advantage of the three-knot, northward-flowing
Florida current, bad weather or adverse winds could quickly imperil the
whole fleet. In fact, in view of all these hazards, it is a wonder so many
convoys survived the voyage intact.

Of the ships participating in the early phase of exploration and
colonisation after 1492 very few remains have been found. Any vessels
from this period would be of prime importance, since naval architecture
was still evolving at this time; there is likely to have been a wide variation
of types and designs among these pioneering ships. The earliest recorded
shipwreck in American waters in fact comes from Columbus's first

voyage, when his flagship, the *Santa Maria*, ran aground on the north-west coast of Haiti. Despite predictably frequent attempts to relocate this wreck, her remains have not yet been found, and there continue to be considerable doubts as to how much of her was left in the sand, since her hull is known to have been extensively looted for the building of a small fort nearby (Peterson 1972, 254). Two Columban ships whose remains have been located, although not yet thoroughly investigated, relate to his last voyage, 1502–4. After a year of cruising around the Caribbean, Columbus was left with only two of his four ships, and they were in a sinking condition, so that he was eventually forced to run them ashore in St Ann's Bay, on the north coast of Jamaica, where they immediately sank. In 1968 Robert Marx, using a sub-bottom profiler and extensive coring, located at least one wreck in the expected position, and retrieved sufficient artefacts to indicate a date of *c.* 1500 (Marx 1973*a*, 254–77). The remains are lying at least 3 metres below the bottom sediment, and include an extensive area of wooden structure.

The earliest remains relating to the trans-atlantic shipment of gold, silver, and other valuables to Spain so far discovered concern the 1553/4 Plate Fleet, which was driven by a tropical storm onto the sandy coast near Padre Island in what is now Texas. Three vessels are believed to lie in this area, one of which (possibly the *Santa Maria de Iciar*) was

Fig. 3.25 A map of the Caribbean basin and Bermuda, showing early historic wreck-sites.

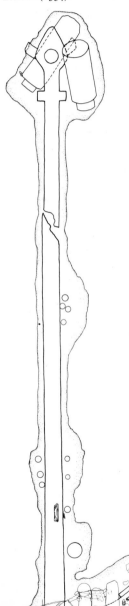

Fig. 3.26 Drawing of an encrustation (no. 81) built up around an iron anchor from the site of the *San Esteban* (1554).

located and salvaged by a treasure-hunting firm in 1967, and another (possibly the *San Esteban*) has been systematically excavated by the Texas Antiquities Committee since 1972 (Arnold & Clausen 1975; Clausen & Arnold 1976; Hamilton 1976). The latter was lying buried in about 1.5 metres of sand and silt with nothing protruding above the sea-bed; it was initially located and surveyed with a magnetometer before excavation began (Clausen & Arnold 1976). By the conclusion of the excavations, over 1500 artefacts had been recovered, although over 85% of them were contained in iron concretion, and almost all the remaining 15% were metal objects of high specific gravity (fig. 3.26). There was considerable evidence to suggest that, in times of severe storms, all the unconsolidated deposits on this site went into suspension, leading to the destruction or removal of all the lighter wreck material. Thus the sample yielded by this site is biassed; nevertheless, the information derived from it has been extensive.

The principal official cargo of the ship was obviously silver, much of it from the Mexico mint which had been opened only seventeen years previously; this collection thus represented an invaluable and closely dated sample of early issues. However, money was also found in smaller quantities associated with other artefacts, possibly representing the contents of chests, boxes, or barrels, in which was stored the personal wealth of the returning adventurers. A surprisingly wide range of foreign items have also been recovered, including English pewter and Cologne stonewares. The armament found included only wrought iron, stave-built guns, which were undoubtedly obsolete by 1554; presumably the more modern cast iron and bronze guns were reserved for use in Europe, while these old types were still adequate for most eventualities in the New World. The same explanation must account for the similar absence of cast iron shot. A particularly fascinating find was a polished iron pyrites half-sphere, possibly an aboriginal Mesoamerican mirror being carried as a souvenir. The painstaking investigation of this site, under water and in the laboratory, has demonstrated what can be learned from even the most scattered of sites.

Centimetres

0   25   50

One of the largest collections of gold and other valuables recovered from one of these wreck-sites was lifted by Teddy Tucker from a wreck of about 1590 in Bermudan waters. It included several gold bars stamped with the word 'PINTO' (indicating that it had come from an area of New Grenada), as well as many spectacular items of jewellery. The ship's armament consisted of both cast- and wrought-iron guns. Other finds illustrated the life of those on board, including their utensils, personal weapons, and navigational instruments, as well as yet another example of an aboriginal souvenir, in this case a collection of Carib palm-wood weapons (Peterson 1972, 257). Another Bermudan wreck investigated by Teddy Tucker illustrated the gradual decrease in the importance of bullion in the exports of the Spanish colonies. This was the site of the *San Antonio* (1621), on which, as well as the inevitable cakes of gold, silver coins, and jewellery, were found bundles of tobacco, jars of cochineal, a chest of indigo, bales of leather, and billets of *lignum vitae* (Peterson 1972, 258–9). However, the carriage of treasure also remained important, as is shown by the *Nuestra Senora de Atoche*, lost in the following year on the Florida Keys, and claimed to be one of the richest wrecks in the Americas (Marx 1972; Lyon 1976).

Perhaps the greatest disasters to strike the Spanish bullion fleets, however, occurred during the eighteenth century, when Spain's control of and profit from her American Empire was beginning to wane. Despite this, the value of her receipts from the Americas was still considerable, and this has been reflected in the treasure recovered from the wrecks of two major fleets which were lost at this period. The earlier catastrophe was in 1715, when the cargoes were exceptionally valuable as a consequence of the resumption of convoys following the peace of 1713. A hurricane struck the fleet of eleven ships in the Florida Straits, and ten of them were cast away on the coasts there. Since 1961, Kip Wagner and his associates have recovered many thousands of gold and silver coins, gold ingots, Chinese porcelain, jewellery, and other valuables, as well as more commonplace items for shipboard use (Peterson 1972, 262–3). An almost identical series of events led to the loss of about twenty-one ships of the 1733 fleet in the second of these disasters and, since the 1940s, a number of these wrecks have been relocated, including the flagship *Rui* (Peterson 1972, 263–4), and the *San José* (Marx 1972).

Most wreck-sites discovered so far in American waters appear to have little in the way of hull remains preserved; as with the Padre Island sites, or those in the Florida Straits, most of them lie in areas of possible violent storms or strong currents. One site with extensive structures was discovered in the Bahamas in 1966; the ship was evidently built for speed, having very fine lines and light timbering. She had two lombards as bow chasers, and eleven swivel-guns along the rails, and the presence of iron-cored lead cannonballs suggested a date before 1580. Everything pointed to this vessel being a pirate ship or privateer, large numbers of which were increasingly attracted to the Caribbean as the sixteenth century progressed (Peterson 1972, 256). Although usually privately financed, the activities of these ships were often covertly supported by the governments of France and, later, England, as an element in their anti-Spanish policies. The structural remains of another ship of about the same date, this time in Bermudan waters, were considerably more massive, and illustrate the kind of bulk carrier against which the pirates operated. All surviving timbers were oak, and the ship is estimated to have been about 120–140 feet long, and to have displaced around 400 tons (Peterson 1972, 256–7).

But the English and French activity in the New World was not limited to piratical attacks; by the end of the sixteenth-century colonies were being established along the eastern seaboard of North America. One of the earliest was the English settlement known as Virginia, on the sea-approach to which lies Bermuda; in 1609 this also became an English colony, when a ship bound for Virginia, the *Sea Venture*, was wrecked there. During the course of the seventeenth-century other English ships came to grief on this island, including the *Warwick* (1619), the *Eagle* (1659), and the *Virginia Merchant* (1660) (Peterson 1972, 259–60). The sites of all these wrecks have recently been located, and yielded a wide range of items illustrating the requirements of the emergent colonies. Axes for forest clearance and lead buckshot for hunting show how close to the frontier and the wilderness these early settlers were living, while the quantities of heavier armaments reflect the continued hostility of both the Indians and the Spanish to the English presence. Increased English commerce and settlement in North and Central America also inevitably drew the Royal Navy into these waters, especially after the British seizure of Jamaica in 1655. Dramatic illustration of this presence is afforded by the wreck of the *Swan*, which was thrown into the middle of Port Royal by the famous earthquake of 1692, and whose remains are still preserved there, including a substantial part of her hull (Marx 1973a, 154–6). The year 1695 saw the loss of two Royal Naval ships whose remains have recently been investigated: the *Winchester*, a Fourth Rate wrecked near Carysfort Reef, Florida (Peterson 1972, 260–1), and the *Sapphire*, a Fifth Rate lying in Bay Bulls Harbour, Newfoundland (fig. 3.27).

A notable feature of the discussion thus far has been the total concentration on vessels outward bound from the Americas, a bias reflecting work on wreck-sites over recent decades, presumably because the remains on such sites tend to be more valuable. However, it also is true that incoming ships, tending to have less substantial cargoes, are likely to be less well preserved and more difficult to locate. Undoubtedly the most valuable import during these centuries was in fact slaves from

Africa, but the archaeological remains relating to this disgraceful traffic will always be slight; slavers had little room for other cargoes, or even extensive armaments (Marx 1971, 92). Evidence of one element in this trade came from the wreck of the *San Antonio* (1621) in Bermuda, on which a large number of cowrie shells were found; having already travelled half-way around the world from the East Indies, they were destined for West Africa, where just a few would buy a healthy adult slave (Peterson 1972, 259). More direct evidence has been found on a wreck near Panama, on which there were hundreds of iron shackles. But for the hull remains of a slave-ship one must look to Western Australia, where the Museum has undertaken a major excavation on the site of an ex-slaver, the *James Matthews* (fig. 3.28) (Henderson 1976). These ships possessed several special characteristics, such as shallow draft, fine lines for speed, and various specialised internal fittings. Few detailed plans of such ships have survived, so that the evidence from this site is invaluable. Having been seized with 433 slaves on board near Dominica in 1837, the ship was renamed and registered in London as a snow brig of 107 tons. She was wrecked while at anchor off Freemantle in July 1841, and the bulk of her hull, along with a cargo of slates and other goods, lies buried in sand in 2 to 3 metres of water.

Fig. 3.27 Iron cannons and ship's timbers from the wreck of *Sapphire* (1695) on the bed of Bay Bulls Harbour, Newfoundland.

The naval vessel *Sapphire* (1695) was an early casualty in a conflict which was to be a recurring theme in North American history down to

1760, the struggle between Britain and France. So far as the war at sea was concerned, British supremacy was finally confirmed in July 1760, at the battle of Restigouche, when the last three ships from a supply convoy dispatched to relieve Montreal were trapped by a small British fleet, and finally scuttled or burned. The remains of one of these ships, probably the *Marquis de Maulauze*, were dragged onto a beach in 1938, while another wreck, the *Machault*, has been the subject of extensive excavations by the Canadian National Historic Sites Service since 1969 (Zacharchuk 1972, 157–63). Parts of the hull of this vessel, the largest in the fleet, have been lifted for study and conservation. The wide range of artefacts recovered, many of which were in extremely fine condition, indicated the supplies thought necessary for the succour of the belea- guered city, and included surprising quantities of luxury goods.

Less than twenty years after the French had been expelled from North America, the colonists turned against the British Government and established the United States of America. The naval aspect of the War of Independence is illustrated by several underwater sites, prob- ably the most extensive and famous of which is that at Yorktown. Before General Cornwallis's surrender in 1781, a number of British ships were sunk in the York River, both as a result of enemy action and as a block- ade, and these have since been the object of many salvage attempts. The first research investigation in modern times was undertaken in 1934–5,

Fig. 3.28 The remains of the slaver *James Matthews* (1841), now lying off Woodman's Point, Western Australia.

using drag-lines and professional divers, during which a wide selection of artefacts were recovered (Bass 1966, 123). Renewed investigations were started in 1976 on this site. Another interesting wreck-site of this period is that of the *Defense*, a brigantine of 170 tons commissioned in June 1779 and scuttled the following August after an unsuccessful attempt by the Massachusetts militia on a new British fort at Castine. Like the rest of the fleet, she was trapped in Penobscot River by a British naval force, and is now lying there in about 6 metres of water on a mud bottom, her hull surviving to a height of over a metre. Her significance lies in the selection from her armament recovered, and in the evidence she affords regarding New England shipbuilding at this period (Mayhew 1974).

With the founding of the U.S.A., the European political domination of the New World was challenged, and within half a century most of the Spanish colonies further south had also achieved independence. During the nineteenth-century, therefore, political and economic relationships across the Atlantic were very different from those which had pertained previously. But on this new order the documentary evidence is considerably more comprehensive, with a consequent contraction in the scope for archaeological research.

3.9 Navigational instruments

There are a number of specialist topics relating to ships and seafaring within which the evidence from wreck-sites has been of importance; subjects such as naval armament, the design of rigging and its fittings, systems of weights and measures, etc. Rather than deal summarily with all of these, this section concentrates on just one study, that of navigational instruments and their development, serving as a representative for them all. In essence, the archaeological contribution in all these fields centres on the fact that such evidence shows what was actually in use on a particular vessel, rather than what contemporary commentators thought should have been there. In the case of navigational instruments, this aspect is particularly valuable, since much of the writing on this topic was done by mathematicians and other academics, many of whom had enough contact with seamen to make their descriptions plausible, and often made insufficient distinction between current practice and original proposals. Even those few practising seamen who wrote books or treatises were not averse to putting forward their own pet ideas for improvements. For a balanced and judicious work of historical synthesis based on such sources, dealing with 'The art of navigation in England in Elizabethan and early Stuart times', see Waters, 1958.

For the student of the history of navigation, the other main source of information until recently consisted of instruments of especial value or with particular associations preserved as heirlooms in museums and private collections. With these, he could check on the veracity of some of the contemporary written descriptions. However, the general failing of all such material is that it is biassed in favour of the more costly, attractive, and prestigious items, representing only weakly the run-of-the-mill articles in everyday use. Fig. 3.29 shows an assemblage representing an early Stuart navigator's instruments of navigation, extracted

Fig. 3.29 An early Stuart navigator's instruments of navigation, assembled from the collections of the National Maritime Museum, Greenwich.

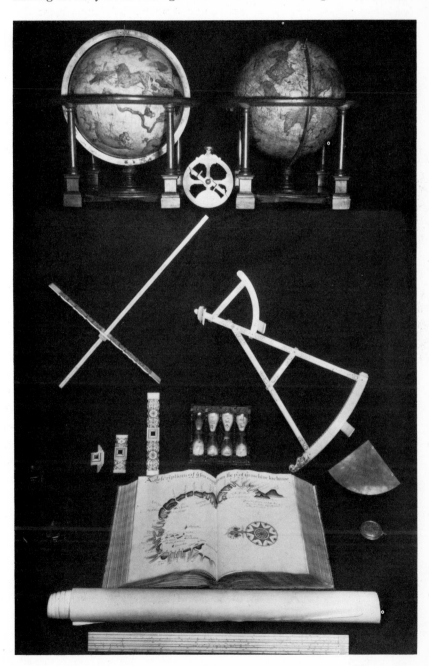

from the extensive collections of the National Maritime Museum, Greenwich. Although the selection of instruments represented is undoubtedly fair, the particular examples shown can hardly be regarded as typical of items in general use during the seventeenth century. The two fine globes at the top of the display are by the great sixteenth-century map and globe maker, Gerard Mercator, while the cross-staff and backstaff in the centre are of ivory, being a presentation set of *c.* 1695 (Waters 1958, xxviii–xxix). Of course, this picture also demonstrates an essential weakness of the archaeological evidence, showing as it does examples of books and charts which are very rarely going to appear in the archaeological record. Ultimately, these two sources of material evidence should be regarded as complementary, in this topic as in most of the others listed above.

The study of navigational instruments is almost entirely restricted to the post-medieval period; the development of position-finding devices during the late medieval period was one of the prerequisites for the subsequent 'expansion of Europe'. On classical wreck-sites, the only specialist instruments apparent are sounding leads, a number of which have been found on various sites of this period (Benoit 1965, 31; Fiori & Joncheray 1973, 86–8). Although the most simple of instruments, there is no denying its importance in navigation in all ages. Ever since the Middle Ages at least, vessels have gauged their progress up the English Channel by reference to the sequence of muds and silts brought up by repeated castings of the lead, while it has been suggested that the failure to adopt the compass generally in the Baltic region until the sixteenth century resulted from the fact that, in those shallow waters, reliance on the lead line remained perfectly adequate (Lane 1963). On any particular wreck-site, there is always a problem of whether any leads found come from the ship concerned, or were lost by other vessels feeling their way across that area. Since the design of sounding leads has not changed for many centuries, intruders cannot be detected on typological grounds. However, in many cases contamination can be excluded either on the grounds that any ship sounding in that situation would most certainly have been cast away herself within seconds, or because a deep-water lead would not usually have been swung in shallow water, or vice-versa.

Until more Viking or medieval wreck-sites have been located and studied, there is also nothing that can be said about what devices, if any, were in use at these periods. The use of the lodestone or the sunstone by the Vikings has been debated, and it would indeed be exciting if any archaeological evidence for their use were found (Gelsinger 1970). Similarly, there is no archaeological evidence for the early evolution of the basic instruments, such as the compass or the astrolabe, before the sixteenth century; the rest of this chapter is concerned with the evidence for the use of these instruments from then until *c.* 1800. In each case the intricacies of the operation of the instruments concerned has been ommitted; readers wishing to pursue these matters are referred to the standard works on this subject (Taylor 1956; Waters 1958; May 1973).

One item which has been recovered from a very large number of wreck-sites, and whose design appears to have changed little over these centuries, or between the ships of different nations, is one-handed navigational dividers, or chart compasses (fig. 3.30). With an interlocking bow at the top, these instruments could be opened and closed with one hand, making them particularly useful for chart work. Examples of practically identical design have been found from ships of the Spanish Armada, including the *Girona* and the *Trinidad Valencera*, from Dutch vessels of the seventeenth and eighteenth centuries, including the *Lastdrager* (1652), *Kennemerland* (1664) (fig. 3.30), and the *Curaçao* (1729), and from ships of the Royal Navy, including the *Dartmouth* (1690) (see fig. 3.33). Straight two-handed compasses have also been found on some sites, including the *Batavia* (1629) and the *Kennemerland* (1664); in case of the *Lastdrager* (1652) a box of seventy-two of this type was found, evidently being carried as cargo (Stenuit 1974).

Fig. 3.30 A pair of chart dividers, from the *Kennemerland* (1664) wreck-site. Scale in centimetres.

A number of the more complex and substantial instruments of this period were concerned with measuring the angle of elevation of the sun, from which could be calculated a vessel's latitude, information of evident importance in position finding. During the late fifteenth century,

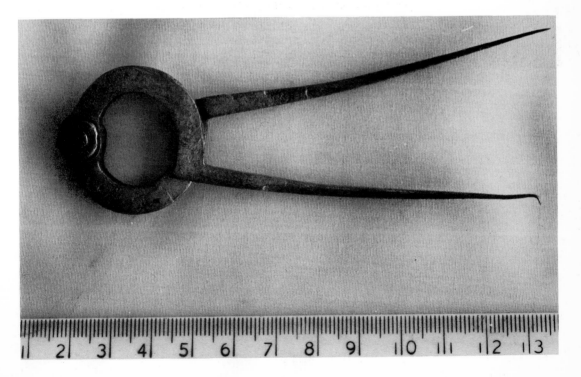

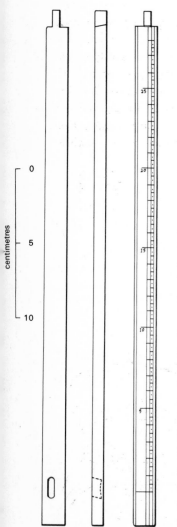

Fig. 3.31 A graduated wooden rule, probably the sight-vane transom of a backstaff, from the *Kennemerland* (1664) wreck-site.

the Portuguese developed a specialist version of the old-established planispheric astrolabe (probably a Greek invention of the second century B.C.), designed specifically for making altitude measurements at sea. This mariner's astrolabe became the standard instrument for measuring altitudes during the sixteenth century, until superseded by the cross-staff and the backstaff at the end of the century. About three dozen examples are known to be in existence, over a third of them being from wreck-sites (Anderson 1972). Three of them were found on one of the ships from the 1554 Plate Fleet wrecked off Texas (Hamilton 1976, 5), and two on the Spanish Armada galleass *Girona* (Stenuit 1972, 237). That they continued in use into the seventeenth century is shown by the four found on the Dutch East Indiaman *Batavia* (1629); although obsolete by then, they were still useful in certain situations, such as when the horizon was obscured. The study of surviving instruments, both from museum collections and archaeological excavations, can reveal a great deal about their design and production; for example, it has been suggested that different units of measurement were used in different countries, so that the precise dimensions of an unmarked example can indicate its country of origin (Destombes 1969, 49–50).

Evidence of a different type of astrolabe has come from the wreck of the Dutch East Indiaman *Lastdrager* (1652) (Stenuit 1974, 226–9), with what was evidently the brass *brachiolus*, or hinged arm, from a catholic or universal astrolabe, and a similar piece has been found on the earlier VOC ship *Batavia*. Also a development from the planispheric astrolabe, this instrument allowed a wide range of astronomical and navigational calculations to be undertaken mechanically anywhere in the world. The *Lastdrager brachiolus* is from an instrument of the 'Gemma Frisius' type, and Robert Stenuit has plausibly suggested that it represents part of a cheap simplified variety of this device, made with a wood or card-board body for everyday use (1974, 227–9) – the type of piece which has not otherwise found its way into modern museum collections.

Towards the end of the sixteenth century, new instruments were developed for measuring altitudes. The first was the cross-staff, pro-gressively refined from early sixteenth-century Portuguese models until it became a reliable device (see fig. 3.29, *centre left*). Few examples of this instrument have been reported from wreck-sites; possibly, because of its simplicity, many cross-staff fragments have gone unrecorded. Then, in the 1590s, the English navigator Captain John Davis invented his quadrant, or backstaff, which represented a considerable advance both by cutting out the need to look into the sun when taking a reading, and by creating a device which could receive a finely graduated scale (Waters 1958, 302–6). Although apparently widely used throughout the seventeenth century, only two pre-1700 examples are known from museum collections; one of *c.* 1660 in Skokloster Castle, Sweden

(Losman & Sigurdsson 1974), and one of *c.* 1695, made of ivory, in the National Maritime Museum, Greenwich (fig. 3.29, *centre right*). That the latter, although a special production for presentation purposes, in fact represents the standard design of that time has been shown by an item from the wreck of the *Dartmouth* (1690) – a horizon vane of almost identical form and dimensions to that on the ivory piece (see fig. 3.33).

A more intriguing fragment probably deriving from a backstaff has come from the Dutch East Indiaman *Kennemerland* (1664) (Muckelroy 1977*c*; Price & Muckelroy 1977, 210–12). It consisted of a graduated wooden rule, marked off from 0 to 25 on one face, and with an angled mortice at one end and an angled tenon at the other (fig. 3.31). It has been tentatively identified as the sight-vane transom of an early and unrefined form of backstaff, generally associated with Dutch practice. Unlike the more common type discussed above, the transoms represented chords, rather than arcs, of a circle around the horizon vane, and were thus intrinsically less accurate. In this example, the graduations themselves were also not precisely placed, and there was no attempt to indicate intervals of less than half a degree. Only one representation of this design has been traced, and that is in W. J. Blaeu's *Eerste deel der Seespiegel* (1623), published in English as *The sea mirrour* (1625); a copy of this illustration is shown in fig. 3.32. Rather surprisingly, the *Kennemerland* example appears to have been graduated for reading

Fig. 3.32 The use of a seventeenth century backstaff, as illustrated in Blaeu's *The Sea Mirrour* of 1625; the mariner is sighting the far horizon to measure the angle of elevation of the sun.

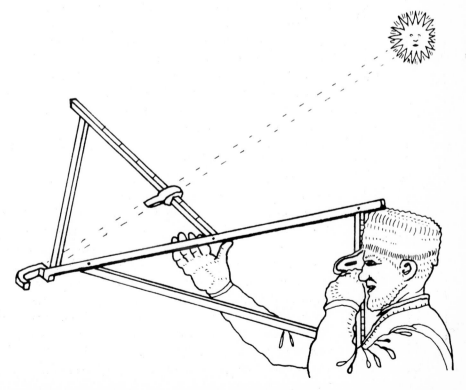

altitude distance rather than zenith, running contrary to the evidence for normal practice for this period from written sources (Waters 1958, 305–6). However, there had previously been no indication that this variant of the backstaff had been used widely, and certainly not that it had remained in use until the 1660s.

The next major step forward in measuring the altitude of heavenly bodies came in the mid eighteenth century, with the invention of the octant and, twenty years later, the sextant; within the following half century these supplanted all previous devices for the great majority of seamen. The octant was apparently invented simultaneously by John Hadley in England and Thomas Godfrey in America in 1730, although the standard pattern of the Hadley octant was not generally available

Fig. 3.33 A collection of navigational instruments from the wreck of the *Dartmouth* (1690) (about 60% full size).

until 1734. It naturally took a few more years for the instrument to gain widespread acceptance; for example, it was not until 1747 that it was specified as standard navigational equipment by the Dutch East India Company. It was thus particularly interesting to find elements of one on the wreck of the Dutch East Indiamen *Hollandia* (1743), including the index arm and its mirror mounting, the mounting for the shade and its two associated mirrors, and the mount for the sight (Cowan *et al.* 1975, 287–9). That this early model was probably being carried for trials is shown by the finding on the same site of parts of two wooden cross-staves.

To conclude this chapter, a complete assemblage of navigational instruments from a wreck-site is illustrated (fig. 3.33) for comparison with the museum display discussed at the beginning (fig. 3.29). This collection is from the wreck of the *Dartmouth* (1690), and includes, along with the backstaff horizon vane already mentioned (*bottom right*), examples of both one-handed bow dividers (*top right*) and double-handed straight dividers (*top centre and left*), along with a protractor, inscribed 'Chas Lucas, Dublin fecit' (*centre*), and some fragments of log-slates (*bottom left*). On these last, the first letter 'H' stands for hours, the letter 'K' for knots, the next 'H' for half-knots, and the final letter 'F' for feet; at two-hourly intervals the log and line were released over-board, and the distance the latter ran out in the prescribed period, as noted down on such a slate, indicated the speed of the ship. This particular assemblage is shown only as an example of the kinds of navigational devices which might be recovered from a moderately well-preserved wreck (Adnams 1974), and is in no way exceptional. Other published collections displaying a similar range of instruments include that from the wreck of the Dutch East Indiaman *Batavia* (1629) (Stanbury 1975), notable for four mariner's astrolabes, two globe meridian rings, and a *brachiolus*, and that from the Russian frigate *Nicholas* (1790) (Ericsson 1975a), notable for a small telescope, a sector, and a couple of protractors. Along with all the other instruments mentioned above, these collections demonstrate the value of being able to study the range and quality of what was actually carried by past sea-farers, setting such information alongside the evidence available from written sources and museum collections.

From bronze-smith's tools on a twelfth-century B.C. merchantman off Cape Gelidonya to navigational instruments on a late eighteenth-century Russian warship is a long jump, but the common theme of ships, seamen, and seafaring has run through all the topics covered in the meantime. The unevenness of current research work is only too apparent, with its emphasis on either the classical period or post-medieval times. Within Europe, the intervening centuries are undoubtedly poorly served, while in the rest of the world periods before the arrival of the Europeans have been almost totally neglected. Within the Mediterranean, it has been amphorae which have attracted attention to sites, while elsewhere it has been cannons; very few of the sites mentioned above (except in section 3.4) have not contained one or other of these objects. While the net result of these researches has been quite respectable for a sub-discipline barely twenty-five years old, it is to be hoped that the next quarter century will see a broadening of interests, alongside both the intensification and expansion of research in the topics described above. The scope for new studies is almost limitless, and chapter 4 is concerned with outlining some of the more obvious additional fields of enquiry.

4.

The unrealised potential of maritime archaeology

In the following outline of the areas of research which may figure in this sub-discipline in the foreseeable future, a certain amount of current work will incidentally be discussed. In all instances, however, the extent of this evidence is so limited or diverse that the overall potential of the field of enquiry is regarded as unrealised, since no coherent synthesis of the data is possible. At the same time, it is frequently the discovery of this material which has indicated the possibilities for future work.

4.1 Prehistoric craft

In the course of chapter 3, only one wreck site concerning the remains of a prehistoric vessel was discussed, the Cape Gelidonya ship, and that figured only in the section on Mediterranean trade. Very few fragments of the vessel itself had survived, and little could be gleaned from them about its mode of construction (section 3.2; Bass 1967). Evidently, archaeological material will always be the prime source for research in this topic, and sufficient has emerged in recent years to indicate the full potential of such studies. In many parts of the world, of course, the prehistoric period continued up until a century or so ago, so that the remnants of indigenous techniques and traditions may be recoverable through a study of local boats still in use, or recently abandoned, although in most areas European influence has effectively masked much of the evidence for earlier practices. But such regions are in a minority; in most cases the archaeological evidence has to stand alone, and in order to demonstrate some of the characteristics of such material, the rest of this section considers boat remains from the prehistoric period in northern Europe.

Amongst the oldest boats found anywhere in the world outside Egypt are three from North Ferriby on the Humber estuary discovered between 1937 and 1963 (Wright 1976). In each case the remains were fragmentary, but enough was recovered to indicate three separate examples of a type of craft not previously encountered, made up of a considerable number of fashioned planks sewn together in a complex and highly sophisticated manner, and caulked with moss; boat 1 is shown in fig. 4.1. Radiocarbon determinations suggest that they were all built somewhere in the range 1800–1000 B.C., and, while they might all be roughly contemporary at around 1350 B.C., they are more likely to have been constructed several centuries apart. They evidently reflect a well established tradition in this part of eastern England which had achieved considerable refinement of technique. Further evidence for continuity can be found in a craft of about a thousand years later, the so-called Brigg raft (McGrail 1975). This lay beside the River Ancolme, a tributary of the Humber, and although possessing evident differences in stitching and planking layout, it had obviously been constructed on similar principles. While it must be assumed that the North Ferriby boats were able to navigate the often turbulent waters of the Humber estuary, it seems very unlikely that they were true sea-going vessels.

However, the majority of prehistoric craft discovered in Europe are dug-outs, or log-boats (McGrail & Switsur 1975; McGrail 1977*b*). These vessels, made by hollowing out a single tree-trunk, were probably first made in Upper Palaeolithic times, and continued in use in some areas until the late medieval period (Lucas 1963); there appear to be no typological characteristics whereby earlier or later examples may be distinguished. Possibly the oldest example recorded in the British Isles was the Scots pine log-boat discovered under carse clay at Friarton brickworks near Perth, and now in the Dundee City Museum, whose reported location suggests a date of 9000–7000 B.C. (Geikie 1879). Among surviving examples of such craft in England, five appear to be of second millennium B.C. construction, with a further three being probably from the first millennium B.C. (McGrail & Switsur 1975, fig. 1). Being essentially vessels for use on inland waterways, they should perhaps be considered primarily in the context of river craft (see section 4.4); there is no evidence from prehistoric Europe of the practice, adopted by later Polynesian seafarers, of lashing dug-outs together to create stable and seaworthy catamarans.

Alongside the log-boat, the inhabitants of prehistoric Europe almost certainly used skin boats, a tradition which continued into modern times with Welsh coracles and Irish curraghs (Hornell 1938). Their use in the second millennium B.C. is suggested by several rock carvings in Norway, such as those at Kalnes (fig. 4.2), which seem to represent people paddling a kind of boat on which the framework is apparent. The skin boat is the only variety which fits this specification, and a recent experimental skin boat built to accord with these drawings at least showed that such a vessel was feasible, and very seaworthy (Marstrander 1976). However, such a construction is unlikely to survive archaeologically in any recognisable form; the only one claimed in Britain is highly dubious (Sheppard 1926, 171). One surviving craft which does bear a superficial resemblance to these carvings is the third-century B.C. boat found in a bog at Hjortspring in Denmark, a wooden clinker-built vessel with sewn planks, but with the distinctive double up-curved prow

Fig. 4.1 The first North Ferriby boat, after clearance in August 1946 on the mudflats of the Humber estuary.

and stern apparent at Kalnes and similar rock-carving sites; this similarity raises the intriguing possibility that, contrary to the standard interpretation given above, these drawings represent wooden craft ancestral to this example.

Thus the totality of evidence to date on prehistoric craft in northern Europe consists of a number of log-boats of limited capabilities, a possible tradition of skin boats, and a highly developed technology of sewn plank boats, so far known only around the Humber estuary. In very few instances have these been found in situations where their function, cargoes, or other indicators of economic significance can be deduced, so that the relationship between these artefacts and the society which produced them must remain predominantly a matter for supposition. The discovery of further remains would seem, on past performance, to be a question of chance reports from dredging, dyke building, or the like. So far, no substantial prehistoric hulls have been recovered from the sea-bed, and many people consider it unlikely that they ever will be. With minimal cargoes and light hulls, it is argued, there would be nothing to pin the structure to the bottom long enough to ensure preservation. But this may be an overpessimistic view. It was

Fig. 4.2 Bronze Age rock carvings, probably representing skin-covered vessels, at Kalnes in Norway.

only the particular topography of the sea-bed off Cape Gelidonya which resulted in only incoherent hull fragments surviving from that Bronze Age vessel; more favourable conditions might have meant a great deal more pinned down by its cargo of bronze and other metals. An even earlier wreck of *c.* 2500 B.C. has recently been found off the island of Hydria in the Aegean, and the survival of some ship's timbers has been predicted for that site. In the long term, therefore, it is not inconceivable that sufficient finds will emerge from underwater sites around Europe to give a more coherent view of both the development of prehistoric boats, and their role in trade. Nevertheless, it remains likely that most boats will continue to be found on land sites, with all the limitations implicit in that situation.

4.2   Medieval shipbuilding in north-west Europe

As demonstrated in sections 3.4 and 3.5, there is a substantial hiatus in knowledge about shipbuilding between the abandonment of the custom of boat burial around A.D. 1000, and the appearance of numerous large and heavily armed trans-oceanic ships in the middle of the sixteenth century. This lacuna is made doubly frustrating by the fact that the second half of this period saw rapid developments in nautical technology, with far-reaching historical consequences. Although several vessels from this period have been investigated, notably in Scandinavia (Crumlin-Pedersen 1972, 182–3), much of this work is inadequately reported, and involves such a variety of types that it is difficult to see any general patterns. At present, the principal evidence available to historians of maritime technology is that afforded by representations of ships on wall-paintings and town-seals. The latter sources are particularly useful since it appears that, until about 1400, engravers consciously sought to depict the most up-to-date craft in use, as a reflection of the mercantile standing of their town. After about 1400, when the pace of innovation began to accelerate, such representations became more stylised and less reliable (see Crumlin-Pedersen 1972; Greenhill 1976, 250–301).

So far as written sources are concerned, a bewildering variety of terms were used for shipping at this period, and there is little general agreement as to how they should be related, if at all, to the ship types found archaeologically. There is also some uncertainty about the consistency with which some of these terms were applied; certainly, by the fifteenth century the same craft was referred to by different names in different ports. However, this may simply be a reflection of the turmoil in techniques associated with the rapid progress achieved in that century, and may not be typical of the whole period. It is also unlikely that the precise meaning of such terms remained constant over several centuries. Nevertheless, there are a couple of names whose meanings are reasonably clear, the *keel* and the cog. The *keel*, as used in England in the eleventh to thirteenth centuries, must surely indicate a vessel of the Scandinavian tradition immediately distinguishable for its keel, and notably different from craft of, say, the Graveney boat type. And the cog is identified in several sources as a beamy, high-sided vessel with a flat bottom, used above all by merchants of the Hanseatic League.

There is some archaeological evidence regarding the development of the Scandinavian tradition after the eleventh century. Dating to a century or so later was a vessel found at Ellingaa in Denmark and investigated in 1968 (Crumlin-Pedersen 1972, 185–6). It was about 17 metres long, and the principal difference between it and the merchant vessels found at Roskilde was somewhat heavier and closer-spaced framing. Recent excavations in the old-port area at Bergen in Norway have yielded the fragmentary remains of a very large thirteenth-century vessel apparently within this same tradition; the completed craft would have been about 25 metres long and 10 wide. However, as the century advanced, the distinction between traditions seems to have become blurred, as, for example, in one of the boats excavated at Kalmar in the 1930s, which shared a general Scandinavian form with the straight stern and central rudder of the cog (Crumlin-Pedersen 1972, 190). So far as warships were concerned, this century also saw the demise of the old Viking-style longship, which was shown to be powerless against the towering sides of cogs and similar vessels. Fighting ships of the later medieval period were more like floating fortresses, with massive bow and stern castles and large numbers of troops on board, a tradition which continued until the time of the *Mary Rose* (1545). That at least some aspects of Scandinavian tradition survived in this epoch is shown by the clinker hull of the *Grace Dieu* (1416). This vessel was rated at 1400 tons, and its hull consisted of a triple thickness of clinker planking, presumably because lighter clinker planking would have been insufficiently rigid or strong (Prynne 1968). It seems likely that this may have been an exceptional essay at producing a large ship within old-established techniques, with few close parallels, but future study of both archaeological and historical sources may prove this to be an unwarranted assumption.

As indicated in section 3.4, the heavy-keeled techniques of the Viking craft were not alone in Northern Europe in the first millennium A.D.; there seems also to have been a tradition of flat-bottomed construction, evidence for which has come from Germany, Holland, and England. It appears that many of the later medieval ship types were derived from these techniques, including the cog and, probably, the hulk. A fine illustration of the continuity of such shipbuilding has come from the excavations on the drained lands of the Zuider Zee in Holland (van der Heide 1956; 1976). A small craft of the eleventh century possessed floor timbers and planking essentially the same as those of similar-sized craft of the Roman period, and the evolution from this into the full range of Dutch inshore craft of the post-medieval period has been clarified by these excavations.

So far as the cog is concerned, the archaeological evidence relies very heavily on one find – that made at Bremen in 1962 and now being prepared for exhibition in the Deutsche Schiffahrtsmuseum at Bremerhaven (fig. 4.3) (Crumlin-Pedersen 1972, 191–2). Uncovered during harbour dredging, the fragments of this vessel were removed despite extremely difficult operating conditions. On investigation it proved to be an unfinished example from about 1400, with a length of about 25 metres, and a breadth and height of about 7.5 metres. The forecastle appeared never to have been built, but a sterncastle supported on a series of stout posts had just that 'stuck-on' appearance shown on contemporary town seals, previously dismissed by many commentators as an artistic convention. Shipbuilders of this period were still thinking of the hull as one item, and the upperworks as a separate problem, rather than considering the whole vessel as a unity. Although this example had a flat bottom, it also had an attached keel, which has been generally taken as a sign of its late date and a merging of shipbuilding traditions. However, until more finds are made of cogs from earlier periods, and the exact features of a 'pure' cog form have been established, this interpretation can be no more than supposition. In this context, the reported discovery of a fourteenth-century example in the Kattegat (Denmark) appears promising.

Fig. 4.3 The Bremen Cog, as found in the banks of the River Weser, West Germany, in 1962.

During the fourteenth century, the type of bulk carrier most frequently mentioned in the records was the 'hulk', a variety whose tech-

nical specifications remain obscure (Greenhill 1976, 283–5). No examples have been recognised in the archaeological record, and the evidence from seals and the like indicates little more than a full-bodied vessel with up-curving ends. There are hints that the hull was formed by drawing all the planks in a great curve from the top of the stern to the prow, but there is no evidence regarding the type of keel used (if any), or the way in which such a vessel might have been framed.

This brief survey has only touched on some of the more obvious questions raised by the limited archaeological and other evidence available on this topic. There can be no doubt that substantial progress can only be made through many more excavated examples; the question is, what are the chances of finding these? The Bremen cog has shown one possible source, from dredging and other waterway improvement schemes, but the supply is likely to be erratic and limited. The great untapped area to date has been the sea-bed, where there must be an almost limitless supply of wrecks. Unfortunately, the North Sea, with its strong currents, shifting sands, and murky water, is not the most favourable situation in which to conduct a search, although any remains found are likely to be well preserved. From the point of view of search by electronic sensing devices, the problem is that most of these operate by registering concentrations of iron, of which there is likely to be very little on a wreck of the pre-cannon age. All in all, the Baltic offers the best prospects, since the fresh waters there allow structural elements to survive in good conditions, proud of the sea-bed, where they can be detected by sonic scanners. That such evidence exists, at least in Swedish waters, is fairly certain (Cederlund & Ingleman-Sundberg 1973, 301), but little work has been done on it.

One enormous gap in the archaeological evidence as available at present is in the British Isles; virtually nothing from the medieval period has been found since the (possibly) medieval boat found at Rye in 1822 (see section 1.2). Practically the only new evidence emerging in recent years has been from reused ship's-timbers which have been built into wharves and the like. Fragments from the thirteenth century have been reported from the Old Custom House site in London (Tatton-Brown 1974), and from Wood Quay in Dublin (Wallace & McGrail 1976). In the latter instance, whole sections of planking still clenched together had been used and, along with many other recognisable fragments, a couple of large Y-shaped timbers were found, which may have been mast-crutches or *mykes*. However, it is very difficult to undertake a full interpretation of such incomplete remains in the absence of comparative material from coherent structures. Again, the most obvious area in which to seek for such evidence is on the sea-bed, but until both the techniques and the organisation of underwater research in Britain has been improved, little progress is likely. In the meantime, knowledge concerning this most important period in the development of naval technology, overseas trade (see section 4.5), and other related matters, will remain fragmentary and unsatisfactory.

4.3   Shipbuilding in Asia

One area of enquiry in which archaeological evidence will in due course have a considerable impact is the study of the history and development of shipbuilding in Asia and neighbouring lands, although at present there is hardly any work going on in this field. As Björn Landström has written: 'We know too little of the sailing vessels whose home waters lie outside of Europe and North America to be able to say anything of their historical development and origin' (1961, 212), and, in view of the paucity of written records and the dying out of many indigenous traditions of ship design, the only hope of greater understanding in the future must lie in the discovery and investigation of the material remains, both on land and under water. The strengths and weaknesses of evidence derived from both environments will be broadly similar to those applying elsewhere, but, at least in the initial stages, until a corpus of information has been built up, the placing of any particular craft in its cultural and technological context will be particularly difficult. At the same time, the broad outlines of some of the relevant traditions can be identified on the basis of the types of vessels produced by local craftsmen in these areas over the past century or so. From this evidence, it is apparent that the blanket heading 'Asian shipbuilding' covers a very wide range of designs and techniques; in the present section there is space to mention briefly only a few of the more noteworthy types.

Operating in the waters of the Red Sea, Persian Gulf, and surrounding coasts for many centuries have been craft of a tradition which may be generally labelled 'Arabian', although strangely enough none of the types involved is known to its owners as a *dhow*. Most modern examples in this area reflect in various degrees the influence of European techniques, but it appears that, before contact was established in the fifteenth century, the indigenous craft were constructed according to a shell-first procedure with the planks sewn together edge to edge. In recent times, the principal ocean-voyaging ship types have been known as the *baggala* and the *bhum* (fig. 4.4). The former possesses a transom stern which appears to reflect the influence of eighteenth-century European merchantmen in its design and decoration (see Greenhill 1976, 148). The homeland of the *bhum* type was the Persian Gulf, and in particular Kuwait, although these vessels traded over long distances to the south along both the Indian and Africa shores, and the example shown in fig. 4.4 belonged in fact to Pakistan. Among inshore craft, as in any area, there was and still is a tremendous variety; examples include the *sambuk* of the Red Sea, or the *zaruk* and *balam* of Aden.

There appears to have been less of a trans-oceanic seafaring tradition among the inhabitants of the Indian subcontinent, and the bulk of the shipbuilding in that area was associated with the demands of coastal or river traffic. Craft intended for the latter could reach considerable proportions, on account of the length of some of these river systems. For example, on the Indus the local type of flat-bottomed craft, the punt, can attain lengths in excess of 15 metres (Greenhill 1976, 106–7). On the Ganges there used to be a quite unusual type of vessel, the *patalia*, having many similarities in design to the medieval European cog, with a flat bottom made of two complete layers of heavy planking set at right angles to one another, and clinker-built sides (*ibid.*, 265–8). Among coasting vessels there was a similar variety, including the *balam* of the Bay of Bengal, of which the lower parts were simply an expanded and extended dug-out (*ibid.*, 137–8).

The one notable exception to this general lack of archaeological data concerning Asian shipbuilding is Chinese craft. As in so many other areas of activity, the craftsmen of China developed their own designs and techniques, owing little if anything to outside influences and having surprisingly little impact on idea in neighbouring lands. Superficially, perhaps the most striking individual feature is the sail of a Chinese boat, designed to concertina up and down, and braced with many horizontal bars. The hull forms are similarly idiosyncratic, being formed without keel, stem or stern-post, square at each end with the floor deeply curved

Fig. 4.4 A Pakistan cargo vessel of a type similar to an Arab *bhum*.

fore and aft, and provided with a series of solid transverse bulkheads, which both determine the overall shape of the craft and render it more watertight (Greenhill 1976, 103–4). Research has not proceeded far enough to identify the stages in the development of these features, but evolution from the idea of the raft is a widely favoured theory, with the concept of watertight bulkheads being copied from the cellular structure of bamboo stems.

The importance of archaeological evidence in this research arises from the fact that, as Dr Joseph Needham has put it, 'systematic nautical treatises did not arise in Chinese culture, or at least did not get into print' (1971, 380). In the relevant section of his monumental investigation into *Science and Civilisation in China* (vol. 4, part 3, 1971, 379–699), Dr Needham makes extensive use of evidence both from old drawings and paintings, and from craft in use in recent times, alongside which the evidence of material remains must be interpreted. Amongst the latter, he mentions the complete hull of a fourteenth-century ship (fig. 4.5) buried in a former tributary of the Yellow River at Liang-shan Hsien (*ibid.*, 479). With transom ends and thirteen bulkheads, it was of typical Chinese build, and was evidently designed for speed, being about 20 metres long and only 3 metres wide. Its contents included an anchor dated 1372, a bronze cannon dated 1377, the remains of several helmets, and other militaria, all tending to the conclusion that it had been a riverine naval patrol boat. Another important recent discovery,

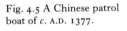

Fig. 4.5 A Chinese patrol boat of *c.* A.D. 1377.

made on the site of one of the Ming shipyards near Nanking, was of a massive rudder-post, nearly 12 metres long (*ibid.*, 481–2). Assuming the usual Chinese proportions for the rudder blade, the latter would have been over 45 square metres in area, and this would in turn imply a ship about 170 metres long. While it is hard to accept this figure literally, it would indicate that the gigantic vessels mentioned in the records as having taken part in the great Chinese voyages to India and Africa, 1405–33, under Admiral Chêng Ho, may not be the literary fantasies they have sometimes been taken to be. More recently still, a vessel built of pine, cedar and camphor wood has been reported from Chuanchow Bay in south-east China, buried under 2 metres of mud, and dating from the Southern Sung period (A.D. 1127–1279) (see *The Times*, 28 September 1976).

Despite regular contacts from at least as early as the first century A.D. between China and Japan, Indo-China, and the East Indies, Chinese naval technology was little imitated elsewhere. In the case of Japan, there was a well-established tradition from early times of building frameless vessels with edge-joined planks, formed in the manner of a built-up dug-out (Greenhill 1976, 141). In Indo-China, however, some Chinese influence can be seen in types such as the *twaqo* of Singapore (Landström 1961, 217). Eastwards, among the Pacific islands, was the area of the dug-out, where great canoes, provided with outriggers or lashed together in catamaran formation, undertook voyages for colonisation or gift-exchange across thousands of kilometres of open sea, at a time when the people concerned had only a Stone Age technology (Johnstone 1974, 56–67). But while much useful data could be gleaned from the excavation of the remains of some of these vessels on land, the chances of finding one of them under water, frozen in time during one of these epic voyages, with its cargo intact, are very remote, since such non-ballasted craft would only sink in very exceptional circumstances.

The area of enquiry skimmed over in this section is a very wide one, both geographically and in terms of the range of shipbuilding traditions involved, but it can reasonably be considered as one large area of unrealised potential because of its lack of current research. It is to be hoped that the future will see adequate resources devoted to these topics, since the technical achievements of the shipbuilders are as much the heritage of all mankind as those of their European counterparts, and are equally deserving of study.

4.4   Inland craft

When discussing the vessels of both India and China in the last section, mention was made of the great number of river boats of all sizes used in those countries, in the case of China to such an abundance that, as western observers from Marco Polo onwards frequently noted, there were probably more boats there than in all the rest of the world (Needham 1971, fig. 948). The vessels of a given lake system or river basin are important both as vital elements in regional culture, and as indicators of relationships between the traditions of different areas. The scope for the discovery and excavation of such craft in all parts of the world is thus very great. So far as land sites are concerned, the beds of abandoned river channels have proved especially productive over the years, ranging from the Rother boat of 1822 through to the recent collection of Roman period craft from Zwammerdam in Holland (Rice 1824; de Weerd & Haalebos 1973). Similarly, a number of boat remains have come from areas of former river bank artificially reclaimed, as with the several craft found at Blackfriars in London (Marsden 1966; 1971). There are few recent examples of relevant underwater discoveries within lakes or rivers, although the extremely favourable conditions for preservation presented by fresh water (see section 2.3) must mean that there is a considerable potential for future discoveries in such situations; one notable recent underwater find was the Gallo-Roman boat lying in 2 metres of water in the Bay of Bevaix in Lake Neuchâtel, Switzerland (Arnold 1974; 1975).

This last craft, which is illustrated in fig. 4.6, represents one of a range of boats of this period found along the rivers of north-west Europe, notably the Rhine and the Thames, which appear to have certain features in common, representing an early tradition of 'continental' boat-building, sometimes labelled 'celtic' (Marsden 1976a; 1977). In section 4.2 on northern European shipbuilding, mention was made of the apparent relationship between some medieval ship types and earlier craft around the Rhine estuaries, so the antecedents of these vessels are of importance if only for this reason. Obviously the details of construction vary between examples, depending on functions, which range from estuarine barge (Blackfriars boat 1), through Rhine ferry (Zwammerdam boat 6), to medium-sized lake boat (Bevaix boat, fig. 4.6). However, there are certain regular features which distinguish this group from

Fig. 4.6 A plan of the Gallo-Roman boat found in the Bay of Bevaix, Lake Neuchâtel, Switzerland.

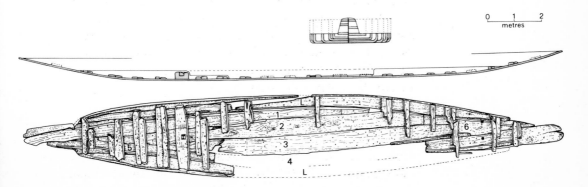

other contemporary traditions in Scandinavia or the Mediterranean, notably the use of clenched iron nails driven through prepared wooden pegs, the flat bottom with angular transition to the sides, and planking set edge-to-edge without being joined. At first sight this last feature would seem to indicate skeleton-first construction, but this may not have been so in every instance; for example, on the Blackfriars boat 1 it has been suggested that the side strakes had been erected on temporary battens (see Hasslöf 1963, fig. 8), and on the Bevaix boat a number of apparently redundant trenails on the bottom planks suggested that they had been lashed together initially, before the frames were set up (Arnold 1975, 125–6). This latter boat also has several other unique features, such as the strange way in which the four massive floor timbers have been set in obliquely to the main axis of the boat (see fig. 4.6).

Evidently well adapted for use on inland waters, this group of vessels appeared in the northern parts of the Roman Empire without any known precursors. The absence of similar techniques of construction in the heartlands of the classical world suggests that the tradition is not simply a result of Roman influences, while the lack of any comparable vessels outside the Roman realms indicates that it is not a purely indigenous technology; as with so many features of Roman life in these areas, it probably represents a conflation of ideas from both sources. The one vessel which might seem to give some clues as to the origins of these techniques, in that it displays nearly all of them and dates from the early Iron Age, is a boat found in the 1880s at Ljubljana in modern Yugoslavia, but, isolated as it is in both time and location, it serves only to demonstrate how limited current understanding is on these matters. Similarly, it is certainly going well beyond the present range of the evidence to suggest that similar techniques were applied in contemporary sea-going craft around Gaul and Britain.

Despite these large areas of uncertainty, this topic of Gallo-Roman and allied craft represents probably the best-studied topic in the whole field of inland boats. Information is considerably more limited regarding earlier river craft in this region; as was suggested above, in section 4.1, the log-boat probably played a major role. For the ensuing medieval period there are a number of surviving boats, but not enough to make out any coherent pattern of evolution or development. One notable find was of a vessel, discovered in 1930 at Utrecht in Holland, about 18 metres long, with a very pronounced fore and aft curve, and formed simply of a series of substantial strakes converging at each end. Although this was undoubtedly a river boat, it has been suggested that the technique involved was in some way ancestral to that used in the later medieval hulk (Crumlin-Pedersen 1972, 186–7).

Even with the post-medieval period there are surprisingly great gaps in knowledge concerning the types of boats in use on different waterways. Contemporary paintings can often be useful sources regarding overall appearance, but are frequently less useful when it comes to constructional details, especially below the waterline. This explains the interest in finds such as that made at Blackfriars in 1969, when a late seventeenth-century brick-carrying barge was excavated (Marsden 1971); clinker-built, with a very flat floor and only a keel plank, it had an extremely medieval appearance. But for most of these now-abandoned local boat types, the most satisfactory evidence lies in examples which were only recently in use, and in the testimony of those older inhabitants who used to work on them; in most parts of the world there is a pressing need for more basic recording of such information, and for the preservation of indigenous craft in working order.

The various craft discovered at Blackfriars in London represent instances where the significance of the find was not limited to considerations of naval technology, but extended to their economic role. The second-century A.D. barge was carrying a cargo of Kentish ragstone, and the seventeenth-century one several thousand red bricks, presumably destined for the rebuilding of the City after the Great Fire of 1666 (Marsden 1966, 39–41; 1971, 97). Furthermore, there are a few circumstances in which attention is focussed solely on cargoes, since no structural elements have survived. A good example of this comes from North America, at the western end of Lake Superior, along the rivers beyond Grand Portage used by European traders seeking furs from the Indians. At various stages along this trail, where the traders' canoes were liable to be upset by rapids, divers have found a wide range of goods representing a cross-section of the items carried for exchange with the Indians (Wheeler & van Gemert 1972; Birk 1975). Craftsmen's tools, guns, knives, kettles and pans, thimbles, and other trinkets were among the objects recovered in this work, which has been continuing on a systematic basis since the early 1960s. While this may represent a somewhat special situation, at the point and period of contact between two very different societies, similar opportunities for such investigations must exist elsewhere in the world.

4.5 Pre-1500 trade outside the Mediterranean

The final point made in the last section, concerning the archaeological evidence for riverine trade, introduces one of the most extensive topics for research in maritime archaeology, that of waterborne trade in general (see sections 6.3 and 7.3). As indicated in the course of chapter 3, there is considerable and growing interest in this topic so far as the Mediterranean world in classical times is concerned, and much of the significance of studies in post-medieval shipping involves economic matters. However, there are a number of other regions and periods in which the potential is as yet unrealised, but for which a handful of maritime finds promise significant future progress.

A specific instance in which this is true concerns economic links between Britain and the Continent, since any goods carried between the two areas in the period between the breaking of the landbridge to south-east England about 8000 years ago and the present century must inevitably have travelled in ships. While there is undoubted indirect evidence for maritime trade in Neolithic times (Bowen 1972, 26–42), the earliest direct evidence lies in a group of bronze blades discovered in the summer of 1977 off the coast near Salcombe in Devon (fig. 4.7). One of them is exceedingly well preserved, and represents a sword with a Rixheim–Monza style blade and a hook-tang, probably manufactured in Central Europe around 1200 B.C.; the other two items are heavily eroded, but still possess a similar lozenge cross-section. Preliminary assessment of the site in October 1977 has indicated that there is probably more material to be found from this assemblage, and the most plausible explanation for their situation is that they are derived from a wreck deposit; an intensive season of search and survey in 1978 may clarify and extend the evidence.

Slightly later in date, but also apparently coming from a wreck deposit, was a collection of bronze implements discovered on the sea-bed near Dover in 1974 (Stevens *et al.* 1976; Coombs 1976). Probably assembled in the period around 1000 B.C., the full significance of this group can never be assessed since unfortunately no records were made of their context on the sea-floor. Another maritime find reflecting over-seas trade at this period was a bronze axe of a Sicilian type dragged up by a fisherman off the Hampshire coast in 1937 (Bass 1966, 86). And finally, the other end of a trade-route leading away from Britain must be suggested by the presence of Hiberno-British bronzes of the late

Fig. 4.7 Three bronze objects recovered from the probable site of a Bronze Age wreck near Salcombe, Devon, in 1977; the top piece is a sword with a hook-tang and a Rixheim–Monza style blade of Middle Bronze Age date, while the other two items are heavily eroded blades with a similar lozenge cross-section. 15 centimetre scale.

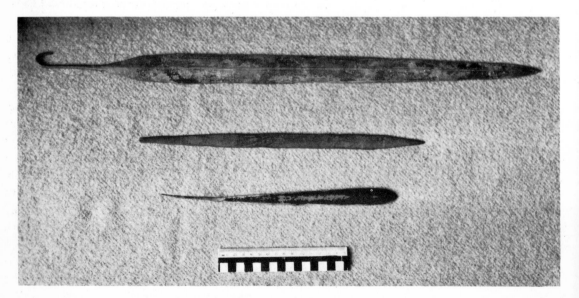

Fig. 4.8 A bronze figurine recovered from the mudflats of the Severn estuary near Aust in Gloucestershire.

Bronze Age dredged up at Huelva in Spain in 1923, and presumably deriving from a wreck-site (Clark 1952, 271). Together, these chance discoveries show that, in time, maritime archaeology should be making a major contribution to an understanding of the mechanics of trade in the northern European Bronze Age, just as the Cape Gelidonya excavation illuminated that of a similar period in the eastern Mediterranean (Bass 1967).

Further maritime finds reflect continuing trade in the pre-Roman Iron Age. Direct contacts with the Mediterranean world may be indicated by the small bronze statuette of apparently Spanish design found in the Severn muds near Aust in Gloucestershire (fig. 4.8) (Cunliffe 1974, 147). An extensive trade in wine and oil is similarly evidenced by a wreck-site found off Belle-Ile, Morbihan, in north-west France, containing amphorae of a type (Dressel 1A) not found in northern France but occurring on several Iron Age sites in southern Britain (Peacock 1971). The major hill-fort of Hengistbury Head in Hampshire seems to have derived its importance from its position alongside Poole harbour, its role as an entrepôt being reflected in the quantities of imported materials found in the limited excavations so far undertaken within its bounds (Bushe-Fox 1915). It must only be a matter of time before a few wreck sites of this period are found in British waters, just as Bronze Age ones have recently been reported, suggesting both these contacts between central southern Britain and north-west France and those operating across the Straits of Dover. It is at the very end of this period that we receive the first documentary evidence for the nature of British exports, listed by Strabo as 'corn, cattle, metals, hides, slaves, and clever hunting dogs'. While few of these items can have left any traces in the conventional archaeological record, they should all be detectable on well-preserved maritime sites.

Strangely, while the absorption of Britain within the Roman Empire must have led to even more extensive cross-Channel contacts, this has not been reflected in numerous discoveries of wreck-sites of this period. At present, the sole representative of this commerce is the site known since the eighteenth century on the Pudding Pan Rock, near Whitstable, in Kent, involving a ship of c. A.D. 170 carrying a cargo of Samian ware from Central Gaul (fig. 4.9) (Smith 1907; 1909; Hartley 1972). And similarly, the continued exchanges of the medieval period have not been matched by the discovery of a single wreck-site. This is presumably because such sites will mostly lie in the dangerous and unattractive waters of the Straits of Dover and the southern North Sea; it probably also reflects the tastes and interests of those currently active in British maritime archaeology.

Alongside the evidence available from particular sites, the author is undertaking more general research into the significance of maritime archaeology for studies in maritime trade in these periods. In recent years, archaeologists have begun to consider the extent of overseas trading, and its main trends, for all periods since Neolithic times, on the basis of finds distributions on both sides of the Channel. The intention is to look at these ideas, develop them where possible, and assess their implications for the mechanics of shipping, trying to correlate them with the evidence for the technical and navigational skills of the people involved. However, this research has only just begun, and it is too soon to indicate even the general tenor of its conclusions.

This brief discussion of early maritime finds around Britain has been given only as an example of the potential for such studies in northern European waters; there are many other areas in which such research may be equally, if not more, productive. Some of the cargoes uncovered within the Zuider Zee polders have already revealed new data about the commodities transported across these waters since the eleventh century (van der Heide 1976). Another area of promise is the Baltic, where already some later medieval sites are known, but not yet investigated, and where the excellent conditions for preservation should lead to almost complete inventories of a vessel's contents. And turning to the Mediterranean between classical and post-medieval times, maritime finds could make a major contribution to the continuing controversies concerning the Pirenne Thesis. This theory, first proposed by the Belgian historian Henri Pirenne, held that there was a severe curtailment of Mediterranean trade and communication consequent on the Islamic conquest of the southern and eastern shores of the Sea, and that this had a profound impact on the subsequent history of western Europe since it caused the area to turn in on itself, both economically and politically (Pirenne 1939). The nature and extent of any maritime trade

Fig. 4.9 A collection of Samian ware of the mid second century A.D. from the Roman wreck-site on the Pudding Pan Rock, Kent.

in these centuries could best be studied through any available contemporary wreck-sites, especially ones lying off the southern coast of France, which formed the contact zone between the two cultures in the early Middle Ages. To date, only two relevant sites have been located and investigated, at Bataiguier in the Bay of Cannes and at Agay (Var), and both of these seem to indicate an extensive and wide-ranging commerce (Joncheray 1976a; Visquis 1973).

At the same time, maritime trade has never been limited to European waters. Since at least the third millennium B.C. there has been a continuous coastal trade around the Indian Ocean (Bass 1972b, 14–15), for which some evidence must have survived. A pressage of future discoveries in this area has come from the fourteenth- or fifteenth-century A.D. shipwreck at Sattahip in Thailand (Weier 1975). This contained a wide range of ceramics of the Sukhothai period (fig. 4.10), including a large number of Thai celadon bowls and other local products, along with brown-glazed jars from China and small plates from present-day north Vietnam. Although pottery apparently constituted the greater part of the cargo, other items recovered included two ivory tusks, a gold ornament set with rubies, and some lead weights. Another foretaste of future developments, this time from Chinese waters, has been given by the cargo found on a wreck of the Southern Sung period discovered in Chuanchow Bay, which included various fragrant woods, betelnuts, frankincense, ambergris, cinnabar, mercury, tortoise shells, and chessmen (*The Times*, 28 September 1976, p. 13). And from Korean waters a wreck has recently been reported coming from the thirteenth or fourteenth centuries A.D. and containing several thousand pieces of celadon porcelain attributable to the Sung Dynasty, presumably Chinese exports to Korea or Japan (Anon 1977).

Fig. 4.10 Ceramics of the Sukhothai period (A.D. 1300–1500) from a shipwreck at Sattahip, Thailand.

4.6 Anchors and anchorages

In addition to the evidence from wreck-sites and artefact distribution maps, past trade and trade-routes can be indicated by clusters of anchors and other jetsam on the sea-bed, betraying those places where ancient shipping frequently took shelter. The archaeological potential of such sites has been recognised for many years by researchers such as Miss Honor Frost (1963a, 29–61; 1973c), although requests for detailed information from divers of all countries have not met with the response they deserved. The theory is that the range and relative frequency of anchors of different periods and origins within such sites should reflect pretty faithfully the relative importance of different routes and seafaring nations at various periods. Without the presence of anchors or other indications of an anchorage, the evidence of stray finds on the sea-bed is unsatisfactory since so many other explanations for their presence are possible alongside that of anchorage jetsam.

An essential element in such studies is an appreciation of the marine environment of the site. Collections of anchors on the sea-bed are generally found in one of two situations. The first is within a safe anchorage in all weathers, where vessels can rest to do business in the region or simply shelter during bad weather. Such havens will not have changed their character over the centuries, except in very unusual geological circumstances, and will thus still be used by modern sailors; a realiable guide to ancient practice can therefore be present-day usage. Thus the presence of permanently sheltered waters behind the island of Jezirat Fara'un hamza at the northern end of the Gulf of Aqaba inspired Mr Alex Flinder to undertake an intensive survey of both the sea-bed and the island itself, so producing evidence for the existence of a major port here from biblical until medieval times (Flinder 1977). The other common situation in which anchors are found is to either side of a particularly dangerous stretch of water, as around a notorious promontory, where vessels have had to wait, sometimes for weeks on end,

Fig. 4.11 A selection of stone anchors from the Temple of the Obelisks at Byblos (Lebanon).

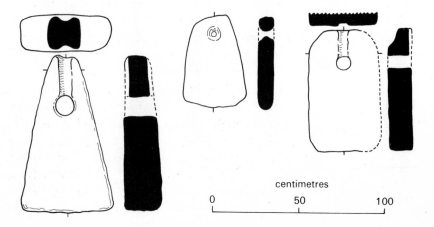

centimetres
0   50   100

before favourable winds allow them to make the passage. Several of the anchorage studies mentioned below have been concerned with such places (e.g. Green 1973b; Fiori 1974; Santamaria 1972). It is very important that any researcher pays close attention to the characteristics of his site from the point of view of sailing vessels before attempting to assess the significance of the anchors or other finds discovered on the sea-bed.

Until the first millennium B.C., ancient shipping appears to have relied on stone anchors. Some types, having only one hole by which to attach a cable, operated by weight alone, while others, possessing up to five holes with pieces of wood rammed through them, were designed to catch on sandy bottoms. The problem with such crude artefacts is dating; the only possible method is by comparison those found in dated land contexts, principally those placed as votive offerings in sacred precincts (Frost 1973c, fig. 1). One such group has come from the Temple of the Obelisks at Byblos, a Bronze Age site in the Lebanon (fig. 4.11), and others of similar date have been found on sacred sites in Egypt, Cyprus, Crete, and Malta. Further dated examples may be found reused in other buildings, as with those incorporated in the seventh century B.C. quays at Sozopol in Bulgaria (Dimitrov 1976; 1977). However, it has yet to be satisfactorily demonstrated that sufficiently distinctive patterns were used at different periods to make such comparisons useful; furthermore, pierced stones have continued to be used into modern times, for purposes such as weighting nets or sounding lines. More progress might be made by an analysis of the stone used within a collection of anchors, in order to identify different regional origins, although this would depend on a very detailed study of rock types around the Mediterranean. While there will always be a few erratics, it is likely that the overall range of sources in any collection will reflect reasonably faithfully the home ports of the vessels using that anchorage.

As indicated above, there have been disappointingly few detailed studies of whole collections of anchors from a given area; furthermore, the potential for such work has been restricted in recent years by the unrecorded lifting of anchors from the sea-bed in areas popular with sports divers. One such survey which showed what could be achieved was undertaken by a team of student divers in north-east Cyprus (Green 1973b), although the conclusions reached were severely limited by the lack of comparative material from other areas (Frost 1973c, 408). One useful fact to emerge from such studies arises from the finding of half-ton anchors both on land and in the sea at Ugarit and other Bronze Age sites in the Levant, showing that Bronze Age ships must have been of considerable size, and certainly too big to have been beached every night (see section 3.3). This deduction arises from the general truth that, while large ships can carry all sizes of anchors, and generally will be equipped with a wide range, a small vessel cannot carry a large anchor.

In the Mediterranean, a large number of bars of lead have been found, being the stocks of anchors from classical times. This identification was finally confirmed by the finding, on the Nemi ships, of huge wooden anchors with such stocks, thus ending a considerable academic controversy. This concentration of weight at the head of an anchor was necessitated by the fact that, until the early centuries A.D. at least, only rope cables were used which could not in themselves act, as chains can, to hold the anchor parallel to the sea-bed (Frost 1963b). The use of specially carved stone stocks to achieve this purpose apparently began in the sixth century B.C., to be superseded a couple of centuries later by the lead variety (Gianfrotta 1977); the latter can thus be seen as a diagnostic feature of shipping in Roman Republican and early Imperial times. They can range in size from just a few kilograms to over 600 (Casson 1959; Rochier 1975). Their presence in any anchorage is thus a good indication of its use at this period, but their absence is less significant, partly because the use of such anchors may not have been universal, and partly because, being both useful and valuable to modern divers, they have been selectively removed from popular diving sites. There have recently been some systematic investigations of major anchorages along the southern coast of France, considering these items along with other surviving jetsam, notably at Cap Gros near Antibes (Fiori 1974) and to the east of Cap Dramont (Santamaria 1972). One single find of undoubted importance was the lead anchor stock, of first-century B.C. pattern, recovered from 15 metres of water near Aberdaron in North Wales, suggesting Roman shipping in the area at a very early, possibly even pre-conquest, date (Boon 1976; 1977).

Iron anchor chains are first mentioned by Caesar, in his famous description of the ships of his maritime adversaries, the Venetii of north-west France (*De Bello Gallico*, III, 13). Archaeological evidence in

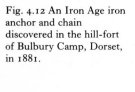

Fig. 4.12 An Iron Age iron anchor and chain discovered in the hill-fort of Bulbury Camp, Dorset, in 1881.

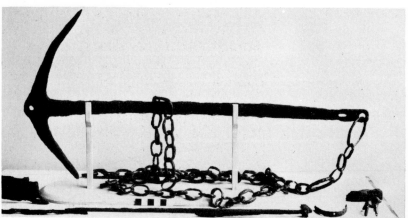

support of his statements has come from an Iron Age hillfort in Dorset, Bulbury Camp, in which an iron anchor and chain were found in 1881 (fig. 4.12) (Cunnington 1884). This was an area in close communication with north-west Gaul; indeed, Caesar implies that the inhabitants of this area were tributary to the Venetii (*De Bello Gallico*, III, 8). The chances of ever identifying an Iron Age anchor in British or northern French waters would seem to be remote, since one will only have survived over such a period in very exceptional circumstances, and in any case it would be superficially indistinguishable from a modern iron one. The idea of the iron anchor was taken up very quickly by the Romans; one was found on the Nemi ships (*c.* A.D. 40), and another has come from an eruption deposit at Pompeii (A.D. 79) (Frost 1963*a*, 59–60). These finds also showed that the idea of the movable stock, hitherto considered a mid-nineteenth-century British invention, was in fact standard Roman practice. During the medieval period, and on through to the early nineteenth century, anchor design remained fairly static, with the fixed stock varying only according to the size of the vessel concerned, thus reducing the scope for anchorage studies of the type above. The possibility of deducing the size of ships involved from the size of anchors recorded has been suggested, on the basis of standard relationships laid down by various authorities (e.g. Witsen 1671, 142–63, on seventeenth-century Dutch ships), but there is considerable doubt as to the extent to which these were generally adhered to.

Thus the only possibilities of any successful anchorage studies would appear to be in the field of classical and pre-classical trade-routes, principally within the Mediterranean. The lack of typological variation within stone anchors would seem to limit their study to certain very specialised varieties, and the greatest potential appears to lie in the recording of lead anchor stocks, with their restricted chronological range. As well as further examples from Atlantic waters, similar lead stocks from the Red Sea or Indian Ocean would be significant indicators of Roman trade in those waters (see Wheeler 1954*b*). However, the depredations of non-archaeological salvage has undoubtedly restricted the usefulness of such research in many areas, thus reinforcing the urgency of detailed investigations of all types of anchors in less popular regions in the next few years.

4.7   Deep-water archaeology

The final area of research to be considered concerns those wrecks lying in waters beyond the range of conventional air-breathing divers. Roughly speaking, this means depths in excess of about 50 metres. The upper part of this zone, down to about 300 metres at present, constitutes the range of commercial and naval mixed-gas-breathing divers, while the waters below that are at present visited only by submersibles, manned or unmanned. The range of the professional diver may be extended for a further few hundred metres by the demands of the offshore oil industry, but there is probably a physiological limit to this process, and the skills required of such persons will always be so specialised and demanding as to limit their application to archaeology. Thus this section will be concerned exclusively with the possibilities of undertaking archaeological investigations at any depth beyond 50 metres using submarines, remote-controlled underwater vehicles, and the like. An assessment of the case for deep-water archaeology, both in terms of the archaeological potential of such areas, and in terms of the technical requirements of such work, has recently been published by Willard Bascom (1976), and the present discussion owes a great deal to his book. The first task is to outline the extent of the archaeological evidence likely to be found in such situations.

Various estimates have been made about the proportion of wrecked ships which have gone down in the open sea well away from any coasts. There can be no doubt that the great majority of all vessels wrecked were sunk as a result of some accident in connection with the shore; just as aircraft are at greatest risk when taking off and landing, so ships are in most danger of collision, casting ashore, or foundering in the more crowded and restricted waters near a coast. Robert Marx has concluded that approximately 98% of all shipping losses in the western hemisphere prior to 1825 occurred in waters less than 10 metres deep (1971, 46), a figure which probably underestimates the potential for deep-water archaeology through not covering losses in mid-Atlantic. On the other hand, Bascom has concluded from a study of nineteenth-century losses at Lloyds of London that about 20% of all sinkings occur well away from coasts (1976, 84). He has proceeded to apply this figure directly to Mediterranean shipping in classical times, a questionable extension in view of the very different sizes and constructions of the vessels involved; nevertheless, it probably represents the correct order of magnitude for all sinkings in the open sea at any period.

However, the potential importance of this area of research is not related to the quantity of vessels involved, but rather to the probability that in many cases the remains will be of a very high quality. The first element in the argument is the fact that any wooden ship reaching the sea-bed is likely to do so reasonably intact. This is because a wooden structure can only be sunk with the aid of its ballast and other contents; if a vessel has broken up on the surface and spilled much of its cargo, etc., far and wide, its constituent parts will wallow about on the surface until eaten by marine creatures. While this consideration means that a large number of the ships lost in the open sea will never have reached the sea-bed in any form, it means that those which have are likely to be of great archaeological significance.

As with shallow-water wrecks, the best guarantee of good preservation of all types of material in deep water is for everything to be buried quickly in stable muds or silts, with a constant reducing environment. There are several factors encouraging such a process in deep water, of which the most important is the fact that the greater part of the ocean floor is composed of muds and oozes, derived from windborne terrestrial dust and the bodies of marine creatures. Furthermore, this sea-floor sediment is generally stable, being out of the range of waves and currents. This latter factor may be a mixed blessing, in the sense that, while it ensures that anything buried remains undisturbed, it may also mean that a wreck cannot act as a trap to waterborne sediments, thus creating its own tumulus, as can happen in shallow water.

However, if a wrecked vessel is not rapidly encapsulated within the sea-bed, but remains standing proud of the bottom, there are factors operating in deep water which can, in the right circumstances, also ensure its preservation in a way not paralleled in shallow water. First of all, the lack of water movement removes the physical stresses and mechanical abrasion which together undoubtedly account for much of the break-up of coastal wrecks. Secondly, the chemical corrosion of many materials, especially metals, is slowed down in deep water, because both salinity and temperature tend to be lower. In the deepest parts of the Mediterranean, the latter is about 13 °C, which is 10 °C less than that on the surface, while that on the ocean floor is a constant 4 °C, at which point many chemical processes are severely inhibited. And finally, destructive biological agents may be restricted or even entirely absent. While the wood borers *Teredo* and *Limnoria* appear not to live below about 100 metres, a third and equally effective destroyer of both wood and calcareous material, the clam *Xylophaga*, seems to thrive down to depths of several thousand metres. However, its effectiveness varies according to region, for reasons which are not fully understood, and it is totally absent, as are all destructive organisms, in waters which are oxygen-free. This very favourable situation can occur when there is no appreciable mixing between the bottom water and the upper oxygenated levels, and where there is sufficient decaying organic matter in the depths to absorb any oxygen diffusing down there; such reducing environments have been found in the Black Sea and the Sea of Marmara, amongst other places. Deep fresh water can be similarly hostile to organisms, which accounts for the spectacular remains recently observed in the Great Lakes of North America (see fig. 2.15, p. 54). Even in oxygenated environments, biological activity may be significantly retarded by the extreme cold at great depths, and it has recently been suggested that great pressure may have similar effects.

Having noted these factors, a proviso must be made to the effect that the study of the ocean deeps is a very new science, in which there remain many imponderables, so that all these suggested archaeological implications remain tentative. This qualification also applies to research in marine biology; for example, in assessing the tolerances of various boring animals it is still not clear whether teredo infestation of ship-timbers will continue to thrive after projection into deep water. Similarly, with the *Xylophaga*, it has been observed that it is most effective within the first metre above the sea-bed, and much less so above that; why this should be is not known.

If it is accepted that many extremely well preserved wrecks of all periods lie in deep water around the world, the question arises as to the feasibility of investigating such remains. The requirement is for methods by which to locate the wrecks, and then for adequate techniques by which they might be examined archaeologically. As a result of the demands of naval authorities, oil companies, and oceanographers, the equipment undoubtedly exists with which to undertake both tasks, and

Fig. 4.13 A surface controlled articulated arm for use in taking samples from deep-water wrecks, as proposed by Willard Bascom (1972).

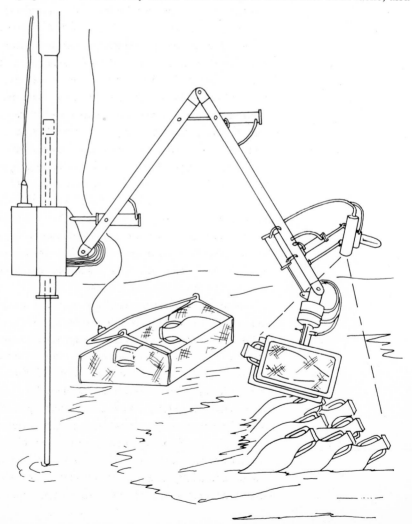

it has been described in considerable detail by Bascom (1976, 119–96).
So far as search is concerned, the problems are essentially the same as
those in shallow water, and the same range of electronic devices can be
used; he especially favoured side-scan sonar. As indicated above
(section 2.2), probably the biggest problem in such work is establishing
the precise location of the sensor at any given moment, but instruments
are available for dealing with this. For the investigation of important
sites, once located, Bascom suggested the use of a remote-controlled
articulated arm extending from a pipe dropped below a specially
designed ship (fig. 4.13) for the initial sampling of a site and the removal
of all loose artefacts, and also a kind of giant grab for the lifting of complete hulls (*ibid.*, 192; see also Bascon, 1972, 183).

Before discussing the merits or otherwise of these proposals, a couple
of major non-archaeological problems must be noted. First, such projects would be tremendously expensive, requiring the sort of budgets at
present only envisaged for oil and mineral exploration on the sea-bed.
Bascom has estimated a budget of over $300 000 for a ten week season
of search and exploration in the Mediterranean, a figure which inflation
has probably already (1977) taken over the half a million mark. This is
between twenty and fifty times the figure required for a similar period
of search and survey along a stretch of coastline. Of course, as Bascom is
anxious to emphasise, the results would be potentially of enormous
significance, but this may be rather beside the point if the proposal
requires resources far beyond the limits of any conceivable sponsorship
for archaeology. And secondly, the legal position of such work is
exceedingly vague, whether it be undertaken in indisputably international waters, or within a nation's zone of economic exploitation (now
generally extending to 200 miles from the coast), making potential
sponsors even more wary, and putting in jeopardy any co-ordinated
archaeological programme. Until international agreement on such
matters has been achieved, attempts to embark on such work would
seem to be highly irresponsible.

Since they constitute the most detailed proposals yet made concerning such research, Bascom's scheme deserves serious consideration.
Where search is concerned, they appear to be quite reasonable, although
limited by the fact that they are geared to identifying objects lying proud
of the sea-bed, while it seems likely that the most significant sites will
be the ones which are totally buried. So far as the hydraulic arm is
concerned (fig. 4.13), its use in obtaining surface samples from a site
would seem unexceptionable, but the undertaking of more extensive
excavation with its appears more debatable. As indicated above, the
principal importance of these sites is likely to reside in the fact that they
are substantially intact, so that meticulous observation and recording of
every artefact will be of even more importance than usual; the sensitive

touch and experienced eye of the trained archaeologist will be very necessary. Certainly, therefore, there is no question of his grab ever being acceptable for the salvaging of complete hulls. It would seem to be infinitely preferable to work towards means of encapsulating such remains and lifting them complete, together with the surrounding sea-bed, for controlled excavation in shallow and sheltered water. Some possible methods are indicated by Bascom (1976, 188–9), but rejected on the grounds of cost. However, since only the most important of these wrecks are ever going to merit attempts at recovery, only the best possible methods will be acceptable.

It thus seems that the archaeological potential of sites in deep water is undoubtedly great, but, while the identification and assessment of such remains is now technically feasible, the financial and legal problems are likely to deter any serious attempts at such work for several years to come. Whether technical advances in three or four decades' time will have led to cheaper and more flexible techniques becoming available, no-one can tell, but it is by no means certain that they will. This being the case, it would be unwise to expect very much from this field in the near future; its potential has been noted but, so far as the present study of maritime archaeology in the late 1970s is concerned, it would appear to have little direct relevance, and will not figure prominently in the discussions in Part Two.

With the exception of this last, all the topics discussed in this present chapter have involved research which has started, or is about to begin, and together they indicate the directions in which maritime archaeology might be expected to expand over the next few years. Although in the last analysis, much of the presentation has been speculative and un-specific, the intention has consistently been to stay within the bounds of what might reasonably be expected in the light of past experience. Taken along with the subjects described in chapter 3, a fairly wide-ranging account of the variety of concerns which might be said to constitute this sub-discipline has emerged, on the basis of which some consideration can be given to the definition of the essential character-istics of maritime archaelogy. Part One of this book has been concerned with describing the subject by investigating its several attributes; Part Two seeks to complete that description by considering its common features and fundamental principles.

PART TWO

Towards a theory of maritime archaeology

5

The archaeology of shipwrecks

5.1 Introduction

Given that maritime archaeology is concerned with the study of ships and seafaring, and that its principal sources of data lie in the remains of such activities preserved on the seashore or sea-bed, it follows that the interpretation of such data is closely bound up with an understanding of what is involved in a shipwreck. The shipwreck is the event by which a highly organised and dynamic assemblage of artefacts are transformed into a static and disorganised state with long-term stability. While the archaeologist must observe this final situation, his interest, as explained in section 1.1 above, is centred on the former, whose various aspects are only indicated indirectly and partially by the surviving material. If the various processes which have intervened between the two states can be identified and described, the researcher can begin to disentangle the evidence he has uncovered.

In the present chapter, an attempt is made to identify the several features common to any shipwreck, and the ways in which they can be assessed on any particular site. Just as the nature of a ship involves certain basic concepts which are common to all periods and places, so the phenomenon of the shipwreck must involve certain regular features common to all instances. If these can be described, then their implications for any analysis of sea-bed remains can be ascertained, and the most appropriate procedures identified. Furthermore, if the latter can be tested and demonstrated on sites for which the evidence, both archaeological and documentary, is extensive, then they can be applied in situations where the evidence is more fragmentary and confused, and the analysis correspondingly more valuable. The validity of any conclusions reached in maritime archaeology depends fundamentally on the understanding of these processes, so that their study must occupy a central place in the sub-discipline. To date, facile and unrealistic assumptions about what happened during and after a wrecking have been a feature of too many wreck-site reports, with a consequent diminution of their value and authority. These considerations account for the concentration on site analysis in the rest of this chapter; it is taken for granted that in any particular project standard archaeological artefactual analysis will also be undertaken.

Compared with equivalent depositional and post-depositional processes on land sites, shipwrecks possess many peculiar features. The environmental factors operating under water are different from those found on land, and are outside the range of normal experience. Furthermore human interference, undoubtedly the most important destructive agent in a terrestrial context, is minimal under water, and limited to a few identifiable activities. Finally, the same factors are operative on every site, although in varying degrees, so that the archaeological evidence is more homogeneous in this sub-discipline than in most others, an attribute which further strengthens its internal cohesion. Thus an investigation into the archaeology of shipwrecks constitutes both the final defining characteristic of maritime archaeology, and the starting point for constructing its general theory.

The flow diagram in fig. 5.1 represents the processes through which that organised assemblage of artefacts comprising a ship and its contents will have passed to produce the collection of items excavated on the sea-floor. This assemblage can be regarded as a system, defined by the necessary characteristics of a ship, which has undergone a series of

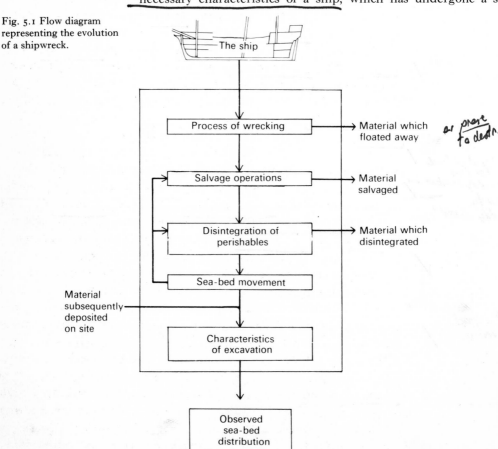

Fig. 5.1 Flow diagram representing the evolution of a shipwreck.

transformations through time, emerging as the results of an archaeological excavation. At the same time, the whole shipwreck process itself constitutes a closed system, with the ship as input, and with a number of different outputs, about which there are varying degrees of knowledge (Clarke 1968, 44). Similarly, the understanding of the several elements within the central box of the system is partial; the hope is that by taking it as a whole the various bits of incomplete knowledge can be integrated in such a way as to increase overall comprehension.

Within the present chapter, consideration of the operation of this system is divided into three parts. First, there is a general discussion (section 5.2) of the natural environment within which it operates, looking for regularities, and supplementing the general ideas presented in section 2.1 above. Then the elements displayed within the central box in fig. 5.1 are divided into two groups, those which act as filters extracting material from the assemblage, and those which operate as scrambling devices, rearranging its patterns. The next part of the discussion is thus concerned with the filtering effects of the process of wrecking, salvage operations, and the disintegration of perishables (section 5.3). The third part, dealing with the scrambling devices, is covered in two sections, one dealing with the rearranging aspects of the process of wrecking (section 5.4) and one with post-depositional sea-bed movement (section 5.5). Having thus described the development of sea-bed distributions, it is possible to proceed to a brief discussion of some of the modes of analysis which might prove valuable in their interpretation (sections 5.6 and 5.7).

While the consideration of this system is presented in general terms, its implications in both interpretation and analysis are illustrated with material derived from a wreck-site with which I have been particularly involved in recent years, and which has proved particularly suitable for testing these ideas. The site is that of the wreck of the Dutch East Indiaman *Kennemerland*, which struck Stoura Stack in the Out Skerries (Shetland Isles, U.K.) on 20 December 1664, while outward bound from the Netherlands to the East Indies; only three men survived by being projected on to the Stack from the look-out post. In addition to the standard archival material from the company records in Amsterdam, there are a number of documents in Scotland referring to the legal disputes over the ownership of material subsequently salvaged, including the treasure. The site was first identified by a student diving team from Aston University in 1971, and since then there have been three major seasons of excavation involving members of Manchester and other British universities. A number of interim and other reports have been issued over the years, from which further information about this work can be obtained (AUSAC 1974; Forster & Higgs 1973; Muckelroy 1976; Price & Muckelroy 1974; 1977).

most idut of
importance of
categories of
remains within
event

+ broder inferences
to be drawn from them

5.2 Wreck-sites and their environments

From the earliest days of archaeological investigations under water it was apparent that, as on land, ancient remains were more likely to have been preserved within soft substrates than within rocky ones. However, it soon became clear that the nature of the sea-bed was by no means the only controlling factor, and so more complex explanations were developed, notably by the French underwater pioneer, Frederic Dumas (see especially Dumas 1962; 1972). Unfortunately, since nearly all the early work in this field concerned wreck-sites in the Mediterranean, the theories developed were heavily biassed by the special characteristics of that Sea. In his discussions, M. Dumas drew a fundamental distinction between sandy shores, rocky shores, and shores with submerged cliffs (Dumas 1972, 32–3), stating that it was only in the last circumstance that coherent archaeological remains were to be found. This feature of submerged cliffs close inshore occurs along much of the northern shores of the Mediterranean, but is not so common elsewhere. Wreck material which had not quickly dropped into deep water was regarded as beyond recovery: 'The sea smashes everything in shallow waters, and such scattered wreckage is of scant interest to the archaeologist' (*ibid.*, 32). From this grew the general rule that nothing of significance would ever be found in shallow water; for example, Miss Frost has written: 'ancient wrecks are necessarily in deepish water' (Frost, 1962, 82).

oven
mid

At the same time, the limitations of these ideas were clearly stated. M. Dumas recognised that his general statements need not be directly applicable outside the Mediterranean (Dumas 1972, 34), while W. D. Nesteroff, a geologist writing in the same volume as Dumas (UNESCO 1972), noted some aberrant sites, such as that at Spargi (Lamboglia 1961). He suggested as additional mitigating factors a heavily fissured sea-bed, offshore islets, and the protection afforded by marine plants (Nesteroff 1972, 176–7). But such instances were seen as exceptions to the general rules, so that it was in terms of the basic distinction between favourable and unfavourable conditions that subsequent workers, both within and beyond the Mediterranean, approached their sites. As will have become clear in the course of chapters 3 and 4 above, however, this is a dangerous oversimplification, since there are a large number of sites on which the remains are neither totally coherent nor totally broken up. The factors producing these intermediate sites are obviously complex and demand further investigation.

One recent study in underwater environmental archaeology, concerning wreck-sites in British waters, has proceeded by appropriating the methods of marine ecology. The idea was to measure the degree of correlation between the quality of the archaeological remains and a number of possibly relevant environmental attributes. These latter were selected on the basis of those which had proved significant in parallel

Table 5.1. *The matrix in which the archaeological survival characteristics (row A) and the eleven environmental site attributes (rows 1 to 11) are ranked across the twenty sites located in Fig. 5.2. The descriptions of the eleven attributes are given in the text*

	1	2	3	4	5	6	7	8	9	10	11	12	13	14	15	16	17	18	19	20
A	5	13	3	17	4	14	11	12	7	10	2	18	16	20	1	8	19	9	15	6
1	11	10	4	13	1	8	12	14	18	15	3	19	9	20	2	17	5	6	7	16
2	3	7	8	10	1	5	2	14	12	9	4	13	11	16	17	15	18	19	20	6
3	8	6	10	12	5	4	2	13	3	19	1	7	17	9	18	14	15	16	20	11
4	14	15	12	8	1	13	20	7	19	3	17	5	10	6	2	18	16	11	9	4
5	12	10	7	19	18	6	14	15	1	16	4	9	5	17	20	2	11	3	13	8
6	2	6	15	10	13	7	18	16	1	19	9	17	8	12	20	3	5	4	14	11
7	14	9	11	15	16	7	19	18	1	17	6	12	5	13	20	2	4	3	10	8
8	10	13	8	4	20	18	17	12	3	15	2	16	14	19	1	9	6	7	5	11
9	6	11	3	18	4	14	16	12	5	7	2	17	9	20	1	8	19	15	13	10
10	9	15	4	13	5	12	16	19	6	7	2	17	8	18	1	3	20	14	11	10
11	5	15	3	18	6	14	9	10	20	12	1	16	8	17	2	4	19	11	13	7

Fig. 5.2 A map showing the locations of the twenty listed wreck-sites in Britain used in the environmental attribute study.

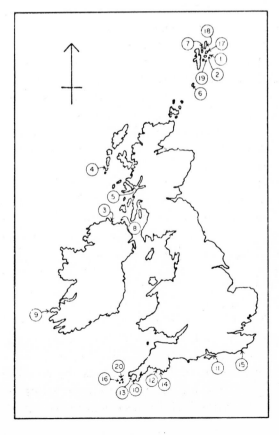

1 *Kennemerland* (1664)
2 *De Liefde* (1711)
3 *Trinidad Valencera* (1588)
4 *Adelaar* (1728)
5 *Dartmouth* (1690)
6 *El Gran Grifon* (1588)
7 *Lastdrager* (1652)
8 *Girona* (1588)
9 *Santa Maria de la Rosa* (1588)
10 *Santo Christo de Castello* (1667)
11 *Mary Rose* (1545)
12 Penlee cannon site (1690?)
13 Low Lee Ledges (?)
14 Mewstone Ledges (?)
15 *Amsterdam* (1749)
16 *Hollandia* (1743)
17 *Wendela* (1737)
18 *Curaçao* (1729)
19 *Evstafii* (1780)
20 *Colossus* (1798)

basis for choosing these elements?

studies in other marine sciences, such as biology (Hiscock 1974) or coastal geomorphology (King 1972), being defined as follows:

1. Maximum offshore fetch, within 30° of the perpendicular to the coast. *(= swell)*
2. Sea horizon from the site; i.e. sector within which there is more than 10 kilometres of open water.
3. Percentage of hours during which there are winds of Force 7 or more from directions within the sea horizon.
4. Maximum speed of tidal streams across site.
5. Minimum depth of site.
6. Maximum depth of site.
7. Depth of principal deposit on site.
8. Average slope of the sea-bed over the whole site.
9. Underwater topography: the proportion of the site over which the sea-bed consists of geologically recent sedimentary deposits.
10. Nature of the coarsest material within these deposits.
11. Nature of the finest material within them. In ordering sites on this attribute and the previous one they were ranked initially according to broad categories of material, and then according to the relative importance of these deposits on the different sites.

look at these.

Twenty wreck-sites were identified for which sufficient environmental and archaeological data were available; their locations and names are given in fig. 5.2. Each attribute was then ranked across the twenty sites, a procedure which allowed both qualitatively and numerically scored ones to be used; the resulting matrix is given in table 5.1. The Kendall Rank Correlation Coefficient τ (*tau*) was then used to quantify these relationships (Siegel 1956, 213–23); fig. 5.3 shows the values produced when correlating archaeological survival against the eleven environmental attributes, together with the 5 % and 0.1 % significance

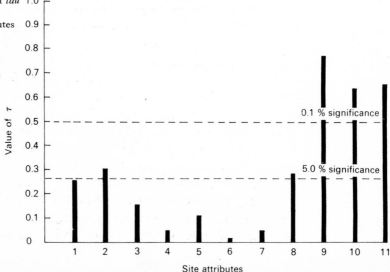

Fig. 5.3 The values of *tau* for the eleven environmental attributes (for list, see text).

levels. For further details of these studies, together with a full discussion of the principal implications, reference should be made to the original papers (Muckelroy 1977*a*, *b*).

As is immediately apparent from fig. 5.3, there can be no doubt that the nature of the sea-bed deposit (described by attributes 9, 10 and 11) is the main determining factor in the survival of archaeological remains under water. While this fundamentally confirms previously established ideas, it also serves to demonstrate that intermediate types of wreck-site are closely related to intermediate types of sea-bed, that there are many gradations between the totally rocky and the totally sandy substrate. The truth of this can be appreciated by looking at several of the illustrations given earlier in this book (e.g. figs. 1.8, p. 21, 2.1, p. 26, 2.3, p. 29, or 2.10, p. 41). Attribute 8, representing slope, also registered a fairly strong correlation, but as this is essentially only another measure of bottom topography it simply reinforces the above conclusions. The implications of the slightly higher figure recorded for attribute 2, representing sea horizon, are more interesting. It suggests that it is the variety of disturbing forces acting on a site, coming from a number of different directions, which is more significant than their force. This idea makes sense if one thinks of a deposit in a gully; once concentrated in a sheltered situation, it can only be disturbed by forces acting in a totally different direction, so that the fewer the number of directions from which disturbance can come, the better the chances of survival for those remains. Similar considerations apply with a sea-bed consisting of sedimentary deposits, in which the substrate is more likely to remain stable if it is not assailed from a number of directions. In terms of the shipwreck flow diagram (fig. 5.1), a restricted sea horizon reduces the significance of the recycling channel on the left-hand side of the box.

At the same time, the low scores registered with respect to certain other attributes are equally interesting. This is particularly the case with those relating to depth (attributes 5 to 7), which markedly contradict previously held convictions. A common denominator in the remaining attributes seems to be water movement across the site, in terms of either the size of the swell, which is a function of fetch (number 1), the frequency of stormy weather (number 3), or the strength of tidal currents (number 4). This would suggest that, once initial deposition has been made, these forces have little impact on the subsequent history of the remains. It seems likely that the influence of algae cover is relevant here, in that it protects material in just those exposed situations which might otherwise prove unsatisfactory for survival. In a way, it reduces the difference in severity between open and protected coasts. It might be felt that water movement is more likely to have affected the distribution of the remains, as opposed to their survival, but a further study, in which the eleven attributes were correlated against a ranking of the *[handwritten margin notes: "they're about this", "need. much redness in environment properties (always notionship between the 2)"]*

twenty sites according to coherence of their distributions, did not support such an interpretation. In fact, the results of this second test showed no appreciable difference from those achieved in the first exercise; what differences there were appeared to be due to special features in the process of the wrecking of some vessels, rather than any environmental considerations (Muckelroy 1977*b*, 53–4).

In the light of these studies, certain general conclusions were reached concerning wreck-sites in British waters. On the one hand, the sites could be divided into five classes, according to their degree of survival, as described in table 5.2. This classification is more discriminating than the simple good/bad dichotomy which has held such wide currency in the past, and, while it must still be regarded as provisional, it has proved useful in a number of contexts, and will reappear later in this chapter. And, secondly, arising from and making use of this classification, a series of general statements regarding the environmental characteristics

Table 5.2 *The five main classes of wreck site at present apparent in British waters*

	Structural remains	Organic remains	Other objects	Distribu- tions	Examples (see fig. 5.2)
Class 1	Extensive	Many	Many	Coherent	*Mary Rose* (11) *Amsterdam* (15)
Class 2	Elements	Some	Many	Scattered ordered	*Dartmouth* (5) *Trinidad V.* (3)
Class 3	Fragments				*Kennemerland* (1) *Colossus* (20)
Class 4	—	Few	Some	Scattered/ disordered	*De Liefde* (2) *Girona* (8)
Class 5	—	—	Few		*Adelaar* (4) *Penlee site* (12)

Table 5.3. *The relevant environmental attributes for each of the five classes of wreck-site described in Table 5.2, derived from an analysis of the data from the twenty British sites*

	Topography	Deposit	Slope	Sea horizon	Fetch
	% of bottom sedimentary deposit	Range of sediments	Average over whole site	Sector of open water for 10+km	Maximum offshore distance
Class 1	100%	Gravel to silt	Minimal	Less than 90°	Less than 250 km
Class 2	More than 70%	Boulders to silt	Less than 2°	Less than 90°	Less than 250 km
Class 3	More than 30%	Boulders to silt	Less than 4°	Less than 150°	More than 250 km
Class 4	More than 10%	Boulders to sand	Less than 8°	More than 30°	More than 250 km
Class 5	Less than 25%	Boulders to gravel	More than 6°	More than 120°	More than 750 km

appropriate to each class in British waters could be proposed; this is given in table 5.3. It was compiled in such a way that every site was accommodated within the specifications for the appropriate class under four of the five headings, and so that the aberrant specification, if there was one, was in one of the last three attributes, for which the correlation scores given above were lower. Whether this table can be used in a predictive sense, in assessing the potential of a site newly discovered but as yet unexcavated, only further testing will tell.

The serious limitations to this study must be very apparent. The sample of twenty sites, although the maximum available at the time, was very small and unevenly distributed around the coasts of Britain, with a strong bias towards the Shetlands and the south-west peninsula (see fig. 5.2). Furthermore, it was limited to just one offshore island in Europe, and is thus no more representative than Mediterranean experience. Similar detailed studies are required for many different parts of the world before any factors common to them all can be isolated. It could also only consider sites on which material remains had actually been found, and thus discounted those situations in which conditions have led to the total eradication of all traces of wreck. As a result, the conclusions given in table 5.3 cannot be used to predict whether any remains will have survived on a site over which a vessel is known to have been wrecked; the possibilities of research into this matter are discussed elsewhere (Muckelroy 1977b, 56). In addition, no account has been taken of the fact that survival conditions can vary enormously across a single wreck-site; in each case, aggregate measurements and overall descriptions have been considered, within which there may have been much significant variation. And, finally, the wrecking process has been looked at as a single event; greater understanding should be possible by considering its constituent elements, and this is the approach pursued in the next three sections.

5.3 Extracting filters

In terms of the flow diagram in fig. 5.1, the three processes which lead to the loss of material from a wreck-site are the process of wrecking, salvage operations, and the disintegration of perishables, each of which thus generates an output shown to the right of the diagram. Essentially, any consideration of this aspect of a shipwreck resolves itself into a matter of simple addition, since the sum total of the outputs must necessarily equal the input (i.e. the original ship). However, the main thesis presented here is that since the operation of each of these processes is limited by a series of constraints, some of which can be identified and described for any particular wreck-site, certain elements in their respective outputs can thus be identified, which in turn amplify the evidence regarding the ship itself.

The process of wrecking, which can act as both an extracting filter and a scrambling device, raises the question of which items on board a ship are likely to have floated away. From first principles one knows that metal objects, for example, cannot float, while most wooden and other organic objects can, at least until they have become waterlogged. Thus on any site there will be a wide range of objects which cannot have disappeared through this process – those in the former category. However, the greater part of a wooden ship is made of materials which can float, so that the process of wrecking must also explain in many cases how these elements came to be held on the sea-bed long enough to become waterlogged and/or buried. One extreme situation is the vessel which sinks intact, dragged down by a combination of ballast, contents, and inflowing water; in this case, everything trapped between decks has a chance to become waterlogged, sink to the bottom and, if favourable circumstances present themselves, become buried. The other extreme is when a vessel disintegrates totally on the surface, spilling all heavy items, and allowing little chance for light objects to reach the sea-floor; here, little will have survived in even the most favourable of environments. But most sites reflect processes intermediate between these extremes, as with the many classical ships pinned down by their amphora cargoes, or with the wreck of the *Dartmouth* (1690), on which part of the hull had been pinned down by the iron and flint ballast (Martin 1978).

Salvage operations obviously vary widely between sites, and are less susceptible to generalisation. In many cases, the assessment of this factor will depend on the evidence of the historical record, but if this is silent, there are certain assumptions which can usually be made. There are some sites on which salvage was inconceivable until modern times, such as those off uninhabited shores or in very deep water. Elsewhere, however, it will generally be safe to assume that, other things being equal, the local inhabitants are more likely to have attempted to raise all they could than leave such a bonanza unexploited. From very early times, many communities will have had the ability to undertake free diving and dragline operations, and since the sixteenth century more sophisticated devices have become available within areas of European influence (Davis 1955, 536–642; Ericsson 1975b). At these later periods, these are records of quite drastic methods being used in salvage, such as trying to drag whole ship sections up the shore with teams of horses. In each instance, the archaeologist must assess both the problems which would have faced any contemporary salvors and their ability to overcome them, and decide which parts of his site are most likely to have been interfered with.

With the disintegration of perishables, the constraints concerning the preservation characteristics of different materials in a marine environment are again more general in application. Here, maritime archaeology must rely on studies of underwater corrosion (e.g. Uhlig 1948), as well as the continuing research specifically concerned with the preservation, and ultimate conservation, of archaeological materials from marine sites (e.g. Weier 1974; Hamilton 1976; Tylecote 1977). It has become apparent from a number of sites that such processes can vary even across quite short distances, depending on the nature of the sea-bed, the extent of marine growths, etc., so that ideally sea-water and deposit samples should be taken from each area excavated, to be chemically and biochemically analysed. Furthermore, the association of different types of wreck-material will itself locally modify the preservative environment; the most extreme example is probably the electrolytic protection of base metal by a neighbouring proud metal. Unfortunately, it is still early days in such research, so that, until a greater understanding has been reached, the maritime archaeologist is probably restricted to only general principles concerning the scale and scope of disintegration of material on any particular site.

In the light of these general considerations, it is worth looking at how they operate in practice on the *Kennemerland* site; table 5.4 shows the system outputs as they are at present understood. This was a vessel which broke up entirely after striking a rocky coast, although a considerable range of fragile organic materials were somehow carried from it onto the sea-bed (Price & Muckelroy 1977, 193–8). Under the heading 'Floated away', the designation 'none' has only been given on materials which in themselves could never have floated. As noted above, a good deal is known about the salvage operations on this site from Scottish Court Records which include long inventories of goods declared; nevertheless, it is to be presumed that considerable quantities totally escaped detection, especially easily secreted but valuable items such as coins, and commodities which were consumed immediately, notably food and drink. One authority mentions that the Out Skerries folk had a wild Christmas that year! (Brand 1701, 140). Within the column headed 'Disintegrated', the entry 'none' has been given only against those materials which could not have so disappeared on the basis of general principles. No specific analysis has yet been conducted on the sea-bed and waters of this area from which to arrive at more detailed conclusions; the variety of conditions across this site is such that consistent trends are unlikely to be present. A summary of material excavated has been included for comparative purposes and in order to indicate the full range of knowledge about the ship to be derived via the system outputs.

A more detailed discussion of the main conclusions arising from this table has been published elsewhere (Muckelroy 1976, 283–6), and only a few outstanding features will be mentioned here. Probably the most striking aspect of the table is that over half of the commodities listed

Table 5.4. *System outputs for the* Kennemerland *site*

	Excavated	Salvaged	Disintegrated	Floated away
Ship's structure	Fragments	—	—	—
Sails	—	69	—	—
Rigging	Pieces rope	7 cables; tackle	—	—
Anchors	8	2	None	None
Ballast bricks	c. 10000	—	—	None
Grindstone	1	—	None	None
Iron	—	Some	None	None
Lead	108 ingots	—	None	None
Nails	c. 400	—	None	None
Cannon	8	7	None	None
Cannon balls	c. 100	—	None	None
Musket shot	c. 2000	1 chest	None	None
Scatter shot	c. 3000	—	None	None
Munitions accessories	9 items	15 lining sheets	—	—
Navigation instruments	3 items	—	—	—
Specie	6 coins	3 chests	None	None
Jewellery	40 pieces	—	None	None
Eating utensils	25 spoons	—	—	—
Personal items	49	—	—	—
Quills etc.	—	1 chest	—	—
Writing paper	—	8 chests	—	—
Clay pipes	c. 200	—	—	None
Bridle bits	—	Some	None	None
Stirrup irons	—	Some	None	None
Tar	Some	19 puncheons	—	None
Tallow	—	9 casks	—	None
Rosin	Some	15 casks	—	None
Mercury	2 flagons	1 chest	None	None
Olive oil	c. 100 bottles	1320 gallons	—	None
Brandy	and c. 100	1604 gallons	—	None
Wine	flagons:	1254 gallons	—	None
Vinegar	c. 3 pints each	145 gallons	—	None
Beer	—	8 casks	—	None
Preserved fruits	1 jar	—	—	None
Butter	—	5 barrels	—	None
Flour	—	2 half-barrels	—	None
Meat	58 bones	2 pieces bacon	—	—
Shoes	—	120 pairs	—	—
Linen	—	337 yards	—	—
Serge	—	300 yards	—	—
Woollen cloth	—	116 yards	—	—
Other cloth	—	236 yards	—	—

cannot have floated away; with the obvious exception of the ship itself, this cannot be the sole cause of the loss of evidence. The position under 'Disintegrated' is less satisfactory, but in this case the areas where this element is particularly important, notably in the lower half of the table, the evidence from salvage records is particularly full, and probably of more than average reliability. The evidence derived from the salvage lists and the excavations themselves is also remarkably complementary, emphasising the importance of integrating the various sources of evidence in this manner. Since the excavations on this site are still far from complete, little can be deduced from the absolute quantities involved, although there are already some interesting implications which can be noted. For example, the collection of coins in the table is very small for the personal moneys held on such a ship (discounting the three official treasure chests salvaged), and strongly suggests extensive unreported salvage. Regarding the ship herself, one suggestion which arises from the quantities of drink indicated in the salvage lists is that it is too much for consumption during the voyage, and must therefore constitute an element in the ship's cargo.

While such a discussion must inevitably deal on the level of probabilities and degrees of certainty, it is undoubtedly worthwhile in that it should help to remove inconsistencies in the deductions being made from the fragmentary evidence available about any wreck-site, and may inspire new ideas about interrelationships and implications within that evidence which, taken in its constituent parts, had not been apparent. There should be very few wreck-sites for which something useful cannot be said about each of these processes, a fact which reinforces the idea that a shipwreck is a particularly worthwhile process to investigate, when compared to other types of archaeological-type.

5.4 Scrambling devices *A*

The process of wrecking

A ship floating or sailing on the surface of the sea is a complex machine containing a large number of constituent parts arranged in a specific order to ensure seaworthiness, ease of handling, and other desirable qualities. From the moment of impact, however, that high degree of organisation begins to break down, until the remains are assimilated into the sea-bed in some degree of disorder, often very extensive. This constitutes the first stage in the rearrangement of the elements of a vessel which interests the researcher, and is covered by the title 'process of wrecking'. This definition is thus a broad one, including the continued break-up of the wreckage on the sea-bed as well as the stages by which it got there, up until the time when it becomes part of the seascape; anything which happens after that can be described as sea-bed movement, and is reviewed in section 5.5. In the present discussion, some of the factors involved are presented by considering a few examples.

The most straightforward wrecking situation is undoubtedly that in which a ship simply fills with water, sinks to the bottom intact, and remains there undamaged for many centuries. In fact, such a sequence of events is very exceptional. Undoubtedly the best known instance is that of the Swedish warship *Wasa*, which sailed from her fitting-out yard across Stockholm harbour on 10 August 1628, heeled over to a squall so that the water entered her open gun-ports, and sank within minutes, with over 200 persons on board (Naish 1968, 5). Injudicious careening of the *Royal George* at Spithead on 29 August 1782, possibly combined with structural weakness, had similar consequences; this time leading to the loss of over 900 lives. Sixty years later, divers reported that her hull remained substantially intact, incidentally showing that the teredo-free waters of the Baltic are not unique in allowing the long-term preservation of complete wooden hulls. However, such sinkings without considerable structural damage onto receptive sea-beds are special cases, bearing little relationship to the majority of shipwrecks.

A more typical situation, which has received much attention in the past, is that of the classical wreck now lying at the foot of a submerged cliff in the Mediterranean. As explained above (section 5.2) this under-water topography is fairly common in the Sea, especially along its northern shores; so far as the best preserved wrecks are concerned, it involves a peninsula, islet or offshore reef surrounded by relatively deep water (40+ metres), as at Cape Dramont, Ile de Planier, or Yassi Ada (Dumas 1972, fig. 4). As Frederic Dumas, who first rationalised the sequence of events in such situations, has written: 'When a boat runs aground on a rock and is holed, it sinks without other damage to the foot of the sea cliff, where it lies sheltered from the sea's violent motions. Often enough it has avoided the *talus* and settled on loose sand, in

Fig. 5.4 A schematised section across an amphora wreck mound.

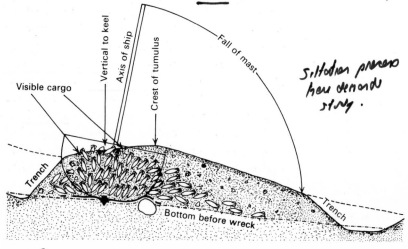

excellent conditions for later study by archaeologists' (1972, 32). Its subsequent slow assimilation within the sea-bed is illustrated in his accompanying diagram (fig. 5.4), with the hull accommodating itself to the sea-bed, the cargo spilling over on one side, and the whole acting as a trap for waterborne sediments, thus creating its own tumulus. This last is the famous 'amphora mound' recognised by modern divers in Mediterranean waters. While the vessel probably reached the sea-bed relatively intact, only the lower part of the hull will be available for study through having been protected by that mound, and the cargo itself will have been considerably displaced from its original arrangements, although in a way which can be understood.

That a similar type of situation is possible with later wrecks not bearing protective amphora cargoes has been demonstrated for Mediterranean waters by the excavations of Peter Throckmorton and his colleagues in the harbour at Porto Longo in Greece (Throckmorton 1970, 20–7). In two cases, with an Austrian brig of 1860 and the *Heraclea* of 1940, the vessels had landed relatively intact on a sandy substrate, worked themselves into the deposit, creating shallow depressions within which the keel, floor timbers, and miscellaneous other pieces had become buried while the rest of the vessels was broken up or eaten away. A somewhat similar process can be seen to have happened with the settlement of the *Mary Rose* into the sea-bed at Spithead after 1545 (see fig. 3.17, p. 93), even though she was a considerably larger vessel, and the marine environment very different from that in the southern Peloponnese. In this instance it seems that a rapid scour took place around the wreck soon after sinking, and that she heeled over into the pit so created, finally reaching an angle of 60°. Her tendency to sink into the sea-bed would also have been assisted by the fact that she was still intact when reaching the bottom, containing all her ballast and contents.

A slightly different process of the same basic nature can be seen with the wreck of the *Dartmouth* (1690) in the Sound of Mull (Martin 1978). Having been swept from her moorings over 3 kilometres away, this warship grounded against a small islet onto a sea-bed consisting of a thin (*c.* 25 centimetres deep) layer of gravel overlying a hard stable clay. The ship appears to have settled on her starboard side, and then to have rocked to and fro on her keel, wearing away a good deal of the latter, and digging a depression in the underlying clay into which the rest of the keel, deadwood, etc., could settle (fig. 5.5). The discovery of a large number of objects from the ship in fine condition within this trench showed that it must have been formed quite rapidly. The shallower depression, into which the starboard planking was to settle, must have been formed by a more gentle fanning action as the ship moved, since the underside of the hull here remained in remarkably fine condition, including the thin pine sheathing, and only a finer, silty deposit containing few artefacts remained below this part of the structure. The vessel seems to have broken her back amidships on a spine of rock and the forward part, apparently less encumbered by iron ballast, broke up *in situ*, leaving a significant pattern of artefacts on the sea-bed (see section 5.6).

However, not all vessels will have reached the sea-bed structurally intact; in fact, the majority do not, since usually either the force of initial impact is sufficient to break the vessel asunder, or it remains stuck fast until it breaks up. In the case of the *Kennemerland* the course of the ship's disintegration is clearly indicated by a combination of local tradition and the spread of the archaeological remains (fig. 5.6). The former was enshrined in a short rhyme current in the islands:

'The Carmelan frae Amsterdam,
Cam on a Maunmas Day,
On Stoura Stack she broke her back,
And in the Voe she ca''
(Forster & Higgs 1973, 292).

Accordingly, the archaeological evidence for initial impact is concentrated around Stoura Stack, including over a hundred lead pigs and many thousand building bricks from the ship's ballast, along with a collection of anchors which had probably been stowed low in the hold around the mainmast step (Glamann 1958, 23). Together, these items suggest that the ship had her bottom torn open. However, there is another local tradition to the effect that the bows of the *Kennemerland* broke away and sank next to the Stack (Bruce 1907, 127), an interpreta-

Fig. 5.5 A section across the structural remains on the *Dartmouth* (1690) wreck-site.

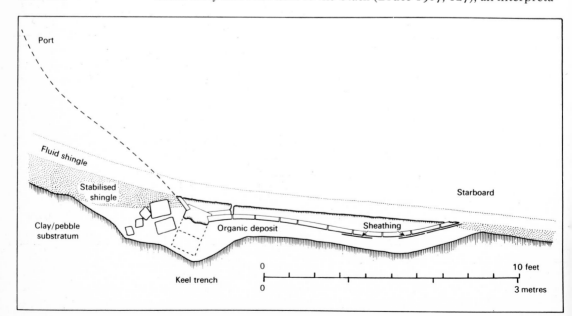

Port

Fluid shingle

Stabilised shingle

Clay/pebble substratum

Organic deposit

Sheathing

Starboard

Keel trench

0   10 feet

0   3 metres

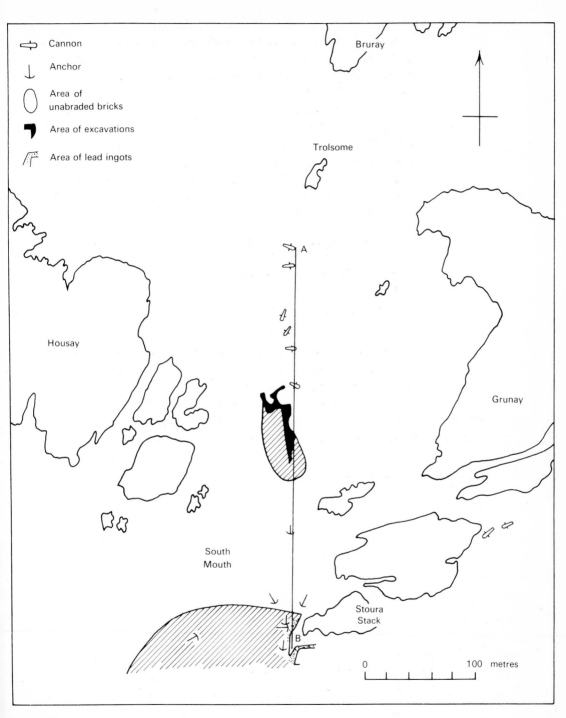

Fig. 5.6 Site plan of the
Kennemerland (1664)
wreck-site in the Out
Skerries, Shetland Isles.

tion not actually contradicted by the evidence. As has already been shown with the *Dartmouth*, it is quite conceivable for a ship to break in two amidships; the main-mast can act as a pile-driver and split the keel.

Either way, having lost a good deal of ballast and possibly her bows, the ship wallowed north for over 150 metres before any substantial further break-up took place, since there is a marked break in the sea-bed distributions (see fig. 5.6). The wreck material reappears at the point where the sea-bed rises to within 10 metres of the surface, as shown in the north–south section across the site (fig. 5.7). This is where the waves would be breaking during a southerly gale, such as is known to have been blowing on this occasion. Presumably, the white water tossed the vessel about and hastened its destruction. However, some structural integrity must have been preserved until it reached the level of the islet Trolsome, where the most northerly of the cannons was dropped. Beyond that the position is less clear, since the area has yet to be thoroughly searched, although it is known that much wreckage was washed up on Bruray.

There is a further tradition, the reliability of which is less certain, that most of the wreckage was soon washed out to sea again by the succeeding tide (Bruce 1907, 127), and this receives a degree of confirmation from the pattern of tidal currents running through the South Mouth that night. High water on 20 December 1664 was at noon, the following high being at 01:00 on the 21st (information courtesy of the Institute of Oceanographic Sciences, Bidston). There are reasons to believe, on the basis of the documentary evidence, that the wrecking took place between dusk (say 16:00) and midnight on the 20th, during which period the currents would have been running weakly northwards before 20:00, and strongly southwards from 21:00. It seems likely, therefore, that the wrecking took place during the evening of the 20th, and that a quantity of remains were swept back across the site around midnight. A further important implication of this interpretation is that the two cannons lying south of Old Man Stack (see fig. 5.6) are likely to have come from the *Kennemerland*, a fact which, in view of their isolation and lack of association with other wreckage, has always been in doubt. This conclusion arises because, during the first half of the four-hour period of northward-flowing currents within the South Mouth, a strong current

Fig. 5.7 A north–south section across the *Kennemerland* wreck-site (see fig. 5.6).

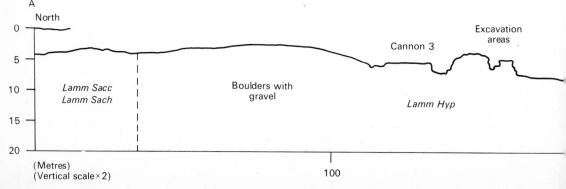

also flows eastwards along the face of Stoura and Old Man stacks which could have carried a part of the wreckage (most likely, a section of the bows) in a semi-submerged state in that direction. The sea-bed in this area is very rocky and heavily scoured, making it quite likely that any other remains settling there would not survive. The corollary of this is, of course, that the wrecking took place during the first part of the four-hour period, say, between 16:00 and 18:00.

Obviously, the extent of the evidence, both archaeological and documentary, available for the interpretation of the *Kennemerland* wreck-site is exceptional; that is one of the reasons why it is a particularly useful site on which to test these methods of analysis. However, other wreckings can be cited in which the vessel has driven on beyond the point of impact, breaking up as it proceeds, and shedding material in its wake, so that its disintegration can be studied through the trail of remains stretching for hundreds of metres across the sea-bed. Among British wreck-sites, those of the *Santa Maria de la Rosa* (Martin 1975, 23–135), and *Hollandia* (Cowan *et al.* 1975), and *Lovely* (Butland & Stubbs 1976) would appear to be of this type (Muckelroy 1977*b*, 53–4). It may be that this phenomenon is peculiar to large post-medieval ships, with their special techniques of construction and considerable ballast concentrated in one, particularly vulnerable, part of the vessel. With most ships which break up on the surface this linear arrangement of the material does not occur, and the result is usually a site of class 4 or 5, according to sea-bed conditions (see table 5.2 above).

5.5 Scrambling devices *B*

Sea-bed movement

The study of processes within sea-bed sediments is itself in a period of rapid development, spurred on by increasing activity in coastal and continental-shelf areas, and aided by technological developments associated with that work. However, the main thrust of current research is into topics which have little or no bearing on archaeological problems, such as the behaviour of deep-water sediments, or the factors operating in areas of substantial shoreline erosion or accretion. In particular, the behaviour of mobile sediments on rocky and irregular sea-beds has been

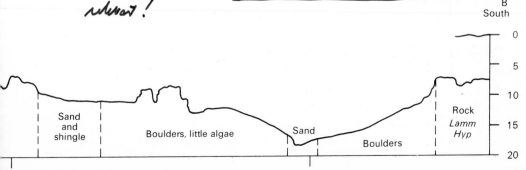

200   300

B
South

0
5
10
15
20

Sand and shingle

Boulders, little algae

Sand

Boulders

Rock
Lamm
Hyp

subject to virtually no systematic study, and several workers in this field have expressed the hope that archaeological data may in time contribute to their studies.

The basic concepts for such investigations can be derived from studies in marine geomorphology (see especially Guilcher 1958; Zenkovich 1967; King 1972). Sediment disturbance is obviously primarily the result of water movement, i.e. by tidal currents or wave action. The former can occur at any depth and with any force, according to circumstances, but the latter has more limited application. The swell reaching any particular location depends on the speed and duration of any onshore wind, together with the distance of open water over which it has travelled (i.e. the fetch) (King 1972, 53–60). But wave energy decreases rapidly with depth, and at a depth of half the wavelength it will be only 1/23 of its surface strength (Guilcher 1958, 19). Thus wave-induced water and sediment motion is principally a feature of shallow-water sites, the exact definition of 'shallow' depending on the maximum wavelength of the swell striking that spot. The next problem is what size of sediment particles are disturbed by a given water velocity; from experience under water, it is evident that a current of several knots is required to move even a coarse sand, and the forces needed to move gravel and shingle appear generally to be operative only in the surf zone. However, the movement of such coarser material seems to be assisted frequently by a phenomenon known as 'kelp rafting', by which marine growths on a stone can act as a kind of sail, enabling it to be swept along by a more moderate current (Jolliffe & Wallace 1973).

Within most marine sediments, there is usually an upper layer of deposit, anything between a few centimetres and several metres thick, which is in a state of semi-suspension, being lubricated by the surrounding water. Heavy objects will obviously tend to drop through this, while less dense items caught in it are likely to be thoroughly jumbled and heavily abraded. The analogy of topsoil on a land site is obvious. One of the few research projects specifically designed to investigate these problems was concerned with the sorting of objects within such a sediment. The area concerned involved deep and accumulating silt in a Norwegian harbour, and the initial hypothesis was that, since this deposit was apparently unconsolidated and presumably in a state of constant flux, objects would be stratified according to specific gravities, with little or no discrimination according to age (Keller 1973). In fact, a test excavation suggested that, on the contrary, the stratigraphy was directly related to chronology. While this conclusion was obviously based on only one location, it does suggest that the re-sorting of objects within such apparently mobile deposits can be overemphasised.

On some sites, it seems that all artefacts simply drop through the upper semi-mobile level, so that it proves to be archaeologically sterile.

This is the case on the *Trinidad Valencera* (1588) site, on which there is a layer of shelly beach sand about 25 centimetres thick, often with small waves formed on its surface, within which there are no artefacts. That objects can fall quickly through it to the stable levels below was shown by the finding of a modern ring-pull beer can alongside a sixteenth-century timber at a depth of about 30 centimetres. The spread of organic remains shown in fig. 2.12 (p. 51) began only a few centimetres below the base of this beach sand. The implication of these observations is, of course, that there is a finite possibility of later contamination within the uppermost archaeological levels on this site. A deeper semi-mobile layer has been identified on the *Mary Rose* (1545) site in the Solent, where the currents are appreciably stronger and the sediment particles finer. Judging from the depth range of post-sixteenth century contamination, later objects could sink to a maximum depth of 70 centimetres, although in this case wreck material was also discovered within this horizon, and no level in it was totally devoid of artefacts. The base of this deposit was marked in some places by a layer of matted organic material, apparently a growth of some kind of sea-grass, which effectively sealed-in the uncontaminated levels below.

On more shallowly buried sites, the matter of continued sediment movement is obviously more critical. With the *Dartmouth* (1690) wreck-site only the area beside and under the hull itself seems to have remained totally undisturbed over the centuries, because it was actually lying below the level of the surrounding clay substrate (see fig. 5.5). That the overlying gravel was semi-mobile was shown clearly by the way it had ground down the upper surface of the surviving structure (see fig. 2.17, p. 55). However, the forces acting on this site must always have been relatively gentle, since the maximum fetch is only 18 kilometres, and it is not scoured by any tidal currents, so that any gravel movement will have been correspondingly moderate (Martin 1978). Furthermore, since there are no reasons for thinking that there has been any long-term gain or loss of sediment, it seems reasonable to suppose that the net result of all the movements has been no change, although there may have been some loss of information in the distributions.

The sediments on the *Kennemerland* site are of a similar thickness, and the question also arises as to whether all or part of them have been subject to periodic reworking over the centuries. Fig. 5.8 shows some sections across one of the excavation trenches (Site G), in which the second horizon down is of particular interest. It consisted of a layer of matted wood splinters, organic remains, patches of wood tar, and other artefacts, which cannot have been substantially disturbed since initial deposition. The origins of this layer are uncertain, but it is likely that it represented at least in part the contents of the ship's bilges (Price &

How to identify wreck? Of cours is this nature no problem - historic.

Muckelroy 1977, 198). The implication is that it, and the horizons below it, have remained undisturbed since the seventeenth century, while the top level, of between 10 and 30 centimetres thickness, was the only one which had been subject to disturbance. The state of preservation of the artefacts from the various horizons supported this interpretation. A similar situation could be detected on four of the other areas excavated (Sites B, D, E, and F; see fig. 5.19), while on two of the others, which lay in more open situations (Sites A and C), there was simply a homogeneous gravel, 20 to 40 centimetres thick, overlying the bedrock. Within this, there was a tendency for artefacts to be found towards its base, and especially around larger rocks and boulders. This last phenomenon has been observed on several sites, and suggests a greater degree of artefact re-sorting over the centuries, the principal characteristics of which demand further investigation.

of all my study sites: layers within gullies.

Fig. 5.8 Three sections through the deposits in Site G, *Kennemerland* wreck-site (for locations, see fig. 5.20 below).

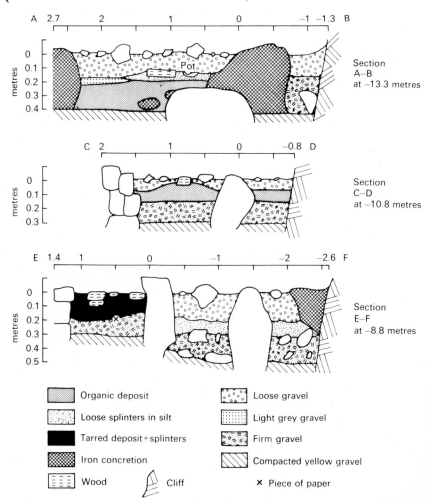

Organic deposit

Loose splinters in silt

Tarred deposit+splinters

Iron concretion

Wood   Cliff

Loose gravel

Light grey gravel

Firm gravel

Compacted yellow gravel

× Piece of paper

Fig. 5.9 illustrates the directions of the main forces acting over this site. Tidal currents are indicated running from the north since this is the situation for over eight hours in every twelve hour cycle, and the reverse current is usually very weak, rarely exceeding half a knot. The south-ward-flowing current can exceed three knots at times. As suggested above, these currents will be dominant in deeper water, and their main thrust may account for the south-western trend of the distribution of bricks and other artefacts off Stoura Stack. For the shallower deposits, however, the reverse wave-induced trend will probably have been more significant. This site is sheltered totally from all directions except the southerly quarter, which is thus the direction marked on fig. 5.9. Furthermore, meteorological observations indicate that storm winds (force 7 or above) blow from these directions for 2.6 % of the time, a far from negligible proportion (hourly observations at Lerwick over the

Fig. 5.9 A diagram summarising the principal natural forces acting on the *Kennemerland* site.

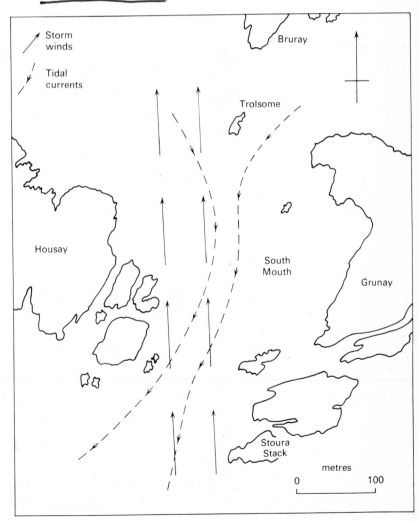

decade 1960–9, courtesy of the Meteorological Office, Edinburgh). The net result of considering these forces is that the distributions may have been 'stretched' in a north–south direction, but not actually scrambled. It is also possible that the contrary trends in shallow and deeper water may partly account for the marked 150 metre gap in the artefact distribution (see fig. 5.6).

On some sites this post-depositional re-sorting has affected the whole deposit, and resulted in a total rearrangement of the remains. A clear example of this is represented by the wreck-site of the *Adelaar* (Dutch East Indiaman, 1728) on the west coast of Barra in the Outer Hebrides (fig. 5.10) (Martin & Long 1975). Exposed to the full force of Atlantic swells, and with a fissured rocky sea-floor, the only artefacts to have survived were those of metal, and many of them were extremely battered and distorted (an idea of the sea-bed conditions can be gained from fig. 2.2, p. 27, and 2.4, p. 30). Experience during excavation showed that the metre or so of shingle filling the gullies was in a state of constant flux, and only those items which eventually became embedded in the layer of concretion below this stood any chance of survival (*ibid.*, fig. 6).

As well as looking at site stratigraphy and general tidal and wave-generated water movement, additional information concerning possible disturbances of the deposits may be gleaned from other ancilliary observations. For localised water movements on any particular part of

Fig. 10 Site plan of the *Adelaar* wreck-site off Barra, Outer Hebrides. (pdr = pounder.)

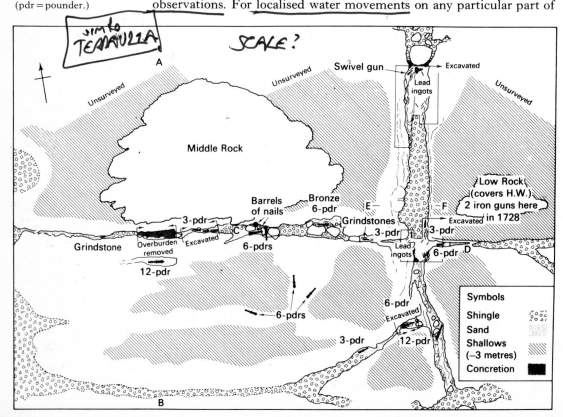

Symbols	
Shingle	
Sand	
Shallows (−3 metres)	
Concretion	

a site, records made by a current-meter may be of assistance, so long as it is left in place for a sufficient length of time. Alternatively, an artificial scatter of specially selected objects representing a range of materials may be placed on the site after excavation is completed, and then mapped at regular intervals in order to see how the distribution evolves. However, both these procedures suffer from the difficulty that they will, if carried on for a sufficient length of time, record average on-site conditions, while there are good reasons to believe that it is the exceptional, once-a-century storm which achieves the most significant reworking of the sea-bed. A third approach, which may partly allow for such eventualities, is to record the flora and fauna in each part of a site, paying particular attention to those species which are tolerant of only a narrow range of conditions, and can thus be regarded as indicators of overall environmental circumstances. Such observations have been made along the depth profile of the *Kennemerland* site (fig. 5.7), and the occurrence of various types of algae, in particular, has supplemented the evidence from other sources about the degree of water movement. However, maritime archaeologists would be deeply indebted to their colleagues in marine biology for more detailed lists of indicator species for different parts of the world.

In addition to that caused by water movement, disturbance of the sea-bed may be occasioned by the activities of marine creatures. The possible impact of crabs has already been noted in section 2.2. In Mediterranean waters, the house-building instincts of the octopus can result in accumulations of potsherds in suitable crannies, including amphorae; this may have been the principal cause of the enigmatic distributions recorded on the Sheytan Deresi site in southern Turkey (Bass 1976, 295–6). At present, there is no evidence suggesting that marine worms might have similar archaeological consequences similar to those of earthworms (Atkinson 1957), and no burrowing creatures analogous to moles or rabbits have been noted.

These observations have together indicated the importance of geomorphological study to the interpretation of any wreck-site, and have shown that the processes involved are very different from those operating in a terrestrial context. Incidentally, they have also shown that an underwater site can possess a complex stratigraphy whose recording and interpretation is essential to the understanding of these processes, and which may, as the experimental work in Mövik harbour has shown (Keller 1973), even have a chronological significance. A further implication for the analysis of sea-bed distributions is that if they have been generated by natural processes, as opposed to the human-inspired ones usually involved on land sites, then the modes of analysis to be used should perhaps be borrowed from the natural environmental sciences. So what.

It was mentioned above that marine geomorphologists were looking to archaeological research under water to furnish data on sea-bed processes, and especially the behaviour of sediments in rocky areas. In this context a great deal of the above discussion is of potential value – above all, the indications of sediment stability over several centuries for some horizons and the suggestion that, in other areas, the net results of any localised disturbances have been minimal. Another type of contribution is illustrated by the late eighteenth-century wreck located in 1974 in the South Edinburgh Channel in the Thames estuary. This channel, whose precise location and configuration is always shifting, has recently begun to move across the wreck-site, with the result that the hull has broken open and begun to disintegrate; its previous pristine state demonstrates that the channel has not occupied this area at any time over the past 200 years, knowledge which the sedimentologists could not have gathered in any other way. Similarly, the remains of the *Mary Rose* (1545) illustrate the geological and biological history of that part of the Solent over the past 400 years (McKee 1973). The next few decades should see an increasingly fruitful exchange of ideas and information between these disciplines.

REPORTS

In concluding this discussion of the various aspects of fig. 5.1, note must also be taken of the extracting and scrambling consequences of the excavation strategy adopted for any particular site, consequent on the considerations outlined in chapter 2. Coming between the sea-bed distribution of remains as it actually exists, and as it appears in the archaeological record, this factor must be taken into account; it is thus the responsibility of any archaeologist to indicate honestly in his report the procedures used, standards of accuracy achieved, precise areas excavated, and so forth, so that their implications can be generally appreciated. Having considered this, and all the other aspects of the wrecking process on a particular site, the researcher is in a position to consider how the observed remains on the sea-bed should be interpreted; the next two sections discuss some of the procedures which might be appropriate.

5.6 The analysis of sea-bed distribution *A*

Continuous sites

In this discussion of modes of analysis for wreck-sites, the presentation is divided into two parts since the problems presented by sites on which the remains are concentrated in one self-contained area are different from those on which they are more scattered. The former have been labelled 'continuous sites' since the artefact distributions are not interrupted by sterile areas whose existence has to be taken into account in any interpretation; the latter variety have accordingly been designated

No of individual

'discontinuous sites'. There is no necessary connection between this distinction in types of site, adopted for purely methodological reasons, and the classification proposed in table 5.2, although class 1 and 2 sites will nearly always be continuous in their distributions. Class 3 sites can be of either type; in this section the Cape Gelidonya wreck is taken as an example of a continuous wreck-site without structural remains, while the *Kennemerland* site will be considered as an equivalent discontinuous site in section 5.7 (Class 4 and 5 sites, being more disturbed, are generally not susceptible to detailed distributional analysis.)

To date there has been remarkably little archaeological work on wreck-sites in which the hull remains substantially intact, and which pose special problems of locational analysis. The most extensive project of this type has undoubtedly been the raising and conserving of the wreck of the *Wasa* (Naish 1968), but in this case the scope of any detailed studies was restricted by the accumulations of mud between decks, and the speed with which this had to be removed after lifting (see fig. 3.18). In the event, the most complex problems of relocation in this project involved those carvings and other fittings from the exterior of the hull which were recovered from the surrounding sea-bed, and which had to be replaced after conservation.

Greater complications arise in those circumstances in which the ship's hull has opened up and partly disintegrated. This is the position with a large number of Mediterranean amphora wrecks (see section 5.4), and consequently there have been several exercises in the interpretation of such remains. In many cases, the principal concern is with establishing the hull's original form, since it has often not only partially disappeared, but also fragmented and distorted, accommodating itself to the contours of the sea-floor (see fig. 5.5). The successful approach to this problem has naturally varied according to circumstances. In the case of the Kyrenia ship (Katzev 1970; 1974; Swiny & Katzev 1973), on which the greater part of the port side had survived, but only a small section of the starboard side broken away from it (fig. 5.11), the wood proved exceedingly soft and pliable; the craft was lifted piece by piece and reassembled after conservation in Kyrenia Castle, a process which involved re-shaping most of the members. With the fourth-century A.D. Yassi Ada boat, the reconstruction, which was done entirely on paper since the vessel was not raised and conserved, proceeded out from a basic framework of the keel and four frames, whose relative positions were quite precisely established (van Doorninck 1976, 115–19) (see fig. 5.13). However, with the seventh-century A.D. ship at Yassi Ada less of the surface curvature had survived, so that the initial reconstruction was done in two dimensions, with every feature being projected onto the plane of the inner surface of the planking. The third dimension was then created by establishing four sections whose general shape could be determined from the way the hull was lying across rock outcrops (fig. 5.12) (van Doorninck 1967, 44).

Very similar problems have arisen in other situations, both above and under water, in which only fragmentary hull remains have survived. In the interpretation of the remains discovered in a drainage ditch at Pantano Longarini (see fig. 3.5, p. 67), Peter Throckmorton relied heavily on the relative position of different sizes and shapes of nail hole as the first stage in reassembling (in the form of a model) the very fragmentary and distorted surviving timbers (Throckmorton 1973*b*, 249–62). Similar difficulties were encountered with the Viking ships at Roskilde (see fig. 3.16, p. 89), where the stones used to sink the hulls as a

Fig. 5.11 The hull of the fourth-century B.C. Greek merchantman found near Kyrenia, after excavation.

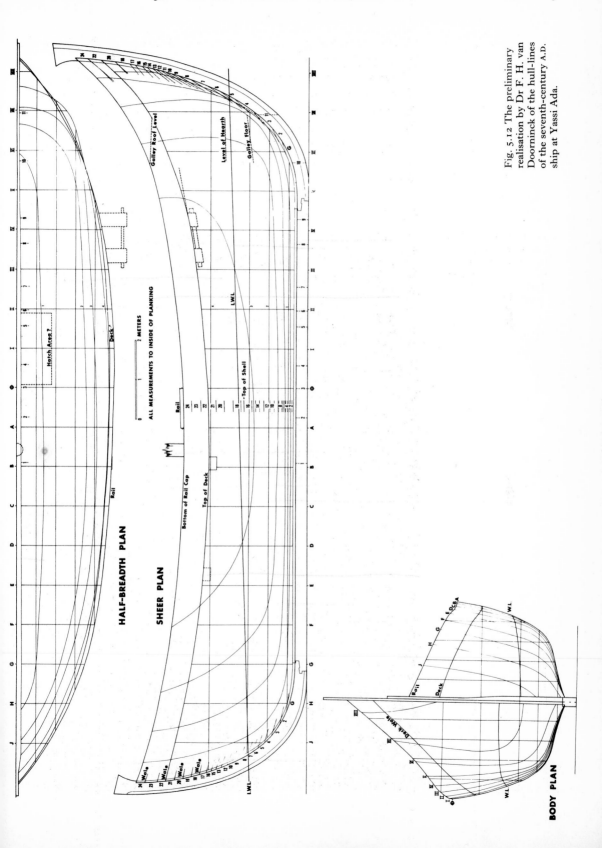

HALF-BREADTH PLAN

SHEER PLAN

BODY PLAN

ALL MEASUREMENTS TO INSIDE OF PLANKING

Fig. 5.12 The preliminary realisation by Dr F. H. van Doorninck of the hull-lines of the seventh-century A.D. ship at Yassi Ada.

blockade had seriously distorted them, and similar methods of reconstruction had to be employed after conservation. A slightly different
problem was presented by the reassembly of the Graveney boat (see
fig. 1.6, p. 18), of which about a third of the fore part was missing, while
the stern was extensively preserved on both port and starboard sides,
although partially flattened (Evans & Fenwick 1971; Fenwick 1972;
Greenhill 1976, 223–6).

While individual treatments have varied according to circumstances,
there are certain general features which are worth noting. Most fundamental of all is the fact that in many cases several alternative arrangements can be proposed on the basis of the evidence, but there is only
one which makes nautical sense. There are certain basic principles of
naval architecture to which a vessel of any period must comply; fundamentally these are that it must be symmetrical in cross-section and that
its lines must constitute a series of fair curves (Throckmorton 1973*b*,
252–5). Thus, no matter what procedure for reconstruction is being
used, the results must be frequently checked to see whether the lines
produced are satisfactory (see, for example, the sequence followed by
van Doorninck on the Yassi Ada fourth-century ship: 1976, 117).
Another common experience has been that models, often of 1 : 10 scale,
offer the easiest way of determining on the correct solution, as with the
Pantano Longarini ship (Throckmorton 1973*b*, 252–5), the Graveney
boat (McKee 1972), the surviving port quarter of the *Batavia* (Baker &
Green 1976, 154 and fig. 12), and others. However, in all this work there
appears to have been a good deal of laborious trial and error; it would
seem likely that in the future the testing of various hypothetical reconstructions will be undertaken via computer programs adapted from
those used in naval architecture (Coates 1977). Another potentially
fruitful area for future development would appear to lie in the modelling
of the processes of sea-bed distortion through the application of com-
puterised transformation techniques (Clarke 1968, 527–30).

Fig. 5.13 A plan of the hull
remains of the fourth-
century A.D. ship at Yassi
Ada (Turkey).

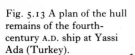

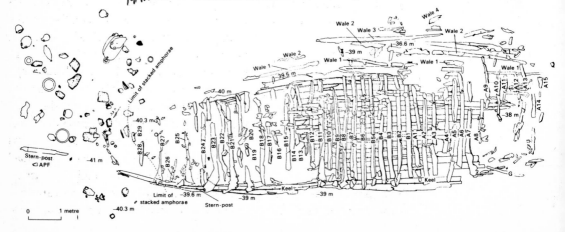

Returning to the problems of Mediterranean amphora wrecks, a second and equally important aspect concerns the interpretation of the distribution of their cargoes, in the light of what is known of the way the vessel fell apart. In many cases the upper parts of the cargo, together with one or both extremities, have become partly scattered, but the lower layers of the cargo remain *in situ*, although leaning over to one side. Thus, with the Kyrenia ship (fig. 5.11), the cargo of amphorae was found to overly a ballast/cargo of grinding stones, while low down towards the bows there was a heap of over 9000 almonds (Swiny & Katzev 1973, 342–4). In the bow and stern areas, concentrations of amphorae made in the island of Samos suggested a different consignment from that stowed amidships, which was probably from Rhodes (*ibid.*, 341–2). The collection of coarse and fine pottery, presumably intended for the use of the crew, was found to be concentrated in two areas, one towards the bows, and one towards the stern, suggesting that crew's stowage space and/or living quarters were provided in both areas (*ibid.*, 344–5).

The potential of a close analysis of sea-bed distributions is clearly shown by recent work on the fourth-century ship at Yassi Ada (Bass & van Doorninck 1971). That the vessel's galley was situated at the stern was clearly shown by the distribution of related artefacts, as shown in fig. 5.13; the shaded objects represent over two dozen stone slabs, which it is thought lined the hearth. The limits of the galley were indicated by the manner in which the pile of stacked amphorae stopped at frame B 29 and the way in which few galley objects were found forward of this line. Since this frame lay approximately 3 metres forward of the vessel's stern, the galley facilities were relatively spacious for a craft of only 50 tons. A similar analysis was undertaken by Dr van Doorninck on the remains of the seventh-century ship at Yassi Ada, where an identical break in the distributions was apparent at frame 8 forward of the stern. Aft of this there was an area of tile fragments associated with cooking utensils, fragments of fired clay, and small iron bars (presumably from the hearth), together with very few amphora fragments (van Doorninck 1967, 107–9). As with the fourth-century wreck (van Doorninck 1976, 130), this galley apparently had a tiled roof, the remains of which were clustered to the port side where they had slid during break-up. Even more detailed deductions were possible in this instance: for example, the distribution of coins and other valuables suggested that they had been stored in a cupboard attached to the bulkhead at frame 8, on the starboard side (van Doorninck 1967, 115–17). A similar analysis was attempted on the remains of the Dramont D wreck near Saint-Raphael in southern France, where the distribution of pottery and other items dissimilar to those constituting the ship's cargo suggested a cabin area at the stern containing food, water, tools, and other supplies, and one forward on the port side where crockery was stored (Joncheray 1973; 1974).

In such instances, very detailed interpretations have been possible because there has not been a great deal of rearrangement of the material since deposition; once the relevant distributions have been plotted out individually (as, for example, in van Doorninck 1967, 287–92, for the seventh-century Yassi Ada ship), their significance can be assessed visually, and requires no more sophisticated analysis to support the conclusions. However, this ceases to be the case with distributions which have suffered slightly more disturbance, or which have lost a greater proportion of the original material. Current experience suggests that this is more likely to occur with the larger and more complex post-medieval wreck-sites; in the present discussion, some of the considerations involved will be demonstrated on the site of the *Dartmouth* (1690). The manner in which the process of wrecking occurred here was described above (section 5.4), where it was explained how part of the hull on the starboard side aft of midships had been preserved (figs. 3.19, p. 96, and 5.5).

The orientation of the vessel was evidenced archaeologically in two separate ways. First, the structural remains themselves, once fully interpreted, showed that the stern had to be to the east, since a massive rising deadwood of that type could not have existed so close to midships in the forward part of the ship (Martin 1978). Secondly, certain artefacts could be taken as indicators of bow and stern, and these were found to be concentrated at the western and eastern ends of the site respectively,

Table 5.5. *A table of 'indicator' artefacts from the three areas of the* Dartmouth *site given in fig. 5.14*

	Area A (aft)	
Navigational instruments	Fine pewter tableware	
Surgical instruments	Fine ceramic tableware	
Flintlock pistol	Leaded mica (for stern windows)	
Balance weights		
	Area F (fore)	
Bosun's stores	Armoury	
cordage	boxes of hand grenades	
parrel and shroud trucks	lead shot	
deadeyes	Highland musket stock	
blocks		
loose sheaves		
	Area S (starboard side)	
Lead scupper liners	Animal bones	
Bricks and tiles	Lead piping (plumbing?)	
Coal and burnt debris	Ship's bell	

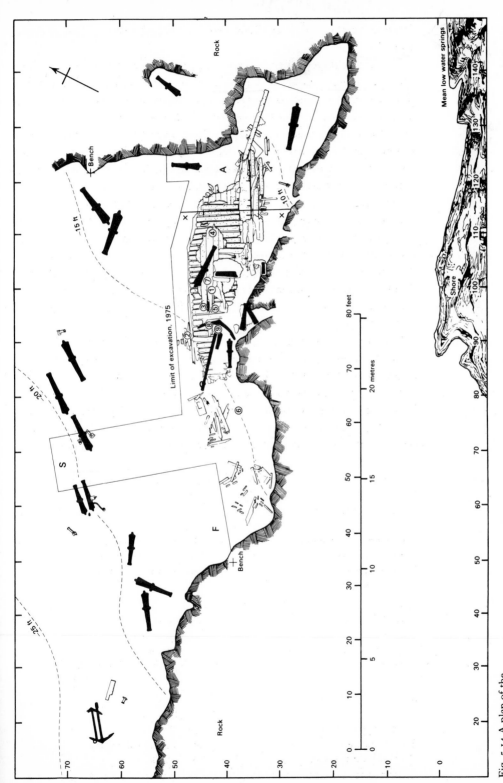

Fig. 5.14 A plan of the
Dartmouth wreck-site in
the Sound of Mull,
Scotland, showing the
arithmetic mean centres
for various classes of
artefacts; for list of classes
see text.

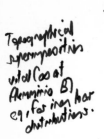

in the areas marked 'F' and 'A' in fig. 5.14. Table 5.5 lists some of these 'indicator' artefacts for each area. Furthermore, there was conclusive evidence from the general bottom topography, the angle of heel of the structural remains, and the line of cannons lying along the northern edge of the site, that the ship had laid over on her starboard side. The cannons had evidently fallen from her upper decks, an interpretation supported by the range of objects found in the same area ('S'; see fig. 5.14). The bricks, tiles, burnt debris, animal bones, etc., were presumably derived from the ship's galley, which would have been situated under the fore-castle at main-deck level, with the ship's bell above it (Martin 1978, fig. 1). A sterile band across the trench driven between areas 'F' and 'S' (fig. 5.14) demonstrated the clear separation between those objects from the upper levels, which had slumped to starboard, and those, such as the bosun's stores and the armoury, which had remained within the lower part of the hull on the alignment of the surviving structure. Thus, although only a small proportion of the hull survived in this instance, a great deal about the layout of the wreck as it disintegrated, and consequently also about the ship as she was originally organised, could be deduced from the archaeological evidence.

However, alongside the 'indicator' artefacts listed in table 5.5, there were a large number of other items whose original locations within the ship were less well known, and whose patterning across the site was less clear cut. In order to facilitate a comparison of their various distributions, their arithmetic mean centres have been calculated, and are given for nine classes of artefact in fig. 5.14. This is undoubtedly the easiest measure to use of those available for aggregating distributions for comparative purposes (Neft 1966; Hodder & Orton 1976, 207–8); it is calculated simply by imposing x and y axes over the site, and then calculating the means of the x and y values across every item, the point (x, y) being the arithmetic mean centre (AMC) for that distribution. The nine classes used in this study were as follows:

Fig. 5.15 A diagram showing the nearest neighbours for the arithmetic mean centres shown in fig. 5.14.

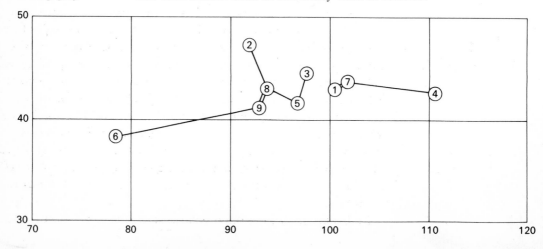

1. Pottery.
2. Glass.
3. Clay pipe bowls.
4. Navigational instruments.
5. Culinary utensils.
6. Rigging fittings.
7. Footware.
8. Personal possessions.
9. Lead patches.

Classes 4 (navigational instruments) and 6 (rigging fittings) were included to test the method, being items associated with the stern and bows, respectively. Clay pipe bowls alone were considered in order to discount the bias towards areas of maximum fragmentation which might have occurred if stems had been included.

The distribution of AMCs given in fig. 5.14 shows immediately that classes 4 and 6 have extreme locations, while the others cluster amidships. The tendencies within this group are perhaps demonstrated more clearly if each is linked to its nearest neighbour, as in fig. 5.15. Some of the trends indicated are reasonably predictable; for example, one would expect leather footware (class 7) and pottery (class 1) to be generally more closely associated with the officers living in the stern than with the men up forward. However, other results give rise to further research, such as the marked forward and upwards trend of the glass distribution (class 2), which gives rise to speculation concerning the location of the drinks store on board. This exercise has principally been undertaken to show the power of the method on a site where the layout of the vessel is already known; a more thorough programme would be required to answer all the problems relating to this specific example, involving the study of additional classes, and of various subdivisions within these classes.

This simple method of aggregating distributions as a preliminary to studies of spatial associations has been surprisingly little used in archaeology, either above or below water, but it would seem to have great potential. Certainly, in the wreck situation, where the site is a continuous one, it would seem to have many attractions especially where the orientation of the wreck is not immediately clear, and an objective measure of its likely trend is required. It should be noted that Neft (1966, 27–36) has put forward a number of reasons why the harmonic mean centre should be considered a preferable statistic for representing an areal distribution, in particular because it is much less sensitive to extreme values, but for most archaeological purposes the greater effort required in its calculation would seem to outweigh its theoretical advantages.

In this last paragraph the discussion has moved to the consideration

I really don't like his applic. of continuous and discontinuous to wreck sites.

very comparable to Flemming's ✓

P.B.

of continuous wreck-sites on which there are no coherent structural remains, a situation which can now be discussed further through a couple of examples. A somewhat special case is represented by the wreck-site at Cape Gelidonya, which was less than 10 metres long overall, the vessel itself being probably of about the same length (see fig. 3.7, p. 69) (Bass 1967, 44–7). Only a few elements from the ship's hull were preserved within the concretion which had formed around the ingots of its cargo; everything not so trapped must have been swept away by the almost constant current in that area. But from the site distribution, Professor Bass was able to reach several conclusions. It appeared that the vessel planed down to the site, and broke its back on a spine of rock, the two ends coming to rest in areas G and P. Although they had partially slid downhill, the packing arrangements of the two piles of ingots were still apparent. The many scrap bronze fragments were found mostly in small groups, suggesting package in bags or baskets, an idea supported by a portion of wicker basket in one such deposit. Nearly all the items of personal possessions were found either in area G or under the boulder to the north of it, where they could have been carried to by the current. From this, it was thought that area G probably represented the stern of the boat. With such a compact site, and a relatively small number of artefacts, all the appropriate results could be gleaned adequately from the visual appreciation of five basic distribution maps (Bass 1967, figs. 37, 41–44).

Another sense in which Cape Gelidonya is, at least at present, an unusual site is that it has been totally investigated and reported on, so that all the relevant facts are available (Bass 1967). Even the *Dartmouth*, the most completely excavated of the post-medieval wrecks discussed in this chapter, has some peripheral areas which have not been uncovered systematically. However, the problems of a partially excavated site are represented most graphically by that of the *Trinidad Valencera* (1588), in Kinnagoe Bay, County Donegal, Eire (Martin 1975, 189–224). Here, the initial indications from the site, as mapped during the first season (1971), consisted of a few objects such as cannons (fig. 3.22, p. 103) or gun-carriage wheels (fig. 3.21, p. 102) protruding from a flat sandy sea-floor, together with a number of metal detector contacts (fig. 5.16). Since then, in three seasons of work, areas within the site have been opened for investigation and, while a wide range of objects have been uncovered, no signs of a coherent ship have so far been found, and it is very difficult to apprehend any pattern in the site distributions. However, the excavators have acquired a strong feeling that the centre of the deposit lies in the centre of the 100 by 200 foot (30.5 × 61.0 metres) area, and, while raw distribution maps can give some indications as to why this impression has been acquired, a simple trend surface analysis demonstrates the position more clearly. The techniques and results of

Good. a serious problem. what does "sampling mean"? can you infer "backwards" from a partially excavated site!

Fig. 5.16 A plan of the
Trinidad Valencera
wreck-site as delimited by
the pre-disturbance
surveys, showing also the
area excavated in the
south-west corner which
was used for the trend
surface analyses.
(pdr = pounder.)

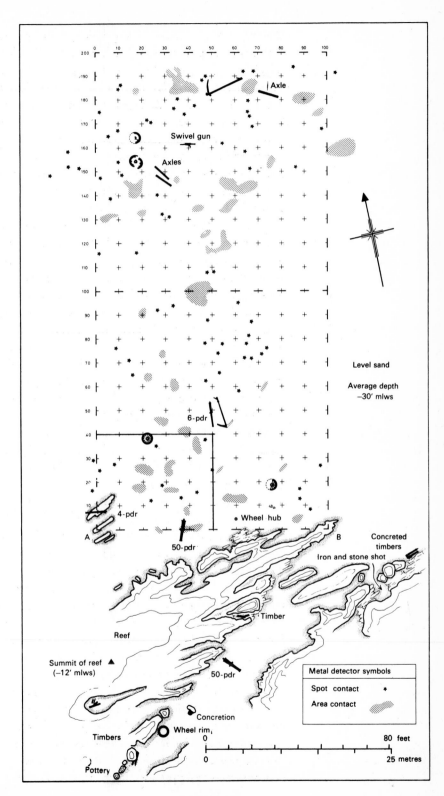

this study are given for one 'window' into this site, an area measuring 40 by 50 feet (12.2 × 15.2 metres) excavated in 1974, working out from datum-point 'A' (fig. 5.16).

The procedure followed in this trend surface analysis was to consider a grid of points over the site, five feet (1.52 metres) apart in each dimension, and to sum for each point the number of objects lying in the four five-foot square quadrats adjacent to that point. Given the density of objects within this area, a five-foot grid was the finest which would produce a reasonable probability of at least one object per quadrat. The results of this first analysis are given in fig. 5.17, representing a fairly low level of generalisation concerning this distribution. To get a higher level, the analysis was repeated, using instead the four ten-foot (3.05 metres) square quadrats around each point; the results are illustrated in fig. 5.18. In each case, the results have been contoured and shaded in order to bring out the main trends more clearly, with appropriate corrections applied to the scores near the borders in order to make them strictly comparable to those in the centre of the grid. While this is a relatively simple form of trend surface analysis, it seems to be adequate for such purposes; for more information on the topic, reference should

Fig. 5.17 The south-west corner of the *Trinidad Valencera* site; trend surface analysis 1.
⬛ = > 4; ⬛ = > 11.

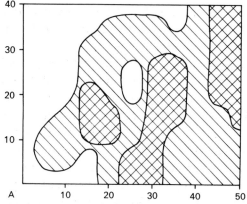

Fig. 5.18 The south-west corner of the *Trinidad Valencera* site; trend surface analysis 2.
⬛ = > 26; ⬛ = > 45.

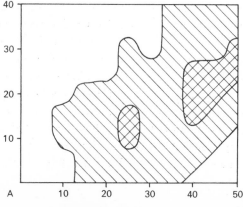

be made to the following (Chorley & Haggett 1965; Cole & King 1968, 375–9; Hodder & Orton 1976, 155–74).

Together, the trend surface maps in figs. 5.17 and 5.18 show quite clearly that the main trend across the site is in a north-east/south-west direction, with a strong suggestion that the greater intensity of artefacts lies off to the north-east. This illustrates precisely the feeling gained during the excavations, and preliminary soundings in the next sector to the north-east of this site suggest that it contains a great concentration of material. The area to the south of the site has yet to be tested. The concentration recorded clearly in fig. 5.17 towards the south-west corner of the site reflects the accumulation of artefacts under and around a broken and heavily concreted wheel-rim, which seems not only to have preserved certain fragile items which would not otherwise have survived (especially leatherwork), but has also attracted to itself a wide range of other objects which could have survived in any case. Complementary to this concentration is a relative scarcity of objects in the zone around the wheel, also reflected in fig. 5.17. It looks as if at some stage the objects have been moving randomly about this area, but that those which became trapped within the concretion of this wheel-rim then ceased to circulate. Once again, this has only been a preliminary exercise to demonstrate the possibilities of the approach, but it would seem to be of some use in such circumstances, involving a partially observed continuous distribution.

With this last example, the discussion has proceeded as far as possible within the definition of a continuous site distribution; the next stage within the progression is a partially observed discontinuous distribution, and that is the subject for consideration in the next section. However, before leaving the topic of continuous distributions, a few points can be emphasised. The most fundamental one is that in all types of analysis, there seems to be a great scope for the increased use of statistical and numerical methods, and for harnessing the powers of modern computers. This applies both to the interpretation of hull remains, where the various hypotheses considered in a reconstruction might be most efficiently modelled by a computer, and to the analysis of artefact distributions (Muckelroy 1975). Within the latter category, some of the simpler and more obvious possibilities have been presented and described briefly above, but many others could be considered; for example, a whole range of techniques based on the nearest neighbour approach have been ommitted (Hodder & Orton 1976, 38–51, 204–7). And finally, the detailed conclusions which have been reached about the construction and organisation of these vessels, using whatever methods, have amply justified the painstaking, expensive, and time-consuming excavation and recording methods which have been used on all the sites considered above.

5.7 The analysis of sea-bed distributions *B*

Discontinuous sites

In the course of the last section, the sophistication of the methods of analysis rose as the degree of reordering of the material on the sea-bed increased, and as the significance of the observed distributions became intuitively less apparent. In the present section, this process moves on a stage further, since with discontinuous sites there has not only been a considerable degree of reordering, but also the loss of any defining structure within which to consider the remains. The distributions on sites such as those at Yassi Ada could be directly related to the framework of the structural remains within which they were formerly contained, and even with the more obscure type of situation such as that represented by the *Trinidad Valencera*, the assumption could still be made that the scatter was related to a single nucleus representing the remains of the vessel. This is no longer true in a situation where the ship has broken up over a considerable distance, or where the sea-bed has presented greatly varying conditions for the preservation of remains within the area of the wreck-site. In this total absence of any defining framework, a discontinuous wreck-site is fundamentally different from nearly all other archaeological situations; perhaps the nearest analogy on land is a midden site.

This presentation of some of the appropriate modes of analysis is concerned exclusively with the *Kennemerland* wreck-site, on which such studies have proved particularly worthwhile; a general plan of the site is given in fig. 5.6. As has already been described, the overall distribution of these remains reflects clearly the break-up of the vessel and the

Fig. 5.19 A plan of the specific areas excavated within the main excavation zone on the *Kennemerland* site (see fig. 5.6 above).

I mean, is not, e.g. Cape Gelidonya strictly 'discontinuous' because there are (or were) no defining structural remains on the wreck-site?

MMMMMM. dut like this

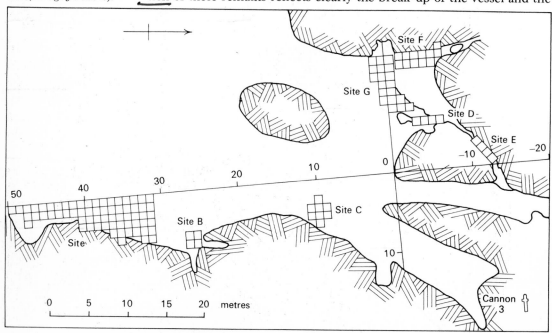

Site F

Site G

Site D

Site E

Site A

Site B

Site C

Cannon 3

50 40 30 20 10 0 -10 -20

0 5 10 15 20 metres

Good stame: determination of the
possibility of synthesis
obligys study

Oad

assimilation of some of its elements into the sea-bed, so there are *a priori* grounds for suspecting that a similar level of significance may lie in the details of these distributions. It is important to be satisfied that such significance is at least conceivable before embarking on any detailed analysis, since no amount of statistical manipulation can extract *any* information from totally scrambled data. Determining that significant patterning is possible does not, of course, guarantee that it will be present, let alone detectable, but it does oblige the archaeologist to search for that pattern, and to so order his excavation and recording processes that the information is available for such a study.

In the case of the site in the South Mouth, discontinuity is imposed not only by the nature of the remains, but also by the limited extent of the areas so far excavated. These have been concentrated in only one part of the site, albeit the central area, in which a good deal of the wreckage was deposited when the foundering ship struck the surf line

*overall
in
detailed
distributions:
references to
and F10?*

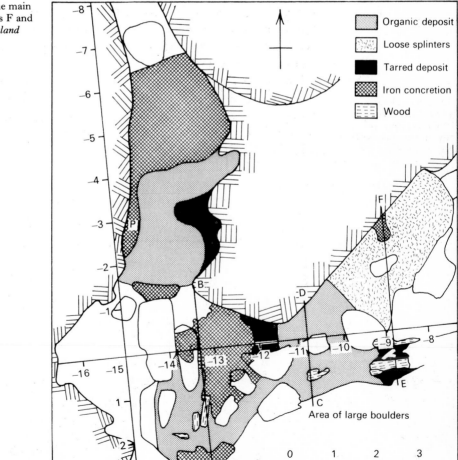

Fig. 5.20 Plan of the main features within sites F and G on the *Kennemerland* site.

Organic deposit
Loose splinters
Tarred deposit
Iron concretion
Wood

Area of large boulders

0   1   2   3
metres

(see fig. 5.7). Furthermore, within this area, only certain sections have been systematically excavated, as shown in fig. 5.19. These seven excavation sites have sampled the main types of sea-bed in this area, including open areas of shingle and boulders (Sites A, C, and G) and enclosed gullies (Sites B, D, E, and F). Similarly, they have sampled a range of deposits, including large expanses of iron concretion (in Sites C, E, and F) and matted organic remains (Sites F and G; see fig. 5.20) as well as clean shingle. Any results emerging are accordingly highly provisional. Nevertheless, the analysis of this information has been proceeding since the end of the first two seasons of excavation (1974), both as a check on the suitability of the excavation methods and as an indication of the kind of questions to tackle in subsequent seasons; a preliminary discussion of some of the initial studies and their findings has already been published (Muckelroy 1975).

they sample 'areas' idea is somehow embedded here, I feel.

Table 5.6. *The incidence of artefacts in the seven main excavation sites on the* Kennemerland *wreck-site; for the definition of classes, see text*

Sites		A	B	C	D	E	F	G	Total
Areas (m^2)		66	4	8	4	4	12	19	117
Class 1	n	185	31	16	33	55	319	313	952
	d	3	7.8	2	8.3	13.8	24.5	16.5	8.1
	p	19	3	2	3	6	34	33	100
Class 2	n	91	134	118	59	72	379	110	963
	d	1.4	33.5	14.8	14.7	18	31.5	5.8	8.2
	p	9	14	12	6	7	39	11	100
Class 3	n	9	5	11	4	7	41	3	80
	d	0.1	1.3	1.4	1	1.8	3.5	0.2	0.7
	p	11	6	14	5	9	51	4	100
Class 4a	n	21	20	8	18	25	117	167	376
	d	0.3	5	1	4.5	6.3	9.8	8.8	3.2
	p	6	5	2	5	7	31	44	100
Class 4b	n	2	8	1	1	5	25	39	81
	d	0.1	2	0.1	0.3	1.3	2	2.1	0.7
	p	2	10	1	1	6	31	48	100
Class 4c	n	23	28	9	19	30	142	206	457
	d	0.3	7	1.1	4.8	7.5	11.8	10.8	3.9
	p	5	6	2	4	7	31	45	100
Class 5	n	1594	0	0	2	1	46	1	1644
	d	24.8	0	0	0.5	0.3	3.8	0.1	14.1
	p	97	0	0	0.1	0.1	3	0.1	100
Class 6	n	13	2	3	10	4	157	25	214
	d	0.2	0.5	0.4	2.5	1	13	1.3	1.8
	p	6	1	1	5	2	73	12	100

Even during the excavation seasons, there were some sea-bed associations which were obviously significant. A particularly clear example concerned a collection of personal possessions (jewellery, thimbles, eating utensils, a small pile of coins, etc.) concentrated in one area of Site F (fig. 5.20: 'P'). These, coming in quantities too great for purely personal use, but too small for Company trading, suggest a spot of (illegal) private trading among the contents of a private chest (Price & Muckelroy 1974, 262). In fact the whole of Site F, and the western part of Site G, was notable for the concentration of such items, perhaps reflecting the part of the ship which ended up in this area close to the western shore of the South Mouth. Within Site G, the almost complete absence of any finds in the eastern part of the site, despite their profusion in the western half and in Site D further east, is equally important for present purposes; since the preservational characteristics of this area were apparently identical to those elsewhere, the paucity of finds must reflect some other factor, presumably related to the process of wrecking.

Sites		A	B	C	D	E	F	G	Total
Areas (m²)		66	4	8	4	4	12	19	117
Class 7	n	9	o	o	o	o	o	o	9
	d	0.1	o	o	o	o	o	o	0.1
	p	100	o	o	o	o	o	o	100
Class 8	n	92	o	o	4	o	o	1	97
	d	1.4	o	o	1	o	o	0.1	0.8
	p	95	o	o	4	o	o	1	100
Class 9	n	389	o	o	o	1	19	1	410
	d	5.9	o	o	o	0.3	1.6	0.3	3.5
	p	94.8	o	o	o	0.3	4.8	0.3	100
Class 10	n	7	o	5	2	o	6	1	21
	d	0.1	o	0.6	0.5	o	0.5	0.1	0.2
	p	33.3	o	23.8	9.5	o	28.6	4.8	100
Class 11	n	5	3	1	o	o	20	20	49
	d	0.1	0.8	0.1	o	o	1.7	1	0.4
	p	10	6	2	o	o	41	41	100
Class 12	n	o	o	7	o	o	8	6	21
	d	o	o	0.9	o	o	0.7	0.3	0.2
	p	o	o	33.3	o	o	38.1	28.6	100
Class 13	n	11	o	22	2	1	42	57	135
	d	0.2	o	2.8	0.5	0.3	3.5	3	1.2
	p	8	o	16	1	1	31	42	100

n, Number of items; d, density (items per square metre); p, percentage within each class

Another marked feature of the distributions which was quickly appreciated was the concentration of lead shot of all types in Site A (Price & Muckelroy 1974, 262). However, a wide range of other items appeared to be irregularly scattered over all the sites, with no patterns immediately apparent.

As a first stage in the analysis, and in order to quantify the variations between sites intuitively felt during the fieldwork, the incidence of different classes of finds in the seven sites was tabulated, in each instance giving the total number of that class in that site, their density (i.e. items per square metre), and the percentage of the total number of that class of find recovered from that particular site (see table 5.6). In every case, the unit of measurement was the smallest identifiable entity, on the grounds that any other approach involved unjustifiable assumptions of relative importance. There was thus no *a priori* weighting, a procedure which, in such contexts, is generally regarded as undesirable (Sneath & Sokal 1973, 109–13). The classes being considered were as follows:

1. Stoneware potsherds, all apparently from Bellarmine flagons (unit: a sherd).
2. Green bottle glass, from square-based glass bottles (unit: a piece of glass).
3. Pewter bottle tops, from the bottles of class 2 (unit: a piece of pewter identifiable as coming from a top).
4. Clay pipes, subdivided into:
   (a) pieces of pipe stem,
   (b) pieces of pipe bowl,
   (c) all fragments of clay pipes.
5. Lead shot, larger than 0.001 metres in diameter; i.e. not scatter shot.
6. Personal possessions (jewellery, thimbles, eating utensils, items of clothing, etc.).
7. Items associated with the ships armament.
8. Fragments of bronze sheeting.
9. Bronze nails.
10. Fragments of lead.
11. Bones.
12. Pieces of rope.
13. Glazed earthenware potsherds (unit: a sherd).

Together, these classes embraced over 80% of all the finds made on this site.

While considerable variations between sites within each class are apparent in table 5.6, it is difficult to make comparisons between the various elements in it, and impossible to bring out any patterns. A simple way of clarifying such a tabulation is to lump together certain units, according to a common feature, so as to bring out the effect of that feature on the overall figures. In table 5.7 this involved aggregating all the open sites (i.e. A, C, and G) and all the enclosed, gully sites (i.e. the remainder), in order to inspect any general trends. While confirming that enclosed sites had a consistently higher density of finds, a fact appreciated during the excavation seasons, it also served to refute another suspicion – that there was a distinction in the relative survivals of clay pipe stems (class 4a) and the more fragile pipe bowls (class 4b) between exposed and protected areas. A similar aggregation bringing together finds from different types of deposit demonstrated no noteworthy trends.

In order to eliminate the effects of the different sizes of the excavation sites, as well as to allow a more detailed investigation of the distributions, a reasonable procedure would seem to be to impose a grid of metre

Table 5.7. *The incidence of artefacts on the* Kennemerland *wreck-site, contrasting open and enclosed sites; abbreviations as in table 5.6*

Sites		Open	Enclosed			Open	Enclosed
Areas (m^2)		93	24			93	24
Class 1	n	514	438	Class 7	n	9	0
	d	5.5	18.3		d	0.1	0
	p	54	46		p	100	0
Class 2	n	319	644	Class 8	n	93	4
	d	3.4	26.8		d	1	0.2
	p	33	67		p	96	4
Class 3	n	23	57	Class 9	n	390	20
	d	0.3	2.4		d	4.2	0.8
	p	29	71		p	95	5
Class 4a	n	196	180	Class 10	n	13	8
	d	2.1	7.5		d	0.1	0.3
	p	52	48		p	61.9	38.1
Class 4b	n	42	39	Class 11	n	26	23
	d	0.5	1.6		d	0.3	1
	p	52	48		p	53	47
Class 4c	n	238	219	Class 12	n	13	8
	d	2.6	9.1		d	0.1	0.3
	p	52	48		p	61.9	38.1
Class 5	n	1595	49	Class 13	n	90	45
	d	17.2	2		d	1	0.9
	p	97	3		p	67	33
Class 6	n	41	173				
	d	0.4	7.2				
	p	19	81				

but on what basis?

problem with this kind of study is that you need variety of artefacts.

MM.

squares over the sites, as in fig. 5.19. This size of square was the smallest justified by the degree of accuracy actually achieved in the recording under water. They were arranged so that the total number of squares on each site equalled the total area (in square metres) of that site, while at the same time ensuring that every artefact could be placed in one square; the parts of each site thus excluded from the grid were those which were sterile. Any items falling on the boundaries between squares were placed in the numerically lower square (i.e. the one nearest the relevant point of origin) on the grounds that a measurement taken by tape is more likely to overestimate a distance than underestimate it, since the tape can be slack and not straight, but it cannot be overstretched. Classes 7 (items of armament), 10 (lead fragments), and 12 (pieces of rope) were omitted from these further stages of analysis, since they were too small to yield significant results. Twenty of the 117 squares were also excluded from further consideration since they contained no finds from any of the classes under consideration; these squares are indicated in fig. 5.21 by underlined numbers. The number of items from each class in the remaining 97 squares is given in table 5.8, following the numeration of fig. 5.21.

Subjectively, it is apparent that there is a strong patterning in the distribution of every class across the 97 squares, an impression confirmed by the extremely high values resulting in every case from a calculation of an Index of Dispersion (Greig-Smith 1964, 63; Hodder & Orton 1976, 34), lying in the range 373.4 (class 3) to 11 224.3 (class 5). Further analysis thus seemed appropriate. The ordering of the squares is obviously arbitrary, and the distances between them vary, so that the problem of determining any pattern within this data in fact resolves itself into a problem of correlation between the twelve classes. For such an analysis, a series of techniques are available within the discipline of numerical taxonomy (Sneath & Sokal 1973), some of which will be explored below.

A common approach to such a problem would be to simplify the data into a table of presence and absence for each class in each area, recording presence for each occasion in table 5.8 when the score is other than zero, and absence when it is zero. A coefficient of correlation can then be produced between every pair of classes relating the number of squares in which they achieve the same state to the number in which they achieve opposite states (Sneath & Sokal 1973, 129–37; Hodder & Orton 1976, 201–4). Considering classes X and Y in table 5.9, this means relating the number of squares in which they are both present (a) or both absent (d) to those in which one is present and one absent (b and c). Such an analysis was attempted on the first batch of data, but the results were not encouraging, since the simplification to presence/ absence states minimised the impact of classes which were highly

Fig. 5.21 Key to the grid square numbers, *Kennemerland* site (for locations, see fig. 5.19).

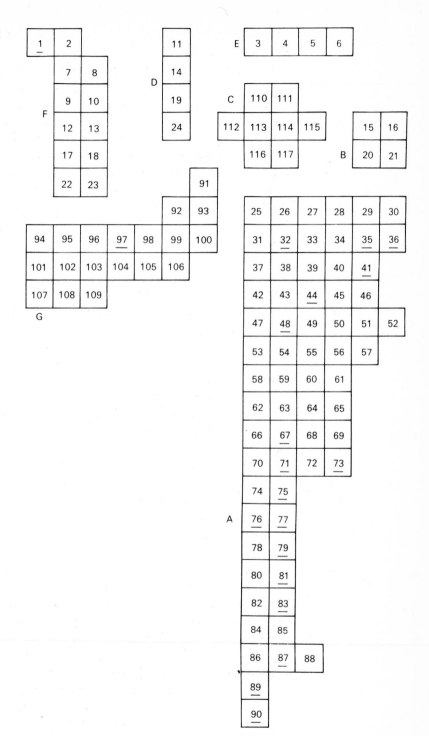

Table 5.8. *The number of items from each of twelve classes occurring in each metre square within the excavation sites on the Kennemerland wreck-site; for a description of the classes, see text; for the location of the squares, see fig. 5.21.*

Class	1	2	3	4a	4b	4c	5	6	8	9	11	13
2	13	70	2	17	2	19	0	3	0	1	0	0
3	13	18	1	6	1	7	0	0	0	0	0	1
4	14	18	2	6	1	7	0	2	0	0	0	0
5	14	18	2	6	2	8	1	2	0	1	0	0
6	14	18	2	7	1	8	0	0	0	0	0	0
7	100	91	10	14	9	23	0	3	0	0	0	3
8	22	0	5	0	0	0	0	0	0	0	0	0
9	1	10	8	0	0	0	1	6	0	0	2	4
10	1	4	2	0	0	0	0	2	0	0	0	0
11	8	14	1	4	0	4	0	2	1	0	0	0
12	50	57	10	20	9	30	21	11	0	0	0	7
13	4	10	1	6	0	5	0	1	0	0	0	2
14	8	15	1	4	0	5	0	2	1	0	0	0
15	8	33	1	5	2	7	0	0	0	0	1	0
16	8	34	2	5	2	7	0	2	0	0	1	0
17	87	46	2	22	5	27	25	100	0	9	4	14
18	3	10	1	1	0	1	0	0	0	0	0	4
19	8	15	1	5	1	5	1	3	1	0	0	1
20	7	33	1	5	2	7	0	0	0	0	0	0
21	8	34	1	5	2	7	0	2	0	0	1	0
22	34	67	0	31	0	31	0	29	0	9	14	5
23	4	14	0	6	0	6	0	2	0	0	0	3
24	9	15	1	5	0	5	1	3	1	0	0	1
25	2	0	0	0	0	0	0	0	0	0	0	0
26	0	4	0	0	0	0	0	0	0	0	0	0
27	0	5	0	1	0	1	0	0	0	0	0	0
28	0	0	1	0	0	0	1	0	0	0	0	0
29	0	4	4	0	0	0	0	10	2	0	0	0
30	2	0	0	0	0	0	0	0	0	0	0	0
31	4	0	0	0	0	0	0	0	0	0	0	0
33	6	2	0	0	0	0	0	0	0	0	0	0
34	0	7	0	0	0	0	10	1	3	6	0	0
37	7	7	0	1	0	1	0	0	0	0	0	0
38	0	5	0	0	0	0	1	0	0	0	0	0
39	0	0	0	5	0	5	1	0	2	6	0	0
40	0	0	1	4	0	4	12	1	1	0	0	0
42	3	6	0	2	0	2	1	0	2	0	0	0
43	3	5	0	0	0	0	0	1	0	0	0	1
45	0	1	0	0	0	0	0	0	0	0	0	0
46	0	0	0	0	0	0	23	0	1	3	0	0
47	7	5	0	2	0	2	7	0	0	3	0	3
49	3	0	0	0	0	0	0	0	1	0	0	0
50	15	6	1	3	0	3	71	0	0	0	3	0
51	17	4	0	0	0	0	41	0	4	95	0	1
52	6	0	0	0	0	0	0	0	0	0	0	0
53	0	1	0	0	0	0	0	0	0	0	0	0
54	10	1	0	1	0	1	54	0	5	4	0	0
55	4	0	0	0	0	0	142	0	25	0	1	1

Class	1	2	3	4a	4b	4c	5	6	8	9	11	13
56	1	0	0	0	0	0	120	0	3	1	0	0
57	0	0	0	0	0	0	218	0	0	0	0	0
58	6	1	0	0	0	0	30	0	1	0	0	0
59	7	1	0	0	0	0	100	0	2	5	0	1
60	5	3	0	0	0	0	67	0	0	13	0	0
61	0	3	0	0	0	0	28	0	9	11	0	0
62	7	2	1	0	0	0	0	0	0	2	0	0
63	6	0	0	0	0	0	6	0	0	2	1	0
64	30	0	0	0	0	0	83	0	1	18	0	0
65	2	0	0	0	0	0	30	0	0	0	0	0
66	6	3	0	0	2	2	30	0	10	28	0	0
68	1	0	0	0	0	0	6	0	0	8	0	0
69	0	0	0	0	0	0	60	0	0	0	0	0
70	12	3	0	0	0	0	6	0	4	0	0	1
72	3	0	0	0	0	0	8	0	0	8	0	0
74	0	3	1	1	0	1	0	0	0	0	0	0
78	2	0	0	0	0	0	0	0	0	0	0	0
80	3	1	0	1	0	1	225	0	14	35	0	0
82	1	7	0	0	0	0	213	0	2	69	0	3
84	1	0	0	0	0	0	0	0	0	0	0	0
85	0	1	0	0	0	0	0	0	0	0	0	0
86	1	0	0	0	0	0	0	0	0	71	0	0
88	2	0	0	0	0	0	0	0	0	0	0	0
91	3	4	0	2	0	2	0	1	0	0	1	0
92	6	9	0	3	1	4	1	0	0	0	0	0
93	3	3	0	7	3	10	0	1	0	0	0	0
94	50	0	0	2	1	3	0	0	0	0	0	0
95	89	20	1	18	0	18	0	6	0	0	2	5
96	2	8	0	4	3	7	0	4	0	0	1	8
98	1	0	0	0	0	0	0	0	0	0	0	0
99	5	8	0	25	9	34	0	0	0	0	0	2
100	24	15	0	28	1	29	0	1	0	0	5	6
101	24	6	0	5	3	8	0	0	0	0	1	2
102	93	24	0	38	11	49	0	9	1	1	0	20
103	6	3	1	14	4	18	0	1	0	0	6	11
104	0	0	0	0	0	0	0	0	0	0	1	0
105	0	0	1	0	0	0	0	1	0	0	0	0
106	1	0	0	0	0	0	0	0	0	0	0	0
107	3	0	0	4	2	6	0	0	0	0	0	0
108	1	5	0	16	3	19	0	1	0	0	3	2
109	2	5	0	5	0	5	0	0	0	0	1	1
110	2	18	2	5	0	5	0	1	0	0	0	6
111	1	5	2	0	0	0	0	0	0	0	0	5
112	2	28	0	0	0	0	0	0	0	0	0	1
113	3	21	3	3	1	4	0	2	0	0	0	8
114	1	13	1	0	0	0	0	0	0	0	0	2
115	4	13	2	0	0	0	0	0	0	0	1	0
116	3	9	1	0	0	0	0	0	0	0	0	0
117	0	11	0	0	0	0	0	0	0	0	0	0

huge problem
here: on cta sites,
ep. amph wrecks,
evidently way
more approach.

concentrated in a small number of squares, and the introduction of an abundance state in addition to presence and absence did not totally solve the problem (Muckelroy 1975, 178–85). However, the study showed clearly that with such material the Simple Matching Coefficient, calculated on the formula $(a+d)/(a+b+c+d)$ (see table 5.9), performed badly since it registered unreasonably high scores between rare classes whose only similarity lay in the facts that they were mutually absent from most of the site and that the Coefficient of Jaccard, calculated on the formula $a/(a+b+c)$ and thus totally discounting the effects of d (mutual absence), was much more satisfactory. Since this characteristic of some rare and some common classes is likely to be typical of many archaeological situations, this conclusion will be widely applicable. The similarity matrix calculated on the Coefficient of Jaccard for this simplification of table 5.8 is given in table 5.10; general inspection of it readily shows that there remains an unfortunate tendency for large classes to achieve high scores with each other.

Table 5.9. *A table giving the conventional designation of the four possibilities of presence/absence relationships between two classes in a matrix*

		Class X	
		Present	Absent
Class Y	Present	a	b
	Absent	c	d

Table 5.10. *Similarity matrix calculated on the Coefficient of Jaccard for the presence/absence simplification of the* Kennemerland *distribution data in Table 5.8*

	1	2	3	4a	4b	4c	5	6	8	9	11	13
1	+											
2	0.64	+										
3	0.37	0.44	+									
4a	0.51	0.57	0.44	+								
4b	0.33	0.34	0.32	0.54	+							
4c	0.51	0.64	0.43	0.98	0.55	+						
5	0.30	0.28	0.15	0.19	0.11	0.21	+					
6	0.34	0.43	0.48	0.50	0.38	0.49	0.14	+				
8	0.21	0.23	0.11	0.17	0.06	0.18	0.48	0.17	+			
9	0.24	0.21	0.07	0.15	0.11	0.16	0.48	0.12	0.37	+		
11	0.23	0.23	0.20	0.27	0.25	0.27	0.10	0.28	0.02	0.08	+	
13	0.40	0.46	0.28	0.39	0.29	0.39	0.20	0.39	0.17	0.14	0.28	+

While such presence/absence methods have the advantage of simplicity and can be applied (albeit laboriously) without the aid of a computer, their use inevitably involves the loss of a good deal of information;
if precise figures, such as those given in table 5.8, are available they
should, all other things being equal, be utilised. A simplified data-set
was explored in the preliminary study, using the Robinson–Brainerd
index of similarity (Robinson & Brainerd 1951), and this served to show
the greater potential of numerical analysis (Muckelroy 1975, 181–5).
However, by harnessing the greater speed and power of a computer,
more complex statistics can be investigated, and a wide range of possible
approaches tested. This has been done, using the data presented in
table 5.8, making use of the CLUSTAN package. In order to suppress
the influence of variations in the sizes of the classes, it was found
necessary to express all scores as percentages for each class, and then to
standardise these percentages.

The first requirement in such a study is the production of a similarity
matrix for the twelve classes, similar to that given in table 5.10. For this,
two widely used correlation coefficients have been tested: a measure of
Euclidean distance and the product–moment measure of similarity. The
matrix based on the former measure is given in table 5.11, while that
derived from the latter is shown in table 5.12. Inspection of these shows
that there are only minor differences between them, and there is no
reason to prefer the one before the other. However, the Euclidean
distance measure might be considered the more suitable generally, since
it allows a greater range of subsequent clustering exercises. Eight of
these clustering procedures from the CLUSTAN package were applied
in this instance, of which only the first four could be applied to the
product–moment correlation results. The dendrograms produced by
five of the more satisfactory clusterings are given in figs. 5.22–5.26.

The criteria applied in deciding on whether a given procedure had
produced a satisfactory pattern were two-fold. First, and most fundamental, it had to produce clear and unambiguous patterning, and it is
the fact that several techniques did produce such satisfactory and
essentially identical results which gives rise to confidence in the general
trends so indicated. And, secondly, it had to show a close association of
classes 4*a*, 4*b*, and 4*c* (different aspects of clay pipes), since it could be
assumed that these were originally closely related; again, the fact that
some procedures did behave satisfactorily on this criterion constitutes
grounds for confidence in the approach. A third criterion could be
applied, consisting of a search for close relationships between classes 2
and 3 (glass bottles and their tops), but this appeared in no instance, and
it must be presumed that the different preservational factors affecting
these two classes had obscured any original association.

A simple and intuitively straightforward clustering procedure is that

Table 5.11. *Analysis of Kennemerland data; similarity matrix, using a Euclidean distance measure*

	1	2	3	4a	4b	4c	5	6	8	9	11	13
1	+											
2	2.314	+										
3	3.103	2.508	+									
4a	2.087	1.442	2.137	+								
4b	2.054	1.814	2.290	1.135	+							
4c	1.941	1.599	2.092	0.301	0.831	+						
5	2.773	2.786	3.187	2.350	2.099	2.370	+					
6	2.295	1.912	1.697	1.487	1.132	1.410	1.699	+				
8	2.963	2.831	3.050	2.120	2.107	2.230	1.739	1.397	+			
9	2.763	2.865	3.294	2.206	2.135	2.338	1.417	1.670	1.523	+		
11	2.673	2.570	2.968	1.752	1.382	1.796	1.938	1.334	2.091	2.035	+	
13	2.575	2.064	2.629	1.578	1.528	1.877	2.054	1.162	2.014	2.046	1.564	+

Table 5.12 *Analysis of Kennemerland data; similarity matrix, using product–moment correlation*

	1	2	3	4a	4b	4c	5	6	8	9	11	13
1	+											
2	−0.014	+										
3	−0.177	−0.034	+									
4a	−0.119	0.138	−0.068	+								
4b	−0.019	−0.024	−0.087	0.086	+							
4c	−0.043	0.029	−0.050	0.750	0.362	+						
5	−0.103	−0.236	−0.223	−0.381	−0.261	−0.376	+					
6	−0.181	−0.105	0.280	−0.311	−0.080	−0.192	−0.127	+				
8	−0.180	−0.256	−0.165	−0.250	−0.300	−0.298	0.180	0.046	+			
9	−0.097	−0.274	−0.267	−0.296	−0.294	−0.360	0.341	−0.123	0.275	+		
11	−0.123	−0.217	−0.208	−0.124	0.060	−0.127	0.003	−0.053	−0.114	−0.059	+	
13	−0.142	−0.012	−0.112	−0.075	−0.098	−0.269	−0.097	0.052	−0.108	−0.103	0.048	+

of linking together nearest neighbours; in fact, some statisticians consider this technique to be the only completely valid one (Doran & Hodson 1975, 176). The dendrogram resulting from this approach using the Euclidean distance measure is given in fig. 5.22, while that using the product–moment coefficient appears in fig. 5.23. The former

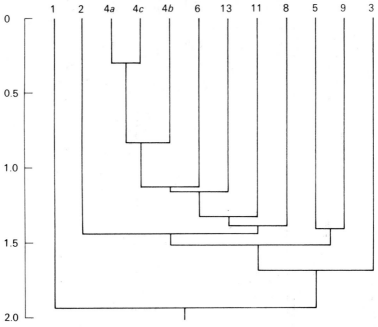

ig. 5.22 *Kennemerland*
te analysis; dendrogram
using distance
rrelation and nearest
eighbour clustering.

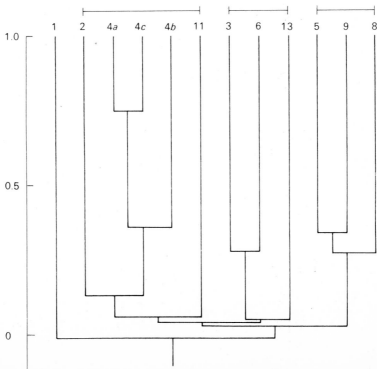

ig. 5.23 *Kennemerland*
te analysis; dendrogram
using product–moment
rrelation and nearest
eighbour clustering.

suffers from undue chaining onto one central cluster initiated by classes 4a, 4b, and 4c, a common failing of this procedure, but the results from the latter are reasonably satisfactory, producing the three discrete clusters indicated along the top of fig. 5.23. A similarly satisfactory couple of dendrograms arose from the use of a related technique, that of group average clustering; the one produced from the Euclidean distance matrix is given in fig. 5.24 and that arising from the product–moment matrix in fig. 5.25. While the former produced a couple of clear clusters, but with still some signs of chaining in the central cluster, the latter displayed a series of very clear groupings, at two distinct levels, as indicated at the top of fig. 5.25. As has been observed in several other archaeological situations, this approach proved in many respects to be the most satisfactory; however, serious mathematical objections have been raised concerning its operation, and complete reliance on it is not recommended (Doran & Hodson 1975, 177). A third related technique

Fig. 5.24 *Kennemerland site analysis; dendrogram 3, using distance correlation and group average clustering.*

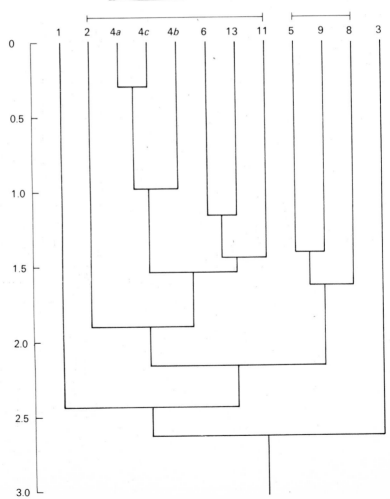

is clustering by considering further neighbours; in the case of the data derived from the Euclidean distance matrix this produced a result which did not cluster all the sub-groups of class 4 together, while the use of the product–moment data produced a dendrogram almost identical to fig. 5.25. The final technique which can be applied to both matrices involves the use of McQuitty's coefficient; in both instances the results were practically identical to those produced by using the group average approach.

Four other procedures were tested which could only be applied to data from the Euclidean distance matrix. Of these, one, the Lance–Williams coefficient, produced a result which did not satisfy the second of the above criteria, while two others, involving the related concepts of centroid and median clustering (Lance & Williams 1967), exhibited undesirable chaining characteristics parallel to those in fig. 5.22. However, the final procedure, known as Ward's Method (Ward 1963),

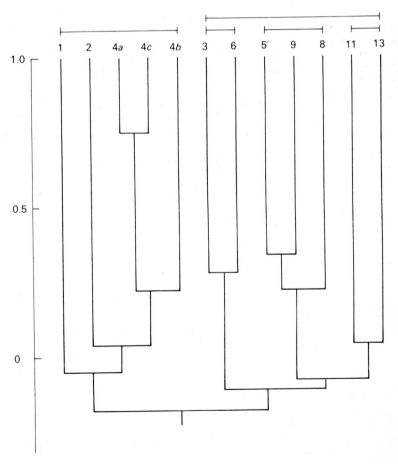

Fig. 5.25 *Kennemerland* site analysis; dendrogram 4, using product–moment correlation and group average clustering.

produced a very satisfactory pattern, as shown in fig. 5.26, although only after a relocation procedure had been applied at several levels, as a result of which class *4b* migrated clusters. This was the result which came nearest to achieving the association of classes 2 and 3, and it is based on a procedure which is widely considered to be particularly satisfactory (Wishart 1969).

If one considers only the first group of four procedures, then there can be no doubt that the product–moment correlation data consistently produced more useful results, being much less susceptible to undesirable chaining. Similar considerations lead to particular faith in the results of using the group average procedure, especially since they are duplicated by those achieved using the McQuitty coefficient, which is not open to the same mathematical objections. However, the satisfactory nature of fig. 5.26 suggests that the distance measure is not to be totally discarded, especially when associated with a clustering procedure to which it is particularly well suited. For a brief discussion of the archaeological consequences of these results given below, attention is focussed on the dendrograms in fig. 5.25 (product–moment correlation plus

Fig. 5.26 *Kennemerland* site analysis; dendrogram 5, using distance correlation and Ward's Method clustering (with relocation).

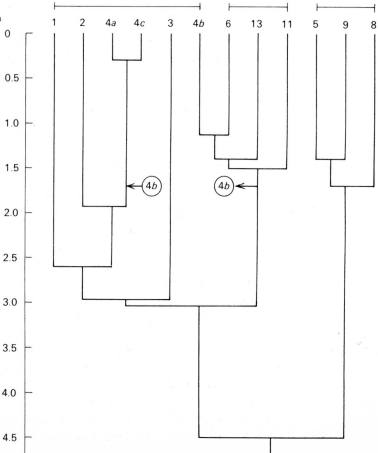

group average clustering) and fig. 5.26 (Euclidean distance measure plus Ward's Method).

In both of these figures, there is a clear association of classes 5, 8, and 9 (lead shot, bronze sheeting, and bronze nails), which might together indicate an origin in the forward part of the ship, where the bosun's stores and the armoury would be situated (see the parallel of the *Dartmouth* discussed above). A similar close association of classes 11, 13, and, in fig. 5.26, 6 (bones, earthenware pottery, and personal possessions) indicates items for use by those on board during the voyage, in the form of salt meat, crockery, and personal valuables and utensils; an interesting point here is that the earthenware might equally well have been considered as cargo if it were not for these results. And finally, there is a consistent, if rather more loose cluster including classes 4 (clay pipes), 1 (stoneware vessels), 2 (glass bottles) and, in fig. 5.26, 3 (bottle tops), which may be taken as indicating items from the ship's cargo. In the case of clay pipes this is a particularly interesting conclusion, since they might otherwise have been regarded as predominantly items for use during the voyage. The stoneware vessels and glass bottles were not themselves the cargo, but rather the containers in which brandy, wine, and other liquids were being carried. The higher level of clustering indicated in fig. 5.25 also suggests a primary division between items in use during the voyage in one context or another, and those permanently consigned to the hold, although this distinction is not so clear in fig. 5.26 or the other dendrograms. This brief summary of some of the possible archaeological implications of this study has obviously not been exhaustive, but it has indicated some of the potential of such an approach.

Despite these relatively satisfactory results, note must be taken of some of the disadvantages inherent in any quadrat technique, arising from the heavy bias imposed on the results by the location, size and shape of the squares (Hodder & Orton 1976, 36–8, 204). In this instance, a few tests comparing the results from different grid sizes, following the procedure for comparing the 'mean square between blocks' (Greig-Smith 1964, 85–93; Hodder & Orton 1976, 34), failed to show that considering larger blocks would improve the discrimination, and suggested that the most satisfactory approach was to consider the smallest possible squares. Furthermore, since the nature of a discontinuous site rules out the use of any measure for distributional analysis depending on the actual distance between items, there are few alternatives to the quadrat method. One other possibility is some form of Runs Test (Hodder & Orton 1976, 208–10), considering the relative ordering of items from two assemblages, and not precise distances, and seeking to reject the null hypothesis that the two assemblages could be derived from the same population. However, it would probably not be valid to use the scores achieved as a detailed measure of association between such groups, and so the approach would seem to be less useful than the quadrat method.

The statistical procedures discussed above have been operating at essentially a descriptive level, seeking to summarise and clarify large bodies of data so that the main patterns within them may be brought out for archaeological interpretation. There are, however, more powerful techniques available, in which the use of the techniques themselves possesses an interpretive potential, in suggesting how the observed pattern came to be generated. For example, useful insights into the processes by which new land may have been colonised by neolithic farmers have been gained by applying procedures developed for the study of epidemics. In the absence of any helpful analogous procedures, a useful technique would seem to be the computer simulation of the shipwreck process in any particular set of circumstances, to be tested for 'goodness of fit' against the observed patterns. In the early stages of such an exercise, the results would undoubtedly be confused and unsatisfactory, but the hope would be that in time the significant factors would become clear, along with any important gaps in current knowledge or understanding. A site such as the *Kennemerland* wreck-site would seem to be particularly suitable for developing such an approach, in the light of the favourable characteristics outlined above, but more general interpretative models should appear in due course, based on those features which are common to all shipwrecks, to be used on sites which are less well evidenced, and especially those from earlier and less well-understood periods. This approach would represent the ultimate consolidation of everything discussed in this chapter, the interpretation of the wrecking system presented in fig. 5.1 and the maximum exploitation of the information contained in the sea-bed distributions; only time will tell whether its promise can be fully realised.

6

The archaeology of ships

6.1 Introduction

At the beginning of the last chapter, a model for the analysis of a ship-wreck was presented in terms of the processes through which it had moved between the time it had been a coherent ship and its ultimate excavation (see fig. 5.1, p. 158). In the present chapter, the purpose is to reverse this sequence, and move back through the system to the original ship itself, in order to examine the limits of what can be learned about it from purely archaeological data. The study of the wrecking process itself is of limited intrinsic significance, its importance lying rather in the link it provides between the remains investigated and the original vessel. Furthermore, the potential and limitations of our understanding of the latter by archaeological means ultimately defines the scope of the whole sub-discipline of maritime archaeology, as discussed in chapter 7.

Ironically, while in any excavation report on an individual wreck site the consideration of what has been learned about the various aspects of the ship constitutes the greater part of the discussion section, in the present work this chapter on the archaeology of ships is relatively short, since there is little generalisation to be made about it. The results of the investigations on particular wreck-sites presented in Part One demonstrate the main elements involved in this topic. However, there are a few recurrent themes which must be discussed in the present context.

A most important point concerns the relationship between archaeological and other sources of evidence about a specific ship, and the great strength of the archaeological data in being more direct than any other. While it is certainly affected by the interpretations of the archaeologist, other sources such as the documentary or the pictorial are subject to two such filters, that of the contemporary recorder and that of their modern interpreter. In the last analysis, the sea-bed remains show what actually existed, rather than what was thought to be there, or should have been there. Furthermore, the survival of that particular body of remains has been totally accidental and unintentional; no-one could have actually intended to end their voyage with a shipwreck. Thus the early and relatively primitive backstaff discovered on the *Kennemerland* (1664) site is clear evidence of the survival of this type several decades later than contemporary writers had implied, and automatically takes precedence over their testimony (see section 3.9). Of course, archaeological evidence possesses its own inherent weaknesses, notably in being unable to shed light on people's motives or ideas, so that the various disciplines should generally be seen as complementary and equal rather than conflicting or in some sort of hierarchy. This situation as it applies to individual ships should become clear in the course of the rest of this chapter.

Another important feature of the subject in recent years has been the way in which the discovery of the ships themselves has acted as a catalyst to further researches into other areas of maritime research. For Peter Throckmorton, the investigation of classical ships around the Aegean led directly to a concern with recording the few surviving examples of old boat types still afloat in that area (Throckmorton 1973*a*). The discovery of the wrecks of the Spanish Armada has led historians of that event to look again at the armaments and other stores actually loaded on those vessels (section 3.6). To some extent, this involves no more than the fruitful tossing backwards and forwards of research problems between disciplines, as described in section 1.1, but in many cases it is more emotional and less scientific than that; the physical remains possess an immediacy which can inspire an interest which begins with no academic justification, but which can lead to genuine progress. Although outside the strict cannons of scientific method, it would be wrong to overlook the impact of this factor.

The framework adopted in this chapter involves a consideration of the three main aspects of a ship involved in its normal activities. In summary, these are:

(*a*) The ship as a machine designed for harnessing a source of power in order to serve as a means of transport.

(*b*) The ship as an element in a military or economic system, providing its basic *raison d'être*.

(*c*) The ship as a closed community, with its own hierarchy, customs, and conventions.

Each of these aspects is discussed in turn, with a particular emphasis on the strengths and weaknesses of archaeological evidence, and its relationship to that available from other sources.

6.2 The ship as a machine

Above all, a ship is designed as a means of transport, both for people and goods, so that her principal features will be constrained by the requirements of this function. There are two basic requisites; first, she must be able to float in all the conditions she is likely to meet, and, secondly, she must be able to move efficiently and in a controlled manner. For the latter purpose she must be able to harness an adequate power source, and for the period under consideration here this has meant either human muscle, through oars, or wind power, through sails. In any particular instance, the understanding of the design and construction of the original ship depends on an appreciation of the methods by which these requirements have been satisfied. As was shown in section 5.6, these essential characteristics can often allow the archaeologist to recover a hull form from only fragmentary remains observed on the sea-bed. The study of ships in this particular sense is the proper concern of nautical archaeology, as defined in section 1.1.

In the course of chapter 3, a number of individual vessels were discussed in these terms, from the fourth-century B.C. Kyrenia ship through the Roskilde Viking ships and the sixteenth-century A.D. *Mary Rose* to the *Dartmouth* of 1690. The fundamental reason for the real progress made in this research, even in these early days, is of course the fact that the marine environment can present particularly favourable conditions for the preservation of wood, the dominant material in pre-industrial shipbuilding. A second positive factor arises from the way a ship's form is principally determined by the design of her keel, stem and stern posts, and to a lesser extent, her lower frames, the parts which are most likely to become buried and preserved within the sea-bed. Examples of the extent of reconstruction which can be achieved have been given above in sections 3.5 (the *Dartmouth*) and 5.6 (the ships at Yassi Ada and other Mediterranean sites). Finally, there is the general point that archaeological remains show the hull as it was actually built, and thus give more direct evidence than any number of plans or drawings. These features, which have already been discussed in considerable detail, together make up the principal strengths of nautical archaeology.

There are, however, a few major drawbacks with this evidence. Possibly the most serious is that, while a concentration on the lower parts of vessels may be very informative, there will always be a bias away from the consideration of topics associated with a ship's upperworks, especially the harnessing of a power source, whether through oars or sails, or details of accommodation for crew and passengers, since such elements will rarely have survived. In fact, as suggested in sections 3.1 and 3.5, this weakness may not always be critical, since it is on just such matters that ship's plans and drawings are often most revealing.

One of the principal strengths of archaeological evidence in general is its strong locational content – that it relates to activities being carried out in the past at a precise spot with given environmental characteristics, in the context of which its former significance may be assessed. This aspect is totally missing from maritime sites, except in the limited sense discussed in section 5.2, since a wreck-site can only have come into being by accident. Lucien Basch (1972, 50–2) considers this to be the most serious weakness in the whole discipline, in particular noting the impossibility of knowing the port of origin of a ship from its remains, let alone its place of construction. Certain probabilities can often be deduced from the cargo, as with the Cape Gelidonya wreck, which is likely to have been of Phoenician origin, and to have called at Cyprus (Bass 1967, 164), but the evidence falls far short of certainty. And there is absolutely no clue as to where the ship may have been built, information of far greater significance when discussing nautical technology. Similar problems with a post-medieval vessel were demonstrated by the Mullion wreck in Cornwall (McBride *et al.* 1972; Larn *et al.* 1974), which appeared from its contents to have been a mid seventeenth-century Dutch ship, but which was eventually shown from documentary evidence to have been a Spanish ship of 1667.

Given these strengths and weaknesses of the evidence within maritime archaeology, how does it relate to that available from other sources? The complementary nature of ship's drawings relating to a vessel's upperworks when set alongside the archaeological data concerning its hull has already been noted. It is particularly well illustrated by the case of the *Dartmouth* (1690), for which there is a fine sketch by William van der Velde (fig. 6.1). This fills in a lot of the detail which could never be gained from the site itself, on which the only structural remains concerned the keel and neighbouring elements (see fig. 3.19, p. 97) (Martin 1978). It is, however, somewhat unusual to have, even for seventeenth-century shipping, a drawing of the particular ship concerned, so that very often the best pictorial evidence available is only of a closely comparable vessel, and part of the problem in interpreting the site will be to identify divergences between the particular ship involved, and the available parallels. This is the situation which arose with the Pantano Longarini ship and the mosaic from Mostra Augustea (figs. 3.4, p. 66, and 3.5, p. 67).

Fig. 6.1 A sketch of a late seventeenth-century Fifth Rate, probably the *Dartmouth*, by William van der Velde the Younger.

If it is unusual to have pictorial representations of particular ships, then it is even more unusual to have detailed documentary descriptions. Even with post-medieval vessels, the best that is usually available will be detailed building accounts or the like, from which a good deal can be gleaned; this is the case with the *Dartmouth* (Martin 1978). Thus once again, the main effort in the interpretation of the remains will be to relate this evidence to the ship under study. The same will be true of any more general accounts of techniques in contemporary naval architecture, which are likely to be somewhat theoretical in content, and will rarely concern themselves with the details of construction, woodworking and carpentry techniques, and the like, on which the structural remains should provide evidence. At the same time, such writings may provide explanations for features whose significance would otherwise have been overlooked or merely guessed at. Once again, the sources are satisfyingly complementary, although the evidence from the structural remains is so direct and comprehensive that it has an almost complete primacy so far as the construction of that individual vessel is concerned.

6.3   The ship as an element in a military or economic system

While the requirements of the ship as a machine define its general features and design, its fundamental purpose will have been to function within a military or economic system, and this should be reflected by the remains on the sea-bed. There is usually less complexity in the assessment of this factor than in the understanding of hull fragments, since, as indicated in section 5.3, recovery of the full range of a ship's contents is ultimately a matter of addition, allowing for the impact of the various 'extracting filters'. In extreme cases these may have been 100 % effective, completely eliminating all indications of the vessel's original purpose, as with craft which have been totally stripped before abandonment or ceremonial burial. However, on any normal wreck-site, it is probably a ship's cargo and heavy equipment (such as armaments) which stand the greatest chance of survival, since they will have been in the lowest parts of the vessel. It is probably true to say that there are very few sites on which there is no evidence relating to this area of enquiry, while there are plenty on which none of the other areas is represented by any significant remains. The consideration of these two main contexts in which a ship might be operating, the military and the economic, obviously excludes a small number of ships, such as pleasure or ceremonial vessels, but it is likely that these will generally be readily recognisable, and will present few problems in interpretation. There can also be no discussion of the potential for research into fishing vessels and their economic role, since no such remains have yet been discovered; it may be that the special nature of the cargoes here positively impedes preservation.

Discussion of the contents of ships, both in terms of cargoes and armaments, arose incidentally in the course of several sections in chapter 3, although in no case was the cargo of any particular ship over-emphasised, for the reason that general discussions of maritime trade, whether in classical (section 3.2) or post-medieval times (sections 3.7 and 3.8), must rely on aggregate figures, and not place too much stress on any one voyage. The dangers of this were stated clearly by Professor Bass (1967, 165) when discussing the importance of the Cape Gelidonya find. Nevertheless, in reporting on any particular ship, her contents at the time of wrecking are as important as any other aspect of the site, although the extent to which they are typical of her usual load must be assessed in every individual case. An extreme case of where they are evidently not representative is merchantmen like the *Trinidad Valencera*, taken into the Spanish Armada of 1588 and armed as warships.

With both warships and merchantmen, the great strength of the evidence from the sites themselves is that it shows, albeit partially, what the ship was actually carrying, as opposed to what the documents say she should have been carrying. In a military context, the importance of such a study is clearly demonstrated by the study of the armament of the flagship of the Armada supply squadron, *El Gran Grifon* (see section 3.6; Martin 1972). A similar situation arises with merchantmen for which the lists of goods loaded are known, when any divergences discovered among the actual remains must be evidence of inadequate recording at the time, fiddling, or unofficial lading by crew members; the last of these has been suggested for certain goods on a number of Dutch East Indiamen, including the *Kennemerland* (1664) (see chapter 5).

In favourable conditions, a great deal can be learned about the total economic role of a merchantman, even in situations where there is absolutely no documentary evidence from which to work. A clear example of this is represented by the large Roman freighter at Madrague de Giens (fig. 3.3, p. 63), where the hull has survived sufficiently intact to allow a fairly secure estimation of the ship's capacity at 400 tons (Tchernia & Pomey 1976). This would have allowed a cargo of around 8000 amphorae full of oil or wine, lying in four layers. In fact, there is only archaeological evidence for three layers, and this in turn has led to a consideration of the position of supplementary cargoes on such a vessel; in this case, the evidence suggests pine kernels, bowls of pigment, and coarse pottery. In many instances it is worthwhile calculating the theoretical capacity of the vessel, and assessing how much of this tonnage can be accounted for by the known cargo; further, more detailed calculations are possible with post-medieval ships where additional documentary evidence is available. It is only through consideration of such practicalities of maritime shipping that the importance of items such as paying ballast can be understood, as, for example, with the building bricks or lead ingots found on a number of Dutch East Indiamen (section 3.7).

While the archaeological evidence relating to the construction of an individual wrecked ship had a considerable significance in itself, the cargo or armament uncovered on such a site is less able to stand alone. If a warship is involved, then the significance of its contents will be related to the prevailing military situation, and this is unlikely to be reasonably understood without some contemporary documentary evidence. If a merchantman's cargo is being studied, then its economic significance is unlikely to be apparent unless there is some supporting documentary evidence, or the assemblage can be related to a number of other archaeological finds, both maritime and terrestrial, which together provide evidence of a continuing economic system. This much should certainly be considered in the final report on any individual ship; the wider implications must be left for discussion in section 7.3.

6.4   The ship as a closed community

Apart from the remains of a ship's structure, fittings and cargo, a wreck-site may also contain items relating to those on board, crew or passengers, shedding light on their circumstances and lifestyles. In the interpretation of such material, considerable assistance can be derived from the several special features of a shipboard society. From earliest times, ships have been run according to strict hierarchies, with one man having ultimate responsibility and authority, and with a marked division between those whose job it is to give orders, the officers, and those who have to obey, the men. This distinction has always been reflected in a considerable difference in rewards between the two classes, and this will in turn be apparent on a wreck-site in terms of the quantity and quality of objects involved. Furthermore, with very few exceptions, it has been customary for ship's crews to be all male.

Despite the apparent promise of this area of enquiry, little research has been devoted to it, and it is only peripherally touched on in some of the sections of chapters 3 and 4. Furthermore, the archaeological evidence concerning the way of life of those on board has not figured prominently in many wreck reports, so a brief summary of what has emerged from those studies which have considered the question is in order. Beginning with the earliest ship, the site at Cape Gelidonya, despite being broken up (see fig. 3.7, p. 69), gave some indications about life on board (Bass 1967). Certain organic remains indicated a supply of food, but there were no signs of any facilities for cooking it; on a vessel only 10 metres long it would, perhaps, have been surprising to find any. Much more could be learned about the crews' facilities on the later ships wrecked off Yassi Ada, and in particular from the seventh-century ship (van Doorninck 1967; 1972; Bass 1971). In this instance, the layout of a well-appointed galley was recovered, set well down in the hull at the stern, and provided with a tiled roof raised about 80 centimetres above main-deck level (fig. 6.2). For cooking, there was a tiled fire-box, well embedded in clay to minimise the fire risk. A wide range of cooking utensils was available and, most surprising of all, there was a fine service of tableware, sufficient for at least three table settings. For a vessel of only about 40 tons, these were remarkably extensive facilities, presumably reflecting the substantial social standing of the self-employed shipowners (the *naukleroi*) of this period; they certainly compare well with the neighbouring and similar-sized fourth-century vessel (see fig. 5.13, p. 186; van Doorninck 1976). Whether the lower ranks of the crew would also benefit from these facilities is not clear, but in such a small vessel it seems possible that they did.

With later and larger vessels, the interpretation of such information is less clear cut, although still revealing. With warships there is no problem of distinguishing utensils from cargo, and such studies can proceed further. For example, as noted in section 3.6, the finding of some Ming porcelain on the *Trinidad Valencera* has suggested an unsuspectedly

Fig. 6.2 A reconstruction by Dr F. H. van Doorninck of the galley in the stern of the seventh-century A.D. ship at Yassi Ada, showing its amenities and relative spaciousness.

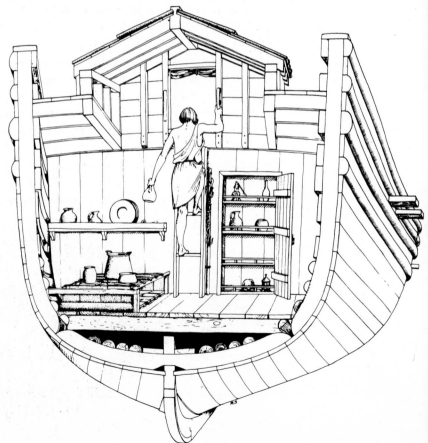

civilised standard of living available to her officers. Similarly, the
collection of objects from the *Dartmouth* (1690) has raised some interesting points respecting the late seventeenth-century Royal Navy. The
range of imported pottery and other utensils has indicated a more
comfortable way of life for the officers than had been anticipated, while
the very large number of clay pipes from a number of different manufacturing centres, confirmed established ideas concerning the comforts
available to the ordinary seamen (Martin 1977). A dipstick for measuring the quantity of a liquid remaining in a barrel reminds one of the
traditional rum ration for the men, while the fine quaich (fig. 6.3)
suggested that the officers were not adverse to sampling the local 'aqua
vitae'. A less pleasant side of naval life was evidenced by the several
pewter syringes, presumably from the surgeon's stores, and apparently
used in the treatment of venereal diseases.

With merchant vessels the isolation of such items from general cargo
is more difficult, although with the material from the *Kennemerland*
(1664) it proved possible to suggest that certain groups of items were
predominantly for shipboard use (see section 5.7). Some of these
objects, such as the dice illustrated in fig. 6.4, reflect directly some of the
activities pursued on board this vessel. Interpretation is more straightforward with a complete Dutch East Indiaman, such as the *Amsterdam*
(1749), from whose preliminary investigation a certain amount of
information has emerged (Marsden 1974). Several items of clothing and
leatherwork could be identified as crew's equipment, along with a large
number of pewter buttons of a type found on a number of VOC ships,
and which apparently come from an early and rudimentary form of
Company uniform. For the higher officers and senior passengers, life
was graced by a wide range of fine pottery and glass objects, including
tea cups and saucers of Chinese porcelain. Particularly noticeable within
this assemblage were those objects belonging to the three lady passengers

Fig. 6.3 A fine quaich
found on the *Dartmouth*
(1690) wreck-site. Scale in
inches.

0   3

known to have been on board, two of whom were described as 'very fine'. These included a high-heeled shoe, pieces of a silk dress with bows, and a beautiful ivory fan. In these instances, only a brief discussion of the available material has been attempted, in view of the present lack of systematic studies on this topic, but enough has been presented to indicate the scope of this aspect of the archaeology of ships.

Until now, the archaeological evidence has been used for little more than illustrating the life of those on board the various ships; however, it is to be hoped that in the long run more comprehensive studies will be undertaken, trying to reconstruct all aspects of such self-contained societies from the evidence of their material culture. The general problems involved in such an approach are central to the whole discipline of archaeology, limited as it is to the direct study of only the material segment of a past society, and the several basic problems involved have been discussed by Dr David Clarke (1968, 119–23) among others. That the problems presented in maritime archaeology may in fact be less severe than in most archaeological situations is suggested by the consideration that all aspects of shipboard life are subordinate to the technical requirements of the ship herself, and that these are directly observable through the material evidence. This, together with its other special characteristics such as a rigid hierarchy and all-male company, should make such societies particularly worthwhile objects of study. On the negative side, however, is the consideration that the material remains from the crew and passengers are likely to be concentrated in the upper parts of a vessel, the area which is least likely to have achieved extensive preservation.

It would be very unusual for any documentary evidence to have survived recording life on board a particular ship on its last voyage; the most that can generally be expected from even quite recent ships is the official log, which is unlikely to be particularly revealing on such

Fig. 6.4 A collection of dice found on the *Kennemerland* (1664) wreck-site. Scale in centimetres.

matters. Even if an officer or passenger did keep a diary, it cannot have been representative of everyone's situation on board, and in particular is unlikely to say much about the lifestyle of the ordinary seamen living in the forecastle. Other contemporary accounts of life at sea are often relevant for comparative purposes, and may assist in explaining the used of objects found for which there are no modern parallels. Nevertheless, the balance of authority between the sources lies in this topic, as with studies in nautical archaeology, firmly on the side of specifically archaeological evidence from the individual ship, reflecting directly all aspects of a self-contained and closed past society.

7

The archaeology of maritime cultures

7.1 Introduction

The tentative theoretical framework for the sub-discipline of maritime archaeology being presented in Part Two involves three distinct levels of investigation and analysis. The lowest level, dealing with the immediate object of study, the shipwreck, was discussed in chapter 5, while the intermediate one, which considers the immediate progenitor of that material, the ship, was discussed in chapter 6. It is now necessary to go beyond the individual and specific events enshrined in these entities, and look at the maritime culture in which they were embedded. Archaeology as a scientific discipline is not just the systematic study of a series of interesting past events in isolation, but must also involve an attempt to understand the development of affairs over periods of time and across regions and continents, as evidenced by those events. The present chapter is thus concerned with the problems and potential of studying a number of related ships and wreck-sites, as well as the relationship between the results of such research and the evidence gleaned from other disciplines which investigate past maritime activities.

Generalisation is fundamental to all academic studies. In the physical sciences, no two experiments or samples are exactly alike in all respects, but the scientist must concentrate on those similarities which appear to him to be significant in the context of his particular study, be it colour, chemical composition, size, shape, or whatever, and overlook the evident differences; the results will be enshrined in hypotheses, theorems, or laws. Similarly, with respect to history, E. H. Carr has written that: 'The historian is not really interested in the unique, but what is general in the unique' (1961, 63), and thus tries to reach conclusions about subjects such as the nature of sixteenth-century warfare in Europe, the lives of the labouring poor in nineteenth-century England, or whatever. Without a corresponding level of generalisation, maritime archaeology would be mere antiquarianism, a fascinating and relatively harmless leisure activity, but not a serious and rewarding academic discipline, demanding of considerable expertise, sophisticated equipment, and support from public funds. That past maritime activities represent a sufficient scope for such research was demonstrated in chapter 1 above; in the current discussion it is necessary to demonstrate that real progress can be made in achieving new insights into them by archaeological means.

One difficulty in establishing the full potential of the archaeology of maritime cultures lies in the lack of currently available studies at this level of analysis. This is hardly surprising, since the number of systematically investigated sites available for consideration is still very limited, and the whole subject is only a few decades old. Possibly the most ambitious attempt to achieve some syntheses at this level was the volume edited by Professor George Bass (1972a) entitled *A history of seafaring based on underwater archaeology*, although some of the contributions emerged as little more than a series of discussions on specific sites, with minimal attention to overall trends and developments. In some respects, the various sections in chapters 3 and 4 above represent further attempts to isolate general themes as they have emerged from current work in this field, and some of these will be cited as appropriate in the detailed discussions below. Nevertheless, a good deal of the case must be presented here in terms of the inherent characteristics of the sub-discipline, and the ways in which they should make this level of analysis particularly rewarding.

The three-dimensional matrix in fig. 7.1 represents a present-day view of a past society, broken up into a number of compartments. Looking at the top of the box, society has been divided up in two ways. First, from left to right, there are various aspects of social life, placed under five arbitrary headings, and analogous to the sub-systems within a society discussed by Dr Clarke in *Analytical archaeology* (1968, 101–23). And, secondly, working from front to back, there are some of the sub-

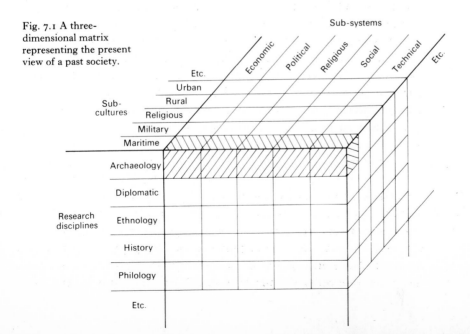

Fig. 7.1 A three-dimensional matrix representing the present view of a past society.

cultures within a complex society, which together allow it to function and earn its living. Within each of them there are special aspects to their economic, political, social, etc., organisation which are different from those in other sub-cultures, although interrelated with them. Thus, for example, within the social sphere, membership of an urban élite may guarantee admission to the officer class within maritime society, although the skills required and the authority exercised in each position may be very different. Maritime culture, as defined in section 1.1 and comprising all the aspects of ships and seafaring (but excluding related communities on shore), has been placed in the front row of the matrix.

However, current views of this past society may be further subdivided by the variety of disciplines through which it can be studied, and these are represented by the vertical component in this matrix. Among these archaeology is only one, placed here (for alphabetical reasons) at the top. The scope of maritime archaelogy as presented in this book is thus contained within the shaded top front row of compartments, while other subdivisions of the subject can be seen in the top rows behind it. This breakdown of archaeology according to the sub-culture studied has not been pursued as thoroughly as the left–right division into social sub-systems (e.g. economic prehistory, industrial archaeology, etc.), although it is a commonplace within history, as with agricultural (rural), military, or maritime history. The initial stages of such subdivisions within British archaeology may be seen in recent definitions of the scope of urban archaeology (e.g. Biddle 1974, 95–8) or rural archaeology (e.g. Fowler 1975), alongside which maritime archaeology should be able to take its place.

This matrix obviously could be given many additional dimensions (artistic conventions permitting) to represent further subdivisions of society, such as the commonly used temporal units of palaeolithic, neolithic, medieval, etc., or regional groupings. The particular view given in fig. 7.1 is an avowedly arbitrary one, illustrating elements which are crucial to the present discussion. This realisation also emphasises that to compartmentalise any society in this way is essentially artificial and potentially dangerous, since there is a danger of overlooking its basic unity. As Dr Clarke has written, 'the "behaviour" of such a unit is more complex than simply the expression of the sum of its components' "behaviours"' (1968, 102). Nevertheless, such subdivisions are essential if any understanding in depth is to be achieved.

While maritime archaeology stands in a similar relationship to seafaring in the past as other subdivisions of the subject do to other aspects of past societies, it possesses certain inherent advantages. Among these, the most fundamental is the fact that the relationship between the original source of the excavated material, the ship, and the society which produced it, is well known and identifiable. It is a sample with known attributes, self-contained in itself, representative in some respects and not in others; the precise ways in which this situation can be used in general investigations will constitute one of the main elements in the detailed sections below. The position in other branches of archaeology is much less satisfactory, since there can be considerable doubts as to the relationship between the sample which is made available for long-term preservation, and the total material culture from which it is drawn. For example, is the range of objects dropped onto the earthen floor of a hut, and thus potentially available for burial and survival, a representative sample of all the objects used in that hut during the period of its occupation? Ultimately, there is no way of telling.

A second, related, strength of this sub-discipline lies in the comprehensiveness of the material remains, and the lack of human interference with them, as outlined in chapter 5 above. The point is made in general terms by Dr Gale Sieveking: 'Examination of short period occupations is most valuable when settlements are untidy or insanitary and rubbish is left to lie where it fell. Where the beginnings of order and tidiness appear in the archaeological record there is always the chance as at Pompeii that the latest event at any rate will be clearly distinguishable' (1976, xxiv). Like the disaster which overtook Pompeii in A.D. 79, a shipwreck is an unforeseen event which engulfs everything, irrespective of the tidiness or otherwise of that society. This consideration is of primary importance with the remains from more recent periods, and sites of this type on which everything has been left where it fell are exceedingly rare. Furthermore, the information from wreck-sites within these more organised and complex societies possesses additional significance in providing dated contexts for assemblages of finds which are otherwise seldom found in their original contexts and are thus difficult to date precisely; this is a specialised and non-maritime aspect of the sub-discipline which should not be overlooked, and is discussed further in section 7.5.

The third and final general consideration again concerns more recent periods, and in particular those for which there is a certain amount of documentary evidence available. As Professor Lynn White of California has emphasised (White 1962), historians relying on documentary evidence for past activities up until the arrival of universal literacy in that society must inevitably produce a one-sided and distorted picture of what happened, since they cannot encompass those groups who left no records. And he points out that: 'until very recently the vast majority of mankind was living in a sub-history which was a continuation of prehistory' (*ibid.*, 7–9), for which the only evidence available, as with prehistoric times, is the archaeological record. Within maritime society this sub-history has continued, if anything, even longer than in other fields, since practical men of affairs, shipbuilders, and ordinary seamen, had little use for writing until the advent of mechanisation. Only in the fields of naval warfare, and to some extent in the control of maritime trade, do written records become available for the Age of Sail, and even then not before the sixteenth century for most European countries. For previous periods, and for other aspects of maritime society up until the nineteenth century, the subject remains 'sub-historic', and therefore one in which the archaeological evidence remains pre-eminent.

This last consideration has raised the question of the relationship between the conclusions emerging from archaeological research and those produced by other disciplines. Reasons have already been put forward in section 1.1 as to why it is necessary that there should be separation of the various approaches right up until this final stage of analysis, since the result will otherwise certainly be gross misunderstandings by the practitioners of one subject of the limitations and constraints of the evidence produced by another. In particular, the archaeological data must not simply be fed into a framework laid down from what documentary evidence is available, or else attention will be focussed only on those areas where the two coincide, and will avoid those topics on which new evidence has become available and which are accordingly much more significant. The other relevant discipline with which maritime archaeology should be related is maritime ethnology; again, the evidence should be assessed separately and only compared once all the internal results have been assessed. The various special considerations involved in integrating these approaches will constitute another main theme of the detailed discussions below.

The main elements in maritime culture can be considered under three headings, each directly arising out of the three areas of enquiry discussed with reference to ships in sections 6.2 to 6.4:

(*a*) Nautical technology.
(*b*) Naval warfare and maritime trade.
(*c*) Shipboard societies.

In each case, these topics will be considered in terms of the scope of the archaeological evidence available, the current state of research, the relationship between it and the evidence available from other disciplines, and the prospects for future progress.

7.2 Nautical technology

In the opening paragraph of chapter 1, it was asserted that the ship was the largest and most complex machine produced by most preindustrial societies, and some illustrations were given in support of this statement. The study of shipbuilding in the past, which may be regarded as the 'leading edge' of the technologies of such societies, is therefore an investigation into the limits of their technical and organisational abilities, and has thus attracted much scholarly attention. However, an appreciation of the potential of archaeological evidence in this field has emerged only recently, for the reasons outlined in section 1.2. In the meantime, general studies on naval architecture through the ages, culled from a variety of disciplines, have been written by Landström (1961), Anderson (1926), and others. With respect to boats and other small craft, the standard work in English has for a generation been *Water transport* by J. Hornell (1946), but this has recently been superseded by *The archaeology of the boat* by Basil Greenhill (1976), probably the first systematic and authoritative study to give precedence to the archaeological evidence, while being, as the author admits, probably the last such study which can encompass the whole field, in view of the rapidly expanding body of information available (*ibid.*, 13).

Among the particular research topics discussed in Part One, a number related specifically to this field of enquiry. In chapter 3, these included the study of Mediterranean shipping in classical times (section 3.1), Viking ships (section 3.4), and post-medieval shipping (section 3.5). From chapter 4, potentially fruitful areas of research can be identified in prehistoric shipping (section 4.1), medieval shipping (section 4.2), Asian shipping (section 4.3) and river craft (section 4.4). In addition, a topic such as navigational instruments (section 3.9) essentially involved the operation of ships as machines, being concerned with one essential for keeping them under control, while the same is true of some aspects of the study of anchors (section 4.6).

The main themes discussed in these sections have illustrated both the strengths and the weaknesses of this research. On the positive side, some significant progress has been made, principally founded on the great advantage of archaeological evidence in showing things as they were actually built. Thus the single most important result of a quarter century of study has undoubtedly been the demonstration of the pre-eminence in classical times of a highly intricate, shell-first technique of hull construction, and its use in many types of vessel in all parts of the Mediterranean. Similarly, with Viking ships, recent excavations have demonstrated the wide range of vessel forms and sizes which existed within the basic northern clinker tradition. At the same time, it is to be hoped that the next few decades of research will lead to further refinements in understanding in these fields, as already presaged by the discoveries of vessels built by modified shell-first techniques from the period of the Roman Empire. The contributions to research in post-medieval ship construction have already been shown to be at this level of refinement, with the evidence they present of substantial variation in techniques within broadly understood traditions, as with the wrecks of the *Mary Rose* (1545; McKee 1973), *Santa Maria de la Rosa* (1588; Martin 1973), *Batavia* (1629; Green 1975), and *Dartmouth* (1690; Martin 1978).

On the other hand, there are some respects in which the source material for maritime archaeology may be regarded as deficient. A particularly serious objection has been raised by Olof Hasslöf (1963), with the suggestion that wrecked ships do not constitute a representative sample of all ships, since they will generally be the older, weaker, and less successful examples of their type and age. That this is true in some instances cannot be denied; the *Wasa* apparently possessed a fundamental design fault (Naish 1968), the *Mary Rose* was overloaded as a consequence of military circumstances (McKee 1973), and the ships of the 1588 Spanish Armada were operating beyond their normal waters (Martin 1975). However, these special cases are readily detectable, and can be allowed for in any general investigation. The majority of wrecks occur as a result of natural or human hazards to which all vessels are vulnerable, regardless of condition, and to which a certain proportion will inevitably succumb. Probably the most important single variable in determining the fate of a ship in a crisis situation is the quality of her crew, and there would seem to be no necessary connection between good crews and good ships, or vice versa.

An undoubted bias in the material remains available for investigation lies in the fact that merchant vessels are more likely to have survived than warships, since the former can be pinned down and protected by their cargoes. This tendency is particularly apparent with Mediterranean warships in classical times, of which very few have been discovered (the notable exceptions being the Punic vessels near Motya in Sicily), and which will generally not have survived because of their very light and insubstantial structure. However, it will also be true of all periods at which the premium was on speed in warships, as a result of which they were very different in design from merchantmen. This restriction obviously does not apply in the post-medieval period, during which warships were heavily ballasted and were generally little different from merchantmen, especially since the latter were usually armed. Finally, maritime archaeology shares in the general restrictions of all archaeological research, in that, since it approaches the past solely through its material culture, it cannot account directly for such intangibles as beliefs, motives, intentions, or the like.

Given these strengths and weaknesses, the question arises as to the relationship between this subject and allied disciplines concerned with the study of nautical technology. The prime parallel is naturally historical research through documentary evidence, an approach which has been pursued for considerably longer than the archaeological; indeed, for the classical period, where the available sources are exceedingly limited, it had pretty well argued itself to a standstill (see section 3.1). The subject of the relationship between history and archaeology is a complex and contentious one (Wainwright 1962; Clarke 1968, 12–14;

Dymond 1974), and cannot be followed through all its ramifications here; all that can be done is to draw together some of the main considerations relative to the study of ship structure. While pictorial evidence may often be most helpful in considering individual ships, for general trends the written sources must be paramount. One of the difficulties met with in such documents is the fact that the writers are frequently not experts in ship construction, and are likely to have oversimplified, or even completely misunderstood, the techniques they were writing about. As noted above, shipwrights generally had no use for literacy until recent times, and only exceptional men were willing or able to disseminate the secrets of their craft. Furthermore, those other authors who did attempt to discuss such technical matters, very often had a propaganda purpose in trying to publicise some new invention or product, and may thus have deliberately given a prejudiced account of the current state of the subject.

A further difficulty with technical treatises on shipbuilding from past ages is that the terms used are often impossible to interpret without actual examples of the features concerned to hand, since they were restricted in use to this particular context. Obviously, this is a greater problem with ancient languages, but it can arise with even seventeenth- and eighteenth-century sources in which now obsolete terms are used. A clear example of this type of problem lies in the section of the *Odyssey* (5.244–5.257) in which the hero builds himself a raft to escape from Calypso's island, and the ways in which the various features of the Cape Gelidonya wreck have clarified this passage (Bass 1967; Casson 1971, 217–19). An even more direct example of technical terms being understood only through reference to archaeological evidence has come from the words and letters painted on the prefabricated sections of the Punic ships from Sicily, whose precise meanings have thus been clarified (Frost *et al.* 1974, 37–8). Finally, these specific problems must be seen as additional to the general weakness of all documentary sources in that they concentrate on the unusual and the unique, and unconsciously overlook the commonplace, which both the original reader and writer will have taken for granted. It should be noted that this is true both of descriptive writings intended to be read by outsiders, such as handbooks or treatises, and internal accounts and memoranda written within a shipyard or admiralty, and not intended for general consumption or the attentions of posterity.

Naturally, there are many areas in which the documentary evidence is invaluable, and without which the archaeological record would make much less sense. The mental approach of shipbuilders and designers may be conveyed more clearly by an essay on principles of naval architecture than a large number of particular hulls. The interplay of influences between different areas and traditions may be only hinted at by the remains, but is made clear by the documents; thus the fact that the architect of the *Dartmouth* (1690) had worked in Dunkirk and Denmark as a young man explains some features of the excavated remains, but could never have been deduced convincingly from them (Martin 1978). In the consideration of such non-material factors, the documentary evidence can complement the archaeological at just the points where the latter is inadequate.

Alongside maritime history, the other main parallel discipline to be considered is maritime ethnology, the study of surviving traditions and modes of behaviour. In nautical archaeology, recourse to such evidence for technical parallels and explanations has been particularly fashionable, especially when considering periods and regions for which the documentary evidence is nonexistent, or nearly so. Within British research, the succession has continued from the work of Hornell (1946) and Lethbridge (1952) up until the present (e.g. Greenhill 1976), while in Scandinavia this approach has been particularly associated with Olof Hasslöf and his colleagues (Hasslöf 1963; Hasslöf *et al.* 1972). Attention has been focussed above all on two aspects of the problem: first, in the identification of different procedures in boat building, such as skin, bark, or plank boats, or shell-first and skeleton-first construction, and, secondly, in the consideration of how a boat may have been handled. In both areas, the standard caveats must apply as in all use of anthropological analogies in archaeology, to the effect that the adoption of certain practices in one society cannot prove that they were followed in another, and that there must be a very close identity between the two social, economic, political, etc., contexts before such a parallelism can be even tentatively suggested.

Fig. 7.2 Fair Isle (Shetland) yoal *Dolphin* and crew, *c.* 1900.

At the same time, consideration of other ethnological material can serve a very useful purpose in freeing the researcher from the restricted

concepts of his own technical tradition; the ways in which modern concepts have been unthinkingly applied to past shipbuilding by earlier workers are a multitude (Hasslöf 1972). Furthermore, the fact that the basic problems are technical and material ones means that close identity of forms and techniques can be established from the archaeological and ethnological material alone. This is less true, however, when considering the question of boat or ship handling, where other factors may apply, and the archaeological evidence may allow a greater range of possibilities, as, for example, with the Sutton Hoo ship, which may or may not have had a sail (Bruce-Mitford 1975, 420–4). In this field, the ethnological evidence undoubtedly carries a great deal more weight when some direct connection can be shown between the past society and the present one, as with recent boatmen around the Shetland Isles, whose practices almost certainly reflect to a considerable extent those of Viking seamen of a millennium ago (fig. 7.2) (Christensen & Morrison 1976, 278).

An allied approach to these problems of construction and boat handling is via experimental archaeology, by which ethnological parallels are, in effect, created artificially to fit a specific set of circumstances. This approach may have the advantage of ensuring a close identity of material forms between the original and the model, but it has the disadvantage of not having the extra veracity conferred by authentic tradition. In practice, there can also be great difficulties in totally eliminating all modern influences, whether it be on tools and techniques, or handling procedures (McGrail & McKee 1974; Greenhill 1976, 232; Coles 1977). Nevertheless, such exercises can be very valuable in demonstrating what is at least possible, as with the successful construction and sailing of a replica of the putative hide-boats of the Scandinavian Bronze Age, which certainly showed that such vessels were prac-

Fig. 7.3 Open-water trials with the replica of the Gokstad *faering* by the staff of the National Maritime Museum, Greenwich.

ticable (Johnstone 1974, 81–6; Marstrander 1976). Viking craft have been favourite subjects for experiments of this type, the earliest being the building of a replica of the Gokstad boat in 1893 which, by sailing the North Atlantic without mishap, effectively dispelled the doubts of those scholars who had questioned the more spectacular of the Viking voyages. Recent, more controlled experiments have included the building and testing of replicas of the Ladby ship by Danish scouts (see section 3.4), and of the Gokstad *faering* (small ship's boat) by the staff of the National Maritime Museum, Greenwich (fig. 7.3) (McGrail & McKee 1974). While such exercises can never prove that anything was actually done in a particular manner, they can at least allow certain possibilities to be eliminated, and produce data on the characteristics of performance and ancilliary requirements relating to a range of other interpretations, some of which may then in turn prove to be testable with reference to the archaeological evidence.

A more refined approach to this problem of testing hypotheses, which holds out great promise for the future, involves the use of computer simulations, borrowing ideas and techniques from current practices in naval architecture. Possible applications include both their use for testing the range of suggested reconstructions of craft from which only fragmentary elements have survived (Coates 1977), and for investigating the uses to which historic craft might reasonably have been put (Graham 1977; McGrail 1977*b*). The advantages of such procedures lie in the fact that they allow the assessment of a far wider range of possibilities than physical reconstructions ever can, as well as in their relative cheapness. In many instances, however, the most satisfactory approach would probably be a combination of the two – the computer testing of the options followed by the building and operation of a replica of the most favoured solution. At the same time, any such artificial models will always lack the ultimate stamp of credibility possessed by those derived from real-life situations.

The general consideration of nautical technologies above and beyond an individual ship, as discussed in this section, can be taken to various levels. At the lowest, it may involve the study of shipbuilding in a particular region over just a few decades, while at the other it may seek to identify certain features of the craft which have endured over millenia and whole continents, such as the traditional conservatism of boat builders, or the role of naval architecture in stimulating economic or technical progress. At all these levels, however, the same considerations apply; the archaeological evidence has a fundamental validity in reflecting directly what was actually built, while at the same time it is subject to the same limitations as all other scientific disciplines in trying to generalise from particular examples. The fact that the subject is barely two decades old means that these problems of generalisation are particularly acute, but it is to be hoped that as the sites and ships multiply, the range of higher-level studies will broaden, and the testimony of nautical archaeology will become as comprehensive as that available from other disciplines.

7.3 Naval warfare and maritime trade

In the conclusion to section 6.3, it was suggested that the indications from one individual site regarding its military or economic significance were less able to stand alone than those referring to its technical or social aspects, since the latter were self-contained and the former were to be understood only in the context of a wider system. In the present section, consideration must be given to the role of maritime archaeology in expanding the understanding of those systems. Since the situation is different in the two main systems involved, they must be considered separately, beginning with the military.

Within chapter 3, few of the topics dealt with problems in naval warfare specifically, with the exception of the discussion on the Spanish Armada (section 3.6), and certain aspects of the overseas expansion of Europe eastwards and into the New World (sections 3.7 and 3.8). With earlier periods, such studies are severely restricted by the lack of wrecks of warships, a feature of the discipline which is unlikely to change markedly in the foreseeable future, while with later centuries the possibilities for study are equally limited by the fact that warfare was an activity which was extensively reported and attracted an unusual level of bureaucracy. The substantial potential for fundamental research in these topics of sixteenth- and early seventeenth-century European history lies in the fact that the documentary evidence relating to them is uneven in its coverage, and often difficult to interpret in technical terms. Thus, while the range and composition of the armaments and other stores carried on board the *Trinidad Valencera* in 1588 is of considerable interest, that carried on a British vessel of barely a century later, the *Dartmouth* (1690), is of little more than illustrative importance, since her general specifications can be established in far greater detail from written sources (McBride 1976). Furthermore, while the disposition of the wrecks from a particular battle of any period may reveal something of the course of that engagement, no amount of archaeological research will ever unravel its political, diplomatic, and military background. At present, therefore, this particular field of research in maritime archaeology is one of the least promising, although in the distant future the prospect of a reasonable sample of naval vessels representing warfare in prehistoric, classical or early medieval times is an exciting one.

The prospects are brighter, however, for the study of maritime trade through archaeological procedures. Already the subject has attracted a good deal of attention, as is shown by the number of related topics discussed in Part One above. In chapter 3, maritime trade constituted the main theme in the discussions on classical trade (section 3.2), harbours (section 3.3), the expansion of Europe eastwards (section 3.7), and the annexation of the New World (section 3.8). In chapter 4, other areas of research into the topic were presented in section 4.5, and it was one of the main themes in the discussion of anchors and anchorages (section 4.6). In every instance, the importance of not overemphasising the contents of one vessel to illustrate a whole trading system became apparent, since one cargo is a very ephemeral assemblage, and may be totally unrepresentative. However, even a small number of sites relating to a regular trade-route can be statistically significant, and begin to give a balanced picture of what was being carried. Furthermore, one particular site may be highly significant if taken together with other evidence not previously considered. Thus, while the results of the investigations on the Cape Gelidonya wreck-site might be severely limited on their own terms, they can inspire a complete reassessment of late Bronze Age trade in the Aegean if considered alongside the distribution of related objects (Bass 1967, 165–7; Renfrew 1973, 233). Similarly, the importance of a wreck-site lying off Belle Île (Morbihan), containing amphorae of a type not found in northern France at that period (first century B.C.), can only be fully assessed when considered alongside the distribution of this type (Dressel 1A) around contemporary sites in southern Britain (Peacock 1971).

These last examples point to a fruitful new area of research, which has yet to be exploited, except in the limited field of the carriage of amphorae around the Mediterranean (Parker 1973), and that is in the integration of traditional archaeological studies of trade and trade networks with the evidence from maritime archaeology. As suggested in section 4.5, the position of the British Isles as an offshore island of Europe presents a fine test-bed for such research, since all exchange between the two areas must have involved shipping. Even without the discovery of any further wreck-sites, there is a good deal of evidence to be collated relating to the size of ships operating at various periods, the frequency of their voyages, and the relative strength of economic links between Britain and the different coastal areas of western Europe. As an example of what is available for the medieval period, fig. 7.4 shows the trading connections suggested by the imported pottery excavated on the site at Stonar in Kent (Dunning 1968). However, care will have to be exercised in relating finds from land contexts with those from wrecks, especially in the matter of quantities. Looking at the pottery directly imported into western Britain in the post-Roman period, for example, the number of pots evidenced would barely fill the hold of a very small merchantman (Thomas 1959). The discovery of the wreck of a vessel employed in this trade could thus double or quadruple the quantity of ceramic material available on this topic, but would the evidence from that vessel be correspondingly more significant than the totality of all the land finds? Almost certainly not. In such studies, it will be necessary to separate the underwater finds from the land ones, since the factors making for survival have been so different in each case.

Another possibly rewarding approach within this topic would be to try to quantify the changing volumes of trade through time by studying the varying quantities of shipwrecks. If the same proportion of voyages are likely to have ended in disaster at each period, then there should be a direct correlation between the two in relative terms. Varying levels of fieldwork across the area concerned should not prove a significant factor, as it might on a similar terrestrial study, since the ships of all periods would presumably have stood an equal chance of being wrecked in any particular locality. The potential of such a study appears to be considerable, although there are two major difficulties which might have to be taken into account. First, there is the possibility that ships of one period were in fact more likely to be wrecked than those of another; factors causing such an imbalance might include continuous naval warfare, endemic piracy, or inherent technical weaknesses. Secondly, it may be that the cargoes of one period are more easily recognised on the sea-bed than those of another; for example, a period in which amphorae were the standard shipboard container is likely to be over-represented as against one in which wooden barrels were used. At present, the Mediterranean is the only area in which sufficient work has been done to indicate such trends, and here there is an apparent bias in numbers of sites towards the second and first centuries B.C., although whether this has any economic significance is at present unclear (Carrazé 1975).

Fig. 7.4 A map of sources of medieval pottery found at Stonar in Kent, and the trade-routes so indicated.

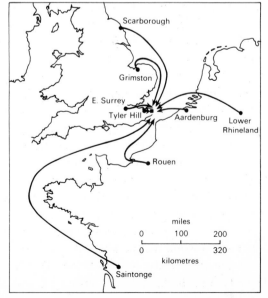

While these possible lines of research apply for periods in which the documentary evidence is virtually nonexistent, the situation is more complicated for more recent centuries in which such written sources are available. Where the manifest of items loaded on board a ship is available, it is likely to be more informative than the range of goods preserved on the sea-bed, since it is more likely to be complete, and will indicate such matters as price, supplier, etc. Thus, with Dutch trade to the East Indies, the basic economic mechanisms have been quite thoroughly investigated through the extensive documentation available (e.g. Glamann 1958; Boxer 1965), and much of the excavated material has little more than illustrative value. However, even here some of the finds have been of interest in revealing matters on which the documents are silent, as with the items being traded unofficially and against Company rules. Furthermore, there were a great number of regular trades (e.g. the coasting trades), even as late as the eighteenth century, which went almost totally undocumented, and on these the sea-bed remains often represent the only evidence.

While the contribution from maritime archaeology to studies in naval warfare has been shown to be limited, the position respecting maritime trade is considerably more promising. Economic affairs have taken a dominant position in archaeology in recent years, replacing the previous concern with migrations and pseudo-political interpretations (Clark 1966); maritime archaeology could take an important place in further progress here, by focussing attention on the mechanisms by which goods are carried over long distances. Even into comparatively late periods, there is scope for research into less well-documented fields. As the number of wreck-sites being investigated is multiplied, progress in this area of research should increase; while the first quarter century of the sub-discipline has undoubtedly seen most attention paid to the problems of naval technology, the second one may see a switch in emphasis to economic ones.

7.4 Shipboard societies

Just as the remains on an individual wreck-site should produce some evidence on the way of life of those on board the ship, so a consideration of the evidence accumulated from a number of sites within a given period or region might produce a general picture of maritime society at that time. To date, nothing in this line has been attempted, although with the steadily accumulating numbers of sites the opportunity will soon be there for at least some areas. As suggested above (section 6.4) certain features will recur through most periods and regions, including a rigid hierarchy and an all-male community. Other features will be more specialised, and should rather be regarded as variants on the customs and conventions of the parent society; these may include peculiar rituals or religious observances, specialised clothes or utensils, or unusual class structure. These may in turn reflect the status of maritime activities within the wider society; for example, the amenities provided for seamen on the seventh century A.D. Yassi Ada ship reflected the importance of sea commerce to the economy of Constantinople (van Doorninck 1972, 139). In most current works of social history, the seafaring community is frequently overlooked, probably for want of extensive documentary evidence; this aspect of maritime archaeology may help to rectify the situation.

In such essays in shipboard social history as have been attempted, the balance of the written material has imposed a bias towards the eighteenth and nineteenth centuries, and towards naval vessels, as in the works of Lloyd (1968) or Kemp (1970). Furthermore, even in such books a great deal of attention has been paid to matters which came to the notice of the authorities, and were thus noted in reports, letters, etc., such as the problems of manning and discipline. When it comes to questions of how seamen actually passed their days, how they felt about their lot, and how they came to be at sea in the first place, there is little to go on before the early nineteenth century. A notable exception is the exceedingly descriptive journal kept by the seaman Edward Barlow concerning his voyages in Dutch and English East Indiamen between 1670 and 1703 (Lubbock 1934). For still earlier periods there is nothing at all apart from passing references in contemporary literature, as in the plays of Shakespeare (Falconer 1964) or the account of St Paul's voyage to Rome given in the Acts of the Apostles. A few additional details concerning the material circumstances of past seamen can be gleaned from paintings and drawings (e.g. Dickens 1957).

More extensive parallel evidence can naturally be derived from studies in maritime ethnology, although the total range of what is available is disappointingly limited. Within this discipline, maritime studies have been, in the words of Olof Hasslöf 'the ugly duckling of the science', since 'it is the early agrarian culture which has been given prominence in the literature and museums' (1972, 15). Furthermore, outside the Scandinavian countries, even that level of recording achieved by Dr Hasslöf and his colleagues has been lacking, and the situation is rapidly becoming irredeemable, since the number of old seamen who can recall even the last days of sail is now rapidly dwindling. Parallel to this failure to record the oral traditions and recollections of the seafaring communities has been the loss of much material evidence concerning their lifestyles; as the Swedish ethnologist Dr Henning Henningsen has written, 'as a rule, however, it is disappointing to see how little even the maritime museums can show in illustration of life aboard ship' (1972, 135). Finally, as with studies in nautical technology, the same safeguards in applying ethnological analogies must apply as in any other archaeological investigation; in particular, it is questionable how representative conditions pertaining during the nineteenth century were of shipboard life in earlier periods. It is in the light of these weaknesses in maritime ethnology as it exists at present that the scope for the social aspect to maritime archaeology would seem to be further enhanced.

7.5 Incidental contributions to archaeology in general

Before concluding this chapter on the higher-level interpretation of the evidence in maritime archaeology, it is necessary to mention some of its peripheral contributions to other aspects of archaeology. Although these do not lie in a strictly maritime context, they can be of some significance, and add to the overall importance of this research.

As mentioned in section 7.1, undoubtedly the most important of these incidental contributions arises from the fact that wreck-sites can provide well-dated and understood contexts for artefacts from periods for which such evidence is otherwise scarce, on account of the orderliness and tidiness of those societies. This statement is subject, of course, to all the qualifications proposed to the concept of the wreck as a closed group in section 2.3, as well as the basic archaeological truth that the date of deposition does not necessarily reflect the date of manufacture. Even if a wreck cannot be precisely dated, the relative contemporaneity of all the artefacts can be of considerable significance. For example, the new information provided on the manufacture and use of amphorae (see section 3.2) is obviously of use both in simple dating terms, and in reflecting a range of economic activities. Within Romano-British archaeology, a similar use of a wreck group to illuminate the dating of a whole class of pottery can be seen in the study of second-century A.D. Samian ware published by Brian Hartley (1972), in which the assemblage from the Pudding Pan Rock constitutes one of the fixed reference points, even though not precisely dated (fig. 4.9, p. 144).

However, as noted above, the prime application of this evidence has been in the study of post-medieval artefacts. Initially, this might seem to be rather surprising, since it would seem likely that the more recent the period, the more archaeological and documentary evidence would be available, but in fact it has generally proved difficult to relate the artefacts to the historical data, and the great bulk of material evidence is from rubbish deposits and other poorly dated contexts. In an attempt to overcome these problems, considerable reliance has been placed in the past on typological studies, but with the variety and volume of production generally involved this approach has been found to be less valid than with earlier material. This situation has been exemplified clearly by the case of salt-glazed stoneware vessels, made from the late fifteenth century in the lower Rhineland around Frechen and later elsewhere, known as Bellarmine flagons. A typological study of these was published

Fig. 7.5 The range of
Bellarmine flagon types
discovered on the
Kennemerland (1664)
wreck-site.

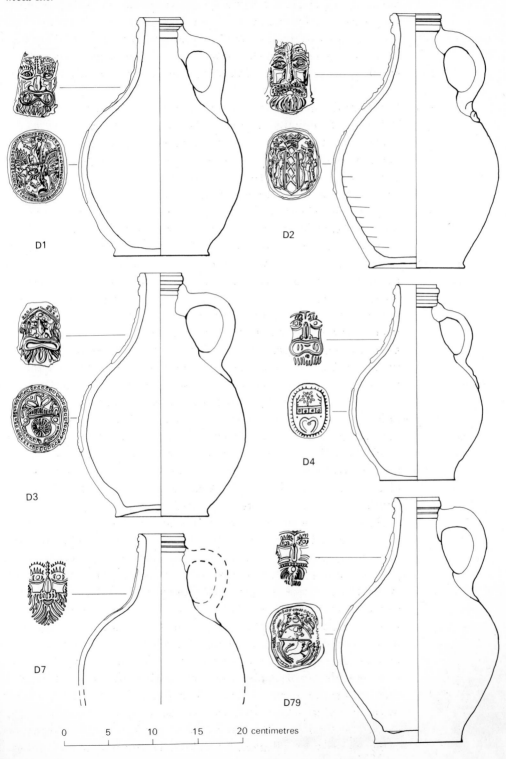

D1

D2

D3

D4

D7

D79

0   5   10   15   20 centimetres

in 1951 (Holmes 1951), tracing the degeneration of the type from the mid-sixteenth century to the end of the seventeenth, and suggesting dates to within a couple of decades for each style. This scheme has now been thoroughly upset by the finds from wreck-sites, especially those of the Dutch East India Company, on which large numbers of such vessels are usually found. The first indication of disagreement came from the excavations on the *Vergulde Draeck* (1656) in Western Australia (Green 1973*a*, 281–2), and further evidence has come from sites such as the *Kennemerland* (1664) (fig. 7.5). On the basis of the 1951 study, this latter group should date from anything between 1600 and 1690, while in fact they are all known to have been in use in 1664, and were almost certainly new at that time.

Similarly important new evidence has come from wreck-sites for another popular artefact for study in the post-medieval period – the clay pipe. Again, the problem has been a lack of dated contexts, so that several assemblages discovered recently under water have had considerable impact. A fine example of this comes from the wreck of the *Dartmouth* (1690), which contained a wide range of types of pipe, mostly from Scottish manufacturing centres, including examples which would previously have been dated anywhere between 1640 and 1720 (Martin

Fig. 7.6 A selection of boots and shoes from the *Kennemerland* (1664) wreck-site. Scale in centimetres.

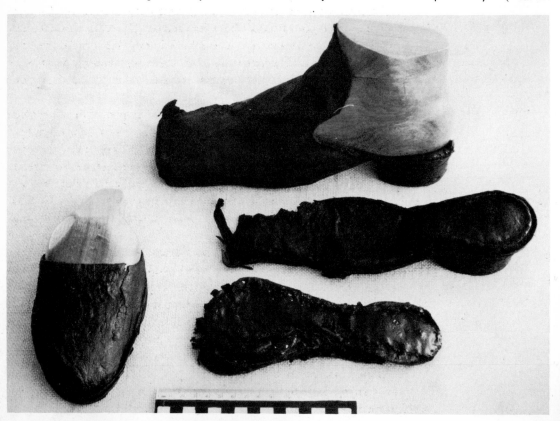

1977). In addition, these post-medieval assemblages have contained groups of artefacts which have not hitherto attracted much attention, but which can now be tackled satisfactorily, within a more secure chronological framework: for example, pewter vessels, treen, or boots and shoes. The footware styles evidenced by the *Kennemerland* collection (fig. 7.6) would on current knowledge have been dated somewhere within the seventeenth century, but probably somewhat earlier than their actual date of 1664 (V. Swann, personal communication). Another specialised aspect of the external application of finds from wreck-sites lies in numismatics, with reference to both classical post-medieval periods, as with the coins from the wreck of the Spanish Armada galleasse *Girona* (Dolley 1974, personal communication).

While this application to problems of artefact dating is undoubtedly the main incidental contribution arising out of studies in maritime archaeology, a few other points should be considered. While most of the specialised excavation equipment used under water has no parallel on land, there may be a link in future between air-lift techniques under water and the use of vacuum cleaners on land sites, as suggested by Philip Barker (1977). In time, there may also be a contribution in the field of excavation strategy, arising from the enforced economy of effort involved on maritime sites, and the greater periods available for consideration and consultation between stages. Currently, underwater investigations can force the director to justify his procedures and standards more explicitly, because of the expense, and because so many of the nautical, diving, and other specialists involved are from non-archaeological backgrounds.

Equally uncertain at present is the potential impact of developments in analytical techniques designed for wreck-sites on similar work on land sites. At present, as was apparent in chapter 5, these techniques rely quite heavily on established approaches within archaeology, but already in the field of quadrat analysis they have gone beyond what has been usual there. The essential point is that on many wreck-sites the distributional patterns are not immediately apparent, since there is no obvious defining framework; while this situation is perhaps not so common in land contexts, it does arise, and in such cases the same techniques may be applicable. Furthermore, the concern with explicating the development of one's site, according to a system such as that given in fig. 5.1 (p. 158) has not so far been common within archaeology in general, and here again work within maritime archaeology may stimulate parallel research in other contexts. Turning to the higher levels of interpretation, research in this topic may again be in the vanguard of procedural developments, this time in the close integration of archaeological studies with parallel investigations in history or ethnology, already a major feature of research into the archaeology of the boat (e.g. Greenhill 1976).

So long as such integration involves the free exchange of ideas and theories between disciplines, it is a practice to be applauded and encouraged, although the danger of conflating and confusing different types of research must always be guarded against.

7.6 Conclusions

In seeking towards a theoretical framework for the new sub-discipline of maritime archaeology, the present discussion has proceeded through a hierarchy of levels of investigation, within which the full significance of any wreck-site might be assessed, and through which the full scope of the subject might be outlined. This hierarchy bears an obvious resemblance to that proposed by Dr David Clarke in his *Analytical Archaeology* (1968, 133), although by analogy rather than by direct application, since his more complex analysis was directed towards extracting the maximum of information from artefacts, assemblages, etc., with less reference to sites and their generation. While such a three-fold analysis might have applications in other branches of the discipline, it is particularly appropriate here because of the way in which the three levels can be related to each other. The links between the ship and its wreck-site have been presented in fig. 5.1 (p. 158), while the intrinsic attributes of the ship in all its aspects were presented in section 6.1, and the necessary relationships between it and the maritime culture in which it was located, as described in section 7.1, tie together the second and third stages in the hierarchy more directly than is usual in archaeology.

In some respects, the division of this book into two parts is arbitrary and unreasonable, since the concepts and ideas discussed in this second part constitute part of the scope of the subject just as much as the more particular and technical matters raised in Part One. Thus, for example, the strengths of the sub-discipline outlined in the last paragraph should by rights have been included in section 2.3 as one of its inherent advantages. Nevertheless, the division can be justified on two grounds. First, maritime archaeology has in the past been frequently thought of simply in terms of its expense, difficulty, and occasional spectacular finds; by isolating the theoretical aspects of the sub-discipline in this way, the fact that these attributes are in fact peripheral can be emphasised. Secondly, the claim of the subject to be regarded as a scientific pursuit has been questioned by many, partly as a result of this popular image; by isolating and expounding at length the theoretical strengths of the sub-discipline, the claim can be justified, past work can be given a proper perspective, and future progress planned.

And what of the future? Many more underwater sites will undoubtedly be found, and it is hoped that most of them will be excavated in the manner of problem-orientated research. In the technical sphere, the emphasis should be on freeing the diver from routine chores so as to allow him the greatest possible time on his principal task of dissecting the material remains. But above all there must be substantial developments in post-excavational procedures through which the interpretation and analysis of wreck-sites can be greatly improved, and the theoretical framework for all this research strengthened. The various elements in the wrecking process (fig. 5.1, p. 158) must be severally investigated by the appropriate specialists, and this, together with more refined modes of sea-bed distributional analysis, should allow the basic stage of interpretation to become considerably more rewarding. And as the number of systematically investigated sites increases in all parts of the world, more attention must be paid to the high-level analysis discussed in chapter 7, from which the principal fruits of all this effort and expenditure might be expected, and which should in turn improve the standing and competence of the whole subject. The extent to which this actually materialises probably depends more on the willingness of communities around the world to support such work than on the enthusiasm and expertise of those individuals directly involved; if the former is forthcoming, then the latter should ensure a worthwhile harvest of knowledge and historical understanding.

8

Theory and practice

In a book significantly entitled *Archaeology under water*, Professor George Bass has written:
'Archaeology under water, of course, should be called simply *archaeology*. We do not speak of those working on the top of Nimrud Dagh in Turkey as mountain archaeologists. They are all people who are trying to answer questions regarding man's past, and they are adaptable in being able to excavate and interpret ancient buildings, tombs, and even entire cities with the artifacts they contain. Is the study of an ancient ship and its cargo, or the survey of toppled harbour walls somehow different?' (1966, 15).
Of course, within the definition of the subject he had chosen, he was quite right, but the result is a subject which lacks any coherence except in terms of basic techniques, as he admits a few pages later: 'A book on archaeology under water must, therefore, be concerned primarily with techniques, just as are those books on aerial surveying for archaeology, physics for archaeology, and conservation for archaeology' (*ibid.*, 20). Even the more methodical approach to underwater archaeological sites proposed by the Norwegian archaeologist Christian Keller (1976) fails, inevitably, to produce a framework of more than operational utility. As has emerged during this present work, general theory, analytical methods, and field techniques are all interconnected; a subject which tries to do without the first two cannot succeed in practising the third alone. By defining maritime archaeology as 'the scientific study of the material remains of man and his activities on the sea' it has been possible to isolate those respects in which ancient ships and their cargoes, along with toppled harbour walls, are different, and so identify a new archaeological sub-discipline.

In order to emphasise the inter-relatedness of every aspect of this research, the discussion must now go full circle and return to the matter of basic techniques of site investigation, for which there are several important implications arising out of the theoretical framework presented above. The flow diagram in fig. 8.1 shows the various stages in a complete investigation within maritime archaeology, and, while the exercise obviously starts at the top and the end results emerge at the bottom, each intervening element is not just a discrete unit to be completed before moving onto the next, but rather an aspect of the whole, to be repeated and reworked in the light of subsequent operations. The requirements of the later stages of analysis and investigation may call for modifications in procedures at earlier stages. This point has already gained wide acceptance in general archaeological theory; for example, Professor L. R. Binford has asserted that 'excavation must be conducted in terms of a running analysis and against a background of the widest possible set of questions to which the data are potentially relevant' (1972, 159). When it was suggested in section 2.3 that the slowness of underwater investigations may make them more elegant and efficient by allowing more regular modifications in tactics, what was being proposed

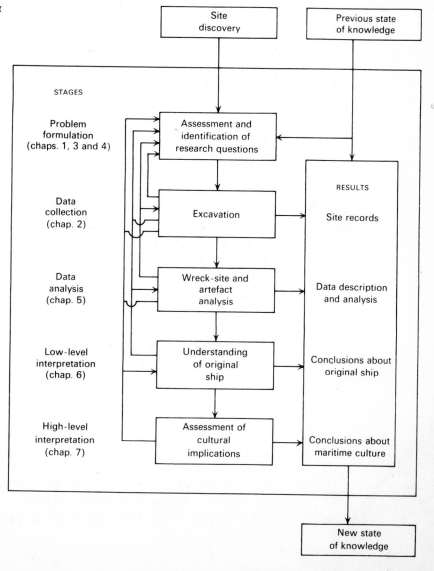

Fig. 8.1 A model describing the process by which a new site adds to the general store of knowledge in maritime archaeology.

was that the feedback channels in fig. 8.1 might have more time to operate.

Many of these practical implications have already been mentioned in the appropriate places, and only a summary need be given here. For example, in the light of preliminary conclusions about the type of site involved (in terms of table 5.2), surveying techniques may have to be altered, while the results of any distributional analyses may lead to a reconsideration of the standards of accuracy required for the particular site (Muckelroy 1975, 173–5). However, the important procedural point to note here is that one must always start with a presumption of great importance and significance in any site, until the results suggest other-wise, rather than make an initial assumption of no particular importance in order to justify slovenly and unsatisfactory working methods. If the appropriate records are never made, no-one can ever tell what has been lost on a site, while it does no harm to have details on file which, on subsequent inspection, prove to be of little significance. However, it is unrealistic to call for 'total accuracy', since there is no such thing: what is needed in 'appropriate accuracy', and this can only be gauged if the excavator is aware of all the ramifications involved in the interpretation of his site.

A further important element in this feedback concerns the decision on whether to undertake any fieldwork in the first place. As explained in section 1.1, an excavation only becomes archaeological if it is 'problem-orientated', but at that stage little could be said about the types of 'problems' towards which a site might be expected to contribute knowledge. The framework propounded above presents three areas in which a site might be able to present significant archaeological data (sections 6.2–6.4 and 7.2–7.4) and on any particular wreck-site the excavator should be able to justify his work in those terms. The situation becomes more complex when the matter of priorities arises, and the solutions are less straightforward. Archaeology under water is un-doubtedly expensive, but with the ever increasing exploitation of the sea-bed there will inevitably be an accelerating discovery rate of new sites. The question of how to distribute limited resources across the field is one which has yet to be solved totally satisfactorily in land archaeology, but in principle the idea should be to concentrate resources on recovering an adequate supply of evidence from those sites which promise to shed light on the most pressing and important questions. Of course, the matter of deciding which are the most important questions is somewhat subjective, and can never be settled to everyone's satis-faction.

The wider questions of finance for maritime archaeology are complex, and essentially ones to be tackled by the whole community, and not within the sub-discipline itself. However, what it can do is present to the public the very real attractions of this area of research – in the immense amount of new information concerning a fascinating aspect of previous societies which it can produce and in the wide range of artefacts which it can make available for display. One point is quite clear in the light of all that has been written in the past seven chapters, and that is that there can be no satisfactory determination of priorities, let alone any solid progress in research, if funds are made available solely on the basis of the commercial value of the artefacts recovered; as General Pitt-Rivers observed in one of his reports: 'the value of relics, viewed as evidence, may . . . be said to be in an inverse ratio to their intrinsic value' (1892, ix). While interesting snippets of information may emerge from salvage operations, no integrated and coherent research can be conducted while the funds are determined by the demands of the sale-rooms.

Allied to questions of finance are obviously those of legal control over such sites. A detailed discussion of this matter would be out of place here, since any particular provisions must relate closely to the legal system operating in any specific country, but a few general points can be made. Obviously, the laws should be so structured as to encourage the responsible investigation of sites, and prevent the raising of objects until such time as an archaeological assessment of their potential can be made. It would seem, human nature being what it is, that the only way of restraining the acquisitive urges of people is to make all historic material on the sea-bed the property of the community, thus removing the financial incentives to proceed in a commercial and non-archaeo-logical manner; this is the approach which has been adopted in most countries. The difficulties of preventing unauthorised interference with underwater sites are frequently overestimated, since coastal communities usually possess a lively awareness of all that is happening at sea, and many of the more deeply buried and better preserved sites cannot be uncovered without bulky and conspicuous machinery on the surface. Nevertheless, there will always be some sites with extensive spreads of material lying on the surface presenting inevitable temptations to souvenir hunters, and which will therefore require excavation immedi-ately after discovery, even though they might not otherwise stand high on the list of research priorities. This presents the standard 'rescue' situation common to all branches of archaeology. Similar provisions must be made for sites lying in international waters, outside the jurisdic-tion of any one state, although the legal and political problems involved will probably delay the achievement of any agreements until after many important sites have been destroyed.

A few general observations can also be made about the organisation of research in maritime archaeology, although the detailed provisions in any one country must obviously depend on the standard provisions for academic work pertaining there. It should go without saying, in the light of all that has been said above, that all involved must have an archaeological training appropriate to their responsibilities. However, the implication of fig. 8.1 and the general theory behind it is that the director, and if possible his deputies or supervisors, should be fully involved in academic research in this subject at all levels, in order that they can appreciate every element in the process, and allow all the feedback channels to operate effectively. Thus the appropriate context from which the senior staff for such excavations should come is that of a university or equivalent institution, or a research unit (perhaps attached to a maritime museum) operating at a similar level. So far as other site-workers are concerned, the standards of competence and experience should ideally be higher than those generally accepted on land excavations, in view of the supervision problems outlined in section 2.2. At the same time, since archaeology is also the most labour-intensive of all the underwater sciences, it should be noted that it will always have to rely to some extent on the involvement of dedicated and experienced amateurs, both in searching programmes and in systematic excavations. Finally, such projects must also depend on the services and skills of a wide range of other specialists – photographers, draughtsmen, diving technicians, conservators, etc. – all of whom must be integrated effectively within a team firmly orientated towards archaeological problem-solving. Professor Grahame Clark has outlined the many academic and

Fig. 8.2 A pictorial integration of the subject; the author excavating within the iron ballast of the wreck of the *Dartmouth*, a drawing board and a survey tape to hand. He is clearing the overburden to reveal further areas of coherent structure, and in the process discovering a range of the ship's former contents, whose distribution has since been analysed (see section 5.6); this spot is near the arithmetic mean centre for culinary utensils (see fig. 5.14).

administrative talents required in a competent archaeologist (1939, 17–20); the barely adequate director of a maritime archaeological project is going to need them all, plus several more!

A final implication of this approach to the subject concerns the presentation of site reports. It should not be necessary nowadays to reiterate that publication is an obligation and that 'an unpublished excavated site has been destroyed or mutilated as surely as if it had been bulldozed' (Barker 1977, 222). It is often thought that reports should consist of a straightforward recitation of the recorded evidence, with a minimum of commentary, on the grounds that this is the only path to complete objectivity. However, if the various stages in the project have been adequately and thoughtfully integrated, as suggested in fig. 8.1, then the 'facts' will owe not a little to the excavator's view of the problems in hand, and the techniques of excavation and post-excavation analysis employed. It is thus essential that all stages in the work be described in detail, so as to place the results in a context which can be appreciated by the reader.

While these few points constitute the most important of the practical implications arising out of what has gone before, it would be wrong to conclude without a mention of the many personal pleasures to be derived from involvement in this work. Any branch of archaeology demands a varied mixture of manual and intellectual work, an alternation between libraries and the open air, but this specialism involves additionally the physical and psychological challenges of working in an alien environment. In addition, there are all the joys and frustrations of any activity on the sea, calling for a degree of seamanship from the archaeologist, and engendering a kinship between him and the past seamen whose moment of disaster he is studying. Above all, there is the intellectual challenge of integrating all these strands in a coherent research design (fig. 8.2), an exercise which for one archaeologist has led to this book. One of the main developments of the next few decades will undoubtedly be the systematic exploitation of the sea-floor, and this will present both great opportunities and heavy responsibilities to those concerned with our cultural heritage under water; it is to be hoped therefore that many more people with relevant skills to offer will wish to become involved in maritime archaeology in the next few years.

BIBLIOGRAPHY

In general, journal titles have been abbreviated according to the forms indicated in the Council for British Archaeology's annual Archaeological Bibliography, or on similar principles. Certain recurring references are, however, abbreviated as follows:

C.A.S.   *Cahiers d'Archéologie Subaquatique*
I.J.N.A.   *International Journal of Nautical Archaeology and Underwater Exploration*

Adnams, J. R. (1974). The *Dartmouth*, a British frigate wrecked off Mull, 1690. *I.J.N.A.*, **3**, 269–74.

Anderson, R. & R. C. (1926). *The sailing ship; six thousand years of history.* Harrap, London.

Anderson, R. G. W. (1972). *The mariner's astrolabe.* Royal Scottish Museum, Edinburgh.

Anon (1977). A thirteenth or fourteenth century A.D. shipwreck near Mokpo. *I.J.N.A.*, **6**, 257.

Arnold, B. (1974). La barque gallo-romaine de la baie de Bevaix. *C.A.S.*, **3**, 133–50.

– (1975). The gallo-roman boat from the Bay of Bevaix, Lake Neuchâtel, Switzerland. *I.J.N.A.*, **4**, 123–6.

Arnold, J. B. & Clausen, C. J. (1975). A magnetometer survey with electronic positioning control and calculator-plotter system. *I.J.N.A.*, **4**, 353–66.

Atkinson, R. J. C. (1957). Worms and weathering. *Antiquity*, **31**, 219–33.

AUSAC (Aston University Sub-Aqua Club) (1974). *The wreck of the 'Kennemerland'.* Aston University, Birmingham.

Baddeley, A. D. (1966). The influence of depth on the manual dexterity of free divers. *J. Applied Psychol.*, **50**(1), 81–5.

Baker, P. E. & Green, J. N. (1976). Recording techniques used during the excavation of the *Batavia. I.J.N.A.*, **5**, 143–58.

Barber, V. (1977). The *Sapphire*, a British frigate sunk in action in Bay Bulls, Newfoundland, in 1696. *I.J.N.A.*, **6**, 305–13.

Barker, P. (1977). *Techniques of archaeological excavation.* Batsford, London.

Basch, L. (1972). Ancient wrecks and the archaeology of ships. *I.J.N.A.*, **1**, 1–58.

Basch, L. & Frost, H. (1975). Another Punic wreck in Sicily: its ram. *I.J.N.A.*, **4**, 201–28.

Bascom, W. (1972). A tool for deep-water archaeology. *I.J.N.A.*, **1**, 180–4.

– (1976). *Deep water, ancient ships.* David and Charles, Newton Abbot.

Bass, G. F. (1966). *Archaeology under water.* Thames and Hudson, London.

– (1967). Cape Gelidonya; a Bronze Age shipwreck. *Trans. American Philosoph. Soc.*, **57**(8). Philadelphia.

- (1971). A Byzantine trading venture. *Scientific American*, **225**, 23–33.
- (ed.), (1972a). *A history of seafaring based on underwater archaeology*. Thames and Hudson, London.
- (1972b). The earliest seafarers in the Mediterranean and the Near East. In Bass, G. F. (ed.), *A history of seafaring, based on underwater archaeology*, pp. 11–36. Thames and Hudson, London.
- (1976). Sheytan Deresi; preliminary report. *I.J.N.A.*, 5, 293–303.
Bass, G. F. & Katzev, M. L. (1968). New tools for underwater archaeology. *Archaeology*, **21**, 165–73.
Bass, G. F. & van Doorninck, F. H. (1971). A fourth-century shipwreck at Yassi Ada. *American J. Archaeol.*, **75**, 27–37.
Baume, D. & Godden, D. (1975). Don't forget the diver. *New Scientist,* 68 **68**(978), 574–7.
Bax, A. & Martin, C. J. M. (1974). *De Liefde*, a Dutch East Indiaman lost on the Out Skerries, Shetland, in 1711. *I.J.N.A.*, 3, 81–90.
Bengtsson, S. (1975). The sails of the *Wasa*; unfolding, identification and preservation. *I.J.N.A.*, **4**, 27–41.
Benoit, F. (1961). *L'épave du Grand Congloué à Marseilles*. XIVe supplément à *Gallia*, Paris.
- (1962). Nouvelles épaves de Provence III. *Gallia*, **20**, 147–76.
- (1965). Mediterranean trade. In Taylor, J. du P. (ed.), *Marine Archaeology*, pp. 24–33. Hutchinson, London.
Biddle, M. (1974). The future of the urban past. In Rahtz, P. A. (ed.), *Rescue Archaeology*, pp. 95–112. Penguin, London.
Binford, L. R. (1972). *An archaeological perspective*. Seminar Press, New York and London.
Birk, D. A. (1975). Recent underwater recoveries at Fort Charlotte. *I.J.N.A.*, **4**, 73–84.
Blackman, D. J. (ed.), (1973a). *Marine archaeology*. Colston Papers No. 23, Butterworths, London.
- (1973b). The harbours of Phaselis. *I.J.N.A.*, **2**, 355–64.
Blundell, Rev. O. (1909). The crannog of Eilean Muireach. *Proc. Soc. Antiquaries Scot.*, **43**, 159–64.
- (1910). Further examination of artificial islands. *Proc. Soc. Antiquaries Scot.*, **44**, 12–33.
Boon, G. C. (1976). A Graeco-Roman anchor-stock from North Wales. *Archaeologia Atlantica*, **1**, 195–9.
- (1977). The Porth Felen anchor-stock. *I.J.N.A.*, **6**, 239–42.
Bowen, E. G. (1972). *Britain and the western seaways*. Thames and Hudson, London.
Boxer, C. R. (1965). *Dutch Seaborne Empire, 1600–1800*. History of Human Society, Hutchinson, London.
Brand, Rev. J. (1701). *A brief description of Orkney, Zetland, Pightland Firth and Caithness*. Edinburgh.
Brøgger, A. W. & Shetelig, H. (1951). *The Viking ships*. Hurst, London.
Bruce, R. S. (1907). Some old-time Shetlandic wrecks, part 2. *Old Lore Miscellany*, **1**(4), 123–8.
Bruce-Mitford, R. (1975). *The Sutton Hoo Ship-burial*, vol. 1. British Museum Publications, London.
Bushe-Fox, J. P. (1915). Excavations at Hengistbury Head, Hampshire, in 1911–12. *Report of the Research Committee of the Society of Antiquaries*, **3**, London.

Butland, W. E. & Stubbs, J. M. (1976). Survey and excavation of the sloop
    Lovely. Maritime Wales, **1**, 51–62.
Callender, M. H. (1965). *Roman amphorae, with index of stamps*. University of
    Durham Publications, London.
Carr, E. H. (1961). *What is History?* Macmillan, London.
Carrazé, F. (1972). Le gisement 'A' de la Jeanne-garde. *C.A.S.*, **1**, 75–87.
– (1975). L'épave 'Grand Ribaud A'. *C.A.S.*, **4**, 19–58.
Casson, L. (1959). *The ancient mariners*. Victor Gollancz, London.
– (1971). *Ships and seamanship in the ancient world*. Princeton University
    Press, Princeton, New Jersey.
Cederlund, C. O. (1977). Preliminary report on recording methods used for
    the investigation of merchant shipwrecks at Jutholmen and Alvsnabben in
    1973–74. *I.J.N.A.*, **6**, 87–99.
Cederlund, C. O. & Ingelman-Sundberg, C. (1973). The excavation of the
    Jutholmen wreck, 1970–71. *I.J.N.A.*, **2**, 301–27.
Chapman, F. H. (1768). *Architectura Navalis Mercatoria*. Stockholm.
Chorley, R. J. & Haggett, P. (1965). Trend-surface mapping in geographical
    research. *Institute of British Geographers, Publications*, No. 37.
Christensen, A. E. (1972). Scandinavian ships to the Vikings. In Bass, G. F.
    (ed.), *A history of seafaring based on underwater archaeology*, pp. 160–80.
    Thames and Hudson, London.
Christensen, A. E. & Morrison, I. A. (1976). Experimental archaeology and
    boats. *I.J.N.A.*, **5**, 275–84.
Cipolla, C. M. (1965). *Guns and sails in the early phase of European expansion,
    1400–1700*. Collins, London.
Clark, J. G. D. (1939). *Archaeology and society*. Methuen, London.
– (1952). *Prehistoric Europe, the economic basis*. Methuen, London.
– (1954). *Excavations at Star Carr*. Cambridge University Press, London.
– (1966). The invasion hypothesis in British archaeology. *Antiquity*, **40**,
    172–89.
Clarke, D. L. (1968). *Analytical archaeology*. Methuen, London.
Clausen, C. J. & Arnold, J. B. (1976). The magnetometer and underwater
    archaeology. *I.J.N.A.*, **5**, 159–69.
Coates, J. F. (1977). Hypothetical reconstructions and the naval architect. In
    McGrail, S. (ed.), *Sources and techniques in boat archaeology*, pp. 215–26.
    British Archaeological Reports, Supplementary Series, No. 29, Oxford.
Cole, J. P. & King, C. A. M. (1968). *Quantitative geography*. Wiley, London.
Coles, J. M. (1977). Experimental archaeology, theory and principles. In
    McGrail, S. (ed.), *Sources and techniques in boat archaeology*, pp. 233–43.
    British Archaeological Reports, Supplementary Series, No. 29, Oxford.
Coles, J. M., Orme, B. J., Hibbert, F. A. & Wainwright, G. J. (1975).
    Somerset Levels Papers, No. 1. Privately published.
Condamin, J., Formenti, F., Metais, M. O., Michel, M. & Blond, P. (1976).
    The application of gas chromatography to the tracing of oil in ancient
    amphorae. *Archaeometry*, **18**(2), 195–201.
Coombs, D. (1976). The Dover harbour bronze find – a Bronze Age wreck?
    Archaeologia Atlantica, **1**, 193–5.
Cowan, R., Cowan, Z. & Marsden, P. (1975). The Dutch East Indiaman
    Hollandia wrecked on the Isles of Scilly in 1973. *I.J.N.A.*, **4**, 267–300.
Crumlin-Pedersen, O. (1970). The Viking ships of Roskilde. *National
    Maritime Museum Maritime Monographs and Reports*, **1**, 7–23.
– (1972). Viking and Hanseatic merchants: 900–1450. In Bass, G. F. (ed.),

A history of seafaring, based on underwater archaeology, pp. 182–204. Thames and Hudson, London.

Cunliffe, B. W. (1974). *Iron age communities in Britain*. Routledge and Kegan Paul, London.

Cunnington, E. (1884). On a hoard of bronze, iron, and other objects found in Bulbury Camp, Dorset. *Archaeologia*, **48**, 115–20.

Daniel, G. (1967). *The origin and growth of archaeology*. Penguin, London.

Davis, R. H. (1955). *Deep diving and submarine operations*. (6th edn). Siebe Gorman, London.

Destombes, M. (1969). Un astrolabe nautique de la Casa de Contratación (Seville, 1563). *Revue d'Histoire des Sciences*, **22**, 33–64. Presses Universitaires de France, Paris.

de Weerd, M. & Haalebos, J. K. (1973). Schepen voor het opscheppen. *Spiegel Historiael* (Bussum), **8**, 386–97.

Dickens, G. (1957). *The dress of the British sailor*. National Maritime Museum, HMSO, London.

Dimitrov, B. (1976). Stone anchors from Sozopol Bay (Bulgaria). *I.J.N.A.*, **5**, 81–3.

– (1977). Anchors from the ancient ports of Sozopol. *I.J.N.A.*, **6**, 156–63.

Doran, J. E. & Hodson, F. R. (1975). *Mathematics and computers in archaeology*. Edinburgh University Press, Edinburgh.

Dumas, F. (1962). *Deep-water archaeology*. Routledge and Kegan Paul, London.

– (1972). Ancient wrecks. In UNESCO, *Underwater archaeology, a nascent discipline*, pp. 27–34. UNESCO, Paris.

Dunning, G. C. (1968). The trade in medieval pottery around the North Sea. In Renaud, J. G. (ed.), *Rotterdam Papers; a contribution to medieval archaeology*, pp. 35–58. Rotterdam.

Dymond, D. P. (1974). *Archaeology and history, a plea for reconciliation*. Thames and Hudson, London.

Ehrenberg, V. (1967). *From Solon to Socrates*. Methuen, London.

Ellmers, D. (1973). The earliest report on an excavated ship in Europe. *I.J.N.A.*, **2**, 177–9.

Ericsson, C. H. (1975a). The instruments from Her Imperial Majesty's frigate *Nicholas*. *I.J.N.A.*, **4**, 65–71.

– (1975b). An eighteenth century diving-suit from Brahestad in Finland. *I.J.N.A.*, **4**, 130–4.

Evans, A. C. & Fenwick, V. H. (1971). The Graveney boat. *Antiquity*, **45**, 89–96.

Falconer, A. F. (1964). *Shakespeare and the sea*. Constable, London.

Fenwick, V. H. (1972). The Graveney boat. A pre-conquest discovery in Kent. *I.J.N.A.*, **1**, 119–29.

Finley, M. I. (1971). Archaeology and history. *Daedalus*, **100**(1), 168;86.

Fiori, P. (1974). Le mouillage antique du Cap Gros. *C.A.S.*, **3**, 81–102.

Fiori, P. & Joncheray, J.-P. (1973). Mobiliers métalliques (outils, pièces de gréement, armes) provenant de fouilles sous-marines. *C.A.S.*, **2**, 73–94.

– (1975). L'épave de la tradelière. *C.A.S.*, **4**, 59–70.

Flemming, N. C. (1965). Apollonia. In Taylor, J. du P. (ed.), *Marine archaeology*, pp. 168–78. Hutchinson, London.

– (1969). Archaeological evidence for eustatic change of sea level and earth movements in the western Mediterranean during the last 2000 years. *Geolog. Soc. America, Special paper* No. 109.

– (1972). *Cities in the sea.* New English Library, London.

Flemming, N. C., Czartoryska, N. M. G., & Hunter, P. M. (1973). Sea level changes in the south Aegean. In Blackman, D. J. (ed.), *Marine archaeology*, pp. 1–66. Butterworth, London.

Flemming, N. C. & Miles, D. L. (1974). *Underwater Association code of practice for scientific diving* (2nd edn). Natural Environment Research Council, London.

Flinder, A. (1977). The island of Jezirat Fara'un. *I.J.N.A.*, **6**, 127–39.

Forster, W. A. & Higgs, K. B. (1973). The *Kennemerland*, 1971; an interim report. *I.J.N.A.*, **3**, 291–300.

Fowler, P. J. (ed.) (1975). *Recent work in rural archaeology.* Moonraker Press, London.

Frank, T. (1933–40). (ed.). *An economic survey of ancient Rome* (6 vols.). The Johns Hopkins Press, Baltimore.

Franzen, A. (1966). *The warship 'Wasa'.* Norstedts, Stockholm.

Frey, D. (1972). Sub-bottom profile of Porto Longo harbour, *I.J.N.A.*, **1**, 170–5.

Frondeville, G. de (1965). Mahdia. In Taylor, J. du P. (ed.), *Marine archaeology*, pp. 39–52. Hutchinson, London.

Frost, H. (1962). Submarine archaeology and Mediterranean wreck formations. *Mariner's Mirror*, **48**, 82–9.

– (1963*a*). *Under the Mediterranean.* Routledge and Kegan Paul, London.

– (1963*b*). From rope to chain. *Mariner's Mirror*, **49**, 1–20.

– (1972*a*). The discovery of a Punic ship. *I.J.N.A.*, **1**, 113–17.

– (1972*b*). Ancient harbours and anchorages in the eastern Mediterranean. In UNESCO, *Underwater archaeology, a nascent discipline*, pp. 95–114. UNESCO, Paris.

– (1973*a*). The first season on the Punic wreck in Sicily. *I.J.N.A.*, **2**, 33–49.

– (1973*b*). The offshore harbour at Sidon and other Phoenician sites. *I.J.N.A.*, **2**, 75–94.

– (1973). Anchors, the potsherds of marine archaeology. In Blackman, D.J. (ed.), *Marine archaeology*, pp. 397–409. Butterworth, London.

– (1975). The pharos site, Alexandria, Egypt. *I.J.N.A.*, **4**, 126–30.

Frost, H., Culican, W. & Curtis, J. E. (1974). The Punic wreck. *I.J.N.A.*, **3**, 35–54.

Fryer, J. (1973). The harbour installations of Roman Britain. In Blackman, D. J. (ed.), *Marine archaeology*, pp. 261–75. Butterworth, London.

Geikie, J. (1879). Discovery of an ancient canoe in the old alluvium of the Tay at Perth. *Scottish Naturalist*, **5**, 1–7.

Gelsinger, B. E. (1970). Lodestone and sunstone in medieval Iceland. *Mariner's Mirror*, **56**, 219–26.

Gianfrotta, P. A. (1977). First elements for the dating of stone anchor stocks. *I.J.N.A.*, **6**, 285–92.

Glamann, K. (1958). *Dutch-Asiatic trade.* Danish Science Press, Copenhagen.

Glob, P. V. (1969). *The bog people; iron-age man preserved.* Transl. Bruce-Mitford, R. Faber and Faber, London.

Godden, D. (1975). Cold, wet, and hostile. *New Behaviour*, **1**, 422–5.

– (1977). Paper presented to Symposium of Underwater Association, 18–19 March 1977.

Godden, D. R. & Baddeley, A. D. (1975). Context-dependent memory in two natural environments; on land and underwater. *Brit. J. Psychol.*, **66**, 325–31.

Graham, J. M. (1977). Quantitative methods and boat archaeology. In McGrail, S. (ed.), *Sources and techniques in boat archaeology*, pp. 137–55. British Archaeological Reports, Supplementary Series, No. 29, Oxford.

Graham, W. (1972). *The Spanish Armadas*. Collins, London.

Green, J. N. (1973a). The wreck of the *Vergulde Draeck*, 1656. *I.J.N.A.*, **2**, 267–89.

– (1973b). Underwater archaeological survey at Cape Andreas, 1969–70. In Blackman, D. J. (ed.), *Marine archaeology*, pp. 141–79. Butterworth, London.

– (1975). The VOC ship *Batavia* wrecked in 1629 on the Houtman Abrolhos, Western Australia. *I.J.N.A.*, **4**, 43–63.

– (1977). *Australia's oldest wreck; the loss of the 'Trial', 1622*. British Archaeological Reports, Supplementary Series, No. 27, Oxford.

Green, J. N. & Henderson, G. (1977). Maritime archaeology and legislation in Western Australia. *I.J.N.A.*, **6**, 245–8.

Green, W. S. (1906). The wrecks of the Spanish Armada on the coast of Ireland. *Geographical J.*, **27**, 429–51.

Greenhill, B. (1976). *The archaeology of the boat*. A. and C. Black, London.

Greig-Smith, P. (1964). *Quantitative plant ecology*. Methuen, London.

Guilcher, A. (1958). *Coastal and submarine morphology*. Transl. Sparks, B. W. & Kneese, R. H. W. Methuen, London.

Guilmartin, J. F. (1974). *Gunpowder and galleys; Mediterranean warfare in the sixteenth century*. Cambridge University Press, London.

Hall, E.T. (1972). Wreck prospecting by magnetometer. In UNESCO, *Underwater archaeology; a nascent discipline*, pp. 285–93. UNESCO, Paris.

Hamilton, D. L. (1976). *The conservation of metal objects from underwater sites; a study in methods*. Texas Memorial Museum, Miscellaneous papers No. 4, and Texas Antiquities Committee, Publication No. 1, Austin, Texas.

Hardie, R. P. (1912). *The Tobermory argosy*. Oliver & Boyd, Edinburgh.

Hartley, B. R. (1972). The Roman occupation of Scotland; the evidence of Samian ware. *Britannia*, **3**, 1–55.

Hartley, K. F. (1973). The distribution of tiles, mortaria and other products of the brickyards of Italy. *C.A.S.*, **2**, 49–60.

Hasslöf, O. (1963). Wrecks, archives, and living traditions. *Mariner's Mirror*, **49**, 162–76.

– (1972). Maritime ethnology and its associated disciplines. In Hasslöf, O., Henningsen, H. & Christensen, A. E. (eds.), *Ships and shipyards, sailors and fishermen*, pp. 9–19. Copenhagen University Press, Copenhagen.

Hasslöf, O., Henningsen, H. & Christensen, A. E. (eds.) (1972). *Ships and shipyards, sailors and fishermen; an introduction to maritime ethnology*. Transl. Knight, M. and Young, H. Copenhagen University Press, Copenhagen.

Henderson, G. (1976). *James Matthews* excavation, summer 1974; an interim report. *I.J.N.A.*, **5**, 245–51.

Henningsen, H. (1972). The life of the sailor. In Hasslöf, O., Henningsen, H. & Christensen, A. E. (eds.), *Ships and shipyards, sailors and fishermen*, pp. 123–50. Copenhagen University Press, Copenhagen.

Hiscock, K. (1974). Ecological surveys of sublittoral rocky areas. *Underwater Association 8th annual report*, pp. 46–65.

Hodder, I. & Orton, C. (1976). *Spatial analysis in archaeology*. Cambridge University Press, London.

Holmes, M. R. (1951). The so-called Bellarmine mask. *Antiq. J.*, **31**, 173–9.

Hornell, J. (1938). *British coracles and Irish curraghs*. Society for Nautical

Research, London.
- (1946). *Water transport*. Cambridge University Press, London.
Hurst, H. (1975). Excavations at Carthage, 1974; first interim report. *Antiq. J.*, **55**, 11–40.
- (1976). Excavations at Carthage, 1975; second interim report. *Antiq. J.*, **56**, 177–97.
Ingelman-Sundberg, C. (1977). The VOC ship *Zeewijk* lost off the Western Australian coast in 1727. *I.J.N.A.*, **6**, 225–31.
Isserlin, B. S. J. (1971). New light on the 'cothon' at Motya. *Antiquity*, **45**, 178–86.
Jameson, M. H. (1973). Halieis at Porto Cheli. In Blackman, D. J. (ed.), *Marine archaeology*, pp. 219–31. Butterworth, London.
Jarman, H. N., Legge, A. J. & Charles, J. A. (1972). The retrieval of plant remains from archaeological sites by froth flotation. In Higgs, E. S. (ed.), *Papers in economic prehistory*, pp. 49–58. Cambridge University Press, London.
Johnstone, P. (1974). *The archaeology of ships*. Bodley Head, London.
Jolliffe, I. P. & Wallace, H. (1973). The role of seaweed in beach supply, and in shingle transport below low tide level. In Flemming, N. C. (ed.), *Science diving international*, pp. 189–96. British Sub-Aqua Club, London.
Joncheray, J.-P. (1973). Contribution à l'étude de l'épave Dramont D, dite 'des pelvis'. *C.A.S.*, **2**, 9–48.
- (1974). Etude de l'épave Dramont D, dite 'des pelvis'. *C.A.S.*, **3**, 21–48.
- (1975). Etude de l'épave Dramont D; les objets métalliques. *C.A.S.*, **4**, 5–18.
- (1976*a*). 1974 excavations at the wreck of Bataiguier. *I.J.N.A*, **5**, 87–8.
- (1976*b*). Le Roche Fouras. *I.J.N.A*, **5**, 107–14.
Jondet, G. (1916). *Les ports submergés de l'ancienne île de Pharos*. Cairo.
Katzev, M. L. (1970). Kyrenia, 1969; a Greek ship is raised. *Expedition*, **12**(4), 6–14.
- (1974). Last harbor for the oldest ship. National Geographic, **146**, 618–25.
Katzev, M. L. & van Doorninck, F. H. (1966). Replicas of iron tools from a Byzantine shipwreck. *Studies in Conservation*, **9**, 133–42.
Kelland, N. (1976). A method for carrying out accurate planimetric surveys underwater. *Hydrographic J.*, **2**(4), 17–32.
Keller, C. (1973). Stratification problems in Norwegian harbours. *I.J.N.A.*, **2**, 187–9.
- (1976). Four methodical groups of underwater archaeological sites. In Adolfson, J. (ed.), *Underwater 75*, pp. 101–10. SMR Committee for Underwater Technology, Stockholm.
Kemp, P. K. (1970). *The British sailor, a social history of the lower deck*. Dent, London.
King, C. A. M. (1972). *Beaches and coasts* (2nd edn). Edward Arnold, London.
Kirkman, J. (1972). A Portuguese wreck off Mombasa, Kenya. *I.J.N.A.*, **1**, 153–7.
Lamboglia, N. (1961). Le navi romana di Spargi. *Proceedings of the 2nd International Congress on Underwater Archaeology*, pp. 124–31. Bordighera.
- (1965). Albenga. In Taylor, J. du P. (ed.), *Marine archaeology*, pp. 53–65. Hutchinson, London.
Lance, G.N. & Williams, W.T. (1967). A general theory of classificatory sorting strategies; 1. Hierarchical systems. *Computer J.*, **9**, 373–80.
Landström, B. (1961). *The ship*. Transl. Phillips, M. Allen and Unwin,

London.
– (1970). *Ships of the Pharaohs; 4000 years of Egyptian ship-building*. Allen and Unwin, London.
Lane, F. C. (1963). The economic meaning of the invention of the compass. *American History Review*, **68**, 601;12.
Larn, R., McBride, P. & Davis, R. (1974). Mid-seventeenth century merchant ship, Mullion Cove, Cornwall. *I.J.N.A.*, **3**, 67–79.
Lethbridge, T. C. (1952). *Boats and boatmen*. Thames and Hudson, London.
Lewis, J. D. (1973). Cosa; an early Roman harbour. In Blackman, D. J. (ed.), *Marine archaeology*, pp. 233–59. Butterworth, London.
Lewis, M. A. (1961). *Armada guns; a comparative study of English and Spanish armaments*. Allen and Unwin, London.
Lewis, N. & Reinhold, M. (1955). *Roman civilisation* (2 vols.). Columbia University Press, New York.
Lightly, R.A. (1976). An eighteenth century Dutch East Indiaman, found at Cape Town, 1971. *I.J.N.A.*, **5**, 305–16.
Linder, E. (1967). La ville Phénicienne d'Athlit. *Archaeologia*, **17**, 25–9.
Linder, E. & Raban, A. (1975). *Marine archaeology*. Cassel, London.
Lloyd, C. (1968). *The British seaman, 1200–1860*. Collins, London.
Long, C. D. (1975). Excavations in the medieval city of Trondheim, Norway. *Medieval Archaeol.*, **19**, 1–32.
Longridge, C. J. N. (1955). *The anatomy of Nelson's ships*. Percival Marshall, London.
Losman, A. & Sigurdsson, I. (1974). *Alde vertenskapliga instrument pa Skokloster*. Skokloster Studies, No. 10.
Love, C. E. (1961). The teredo. *Scientific American*, **204**, 132–40.
Lubbock, B. (ed.) (1934). *Barlow's Journal of his life at sea* (2 vols.). Hurst and Blackett, London.
Lucas, A. T. (1963). The dugout canoe in Ireland. *Varbergs Museum Arsbok*, **68**, 57–68. Varberg, Sweden.
Lundin, E. (1973). Locating objects underwater, using a hydrolite. *I.J.N.A.*, **2**, 371–8.
Lyell, C. (1832). *Principles of geology* (1st edn, 3 vols.). London.
Lyon, D. J. (1974). Documentary sources for the archaeological diver; ship plans at the National Maritime Museum. *I.J.N.A.*, **3**, 3–19.
Lyon, E. (1976). The trouble with treasure, *National Geographic*, **149**, 786–809.
McBridge, P. (1976). The *Dartmouth*, a British frigate wrecked off Mull, 1690. 3. The guns. *I.J.N.A.*, **5**, 189–200.
– (1977). The ship that died on Reefdyke shoal. *Triton*, **22**(5), 220–2.
McBride, P., Larn, R. & Davis, R. (1972). A mid-seventeenth century merchant ship found near Mullion Cove, Cornwall. *I.J.N.A.*, **1**, 135–42.
McGrail, S. (1975). The Brigg raft re-excavated. *Lincolnshire Hist. Archaeol.*, **10**, 5–13.
– (ed.) (1977a). *Sources and techniques in boat archaeology*. British Archaeological Reports, Supplementary Series, No. 29, Oxford.
– (1977b). Searching for pattern among the logboats of England and Wales. In McGrail, S. (ed.), *Sources and techniques in boat archaeology*. British Archaeological Reports, Supplementary Series, No. 29, Oxford.
McGrail, S. & McKee, E. (1974). The building and trials of the replica of an ancient boat: the Gokstad faering (2 vols.). *National Maritime Museum, Maritime Monographs and Reports* No. 11. London.
McGrail, S. & Switsur, R. (1975). Early British boats and their chronology. *I.J.N.A.*, **4**, 191–200.

McKee, A. (1973). *King Henry VIII's 'Mary Rose'*. Souvenir Press, London.

McKee, E. (1972). The Graveney boat; permissable assumptions during reconstruction – A summary. *National Maritime Museum, Maritime Monographs and Reports* No. 6, p. 25. London.

Mainwaring, H. (1644). *The seaman's dictionary*. London.

Marsden, P. (1966). *A Roman ship from Blackfriars*. Guildhall Museum, London.

– (1971). A seventeenth century boat found in London. *Post-Medieval Archaeol.*, **5**, 88–98.

– (1972). The wreck of the *Amsterdam* near Hastings, 1749. *I.J.N.A.*, **1**, 73–96.

– (1974). *The wreck of the 'Amsterdam'*. Hutchinson, London.

– (1976a). A boat of the Roman period found at Bruges, Belgium, in 1899, and related types. *I.J.N.A.*, **5**, 23–55.

– (1976b). The *Meresteyn*, wrecked in 1702, near Cape Town, South Africa. *I.J.N.A.*, **5**, 201–19.

– (1977). Celtic boats of Europe. In McGrail, S. (ed.), *Sources and techniques in boat archaeology*, pp. 281–8. British Archaeology Reports, Supplementary Series, No. 29, Oxford.

Marstrander, S. (1976). Building a hide boat; an archaeological experiment. *I.J.N.A.*, **5**, 13–22.

Martin, C. J. M. (1972). *El Gran Grifon*, an Armada wreck on Fair Isle. *I.J.N.A.*, **1**, 59–71.

– (1973). The Spanish Armada expedition, 1968–70. In Blackman, D. J. (ed.), *Marine archaeology*, pp. 439–59. Butterworth, London.

– (1975). *Full fathom five. The wrecks of the Spanish Armada*. Chatto and Windus, London.

– (1978). The *Dartmouth*, a British frigate wrecked off Mull, 1690. 5. The ship. *I.J.N.A.*, **7**, 29–58.

Martin, C. J. M. & Long, A. N. (1975). The use of explosives on the *Adelaar* site, 1974. *I.J.N.A.*, **4**, 345–52.

Martin, P. F. de C. (1977). The *Dartmouth*, a British frigate wrecked off Mull, 1690. 4. The clay pipes. *I.J.N.A.*, **6**, 219–23.

Marx, R. F. (1971). *Shipwrecks of the Western Hemisphere, 1492–1825*. David McKay, New York.

– (1972). New World Newsletter; Florida. *I.J.N.A.*, **1**, 208–9.

– (1973a). *Port Royal rediscovered*. New English Library, London.

– (1973b). United States news; Florida. *I.J.N.A.*, **2**, 204–5.

Mattingly, G. (1959). *The defeat of the Spanish Armada*. Jonathan Cape, London.

May, W. E. (1973). *History of marine navigation*. G. T. Foulis, Henley on Thames.

Mayhew, D. R. (1974). The *Defense*; search and recovery, 1972–3. *I.J.N.A.*, **3**, 312–13.

Morrison, J. S. (1976). The classical tradition. In Greenhill, B., *The archaeology of the boat*, pp. 155–73. A. and C. Black.

Muckelroy, K. W. (1975). A systematic approach to the investigation of scattered wreck sites. *I.J.N.A.*, **4**, 173–90.

– (1976). The integration of historical and archaeological data concerning an historic wreck site: the *Kennemerland*. *World Archaeol.*, **7**(3), 280–90.

– (1977a). Historic wreck sites and their environments. In Hiscock, K. & Baume, A. D. (eds.), *Progress in underwater science*, pp. 111–20. Pentech Press, London.

– (1977b). Historic wreck sites in Britain and their environments. *I.J.N.A.*, **6**, 47–57.

– (1977c). A possible seventeenth-century Dutch backstaff. *Mariner's Mirror*, **63**, 213–14.

Muhly, J. D., Wheeler, T. S. & Maddin, R. (1977). The Cape Gelidonya shipwreck and the Bronze Age metals trade in the eastern Mediterranean. *J. Field Archaeol.*, 4, 353–62.

Müller-Wille, M. (1974). Boat graves in northern Europe. *I.J.N.A.*, **3**, 187–204.

Naish, G. P. B. (1968). *The 'Wasa', her place in history.* HMSO, London.

Needham, J. (1971). *Science and civilisation in China.* Vol. 4, part 3: *Civil engineering and nautics.* Cambridge University Press, London.

Neft, D. S. (1966). *Statistical analysis for areal distributions.* Regional Science Research Institute: Monograph series, No. 2. Philadelphia, Pennsylvania.

Nesteroff, W. D. (1972). Geological aspects of marine sites. In UNESCO, *Underwater archaeology, a nascent discipline*, pp. 175–83. UNESCO, Paris.

North, N. A. (1976). The formation of coral concretions on marine iron. *I.J.N.A.*, **5**, 253–8.

Ohrelius, B. (1962). *'Vasa', the King's ship.* Transl. Michael, M. Cassell, London.

Olsen, O. & Crumlin-Pedersen, O. (1967). Skuldelev ships, II. *Acta archaeologica*, **38**, 73–174.

Osaki, E. (1973). Seventeenth century Japanese harbour works. In Flemming, N. C. (ed.), *Science diving international*, pp. 66–9. British Sub-Aqua Club, London.

Owen, D. I. (1970). Picking up the pieces; the salvage excavation of a looted fifth century B.C. shipwreck in the Straits of Messina. *Expedition*, **13**, 24–9.

– (1971). Excavating a classical shipwreck. *Archaeology*, **24**, 118–29.

Parker, A. J. (1973). Evidence provided by underwater archaeology for Roman trade in the western Mediterranean. In Blackman, D. J. (ed.), *Marine archaeology*, pp. 361–81. Butterworth, London.

– (1976). Report on Fifth International Congress of Underwater Archaeology. *I.J.N.A.*, **5**, 347–8.

Peacock, D. P. S. (1971). Roman amphorae in pre-Roman Britain. In Jesson, M. & Hill, D. (eds.), *The Iron Age and its hill-forts*, pp. 161–88. Southampton University Department of Archaeology, Southampton.

Pearson, C. (1976). Legislation for the protection of shipwrecks in Western Australia. *I.J.N.A.*, **5**, 171–3.

Peterson, M. L. (1972). Traders and privateers across the Atlantic: 1492–1733. In Bass, G. F. (ed.), *A history of seafaring, based on underwater archaeology*, pp. 254–80. Thames and Hudson, London.

Piercy, R. C. M. (1977). Mombasa wreck excavation, preliminary report, 1977. *I.J.N.A.*, **6**, 331–47.

Pirenne, H. (1939). *Mohammed and Charlemagne.* Transl., Mial, B. from 10th French edn. Unwin University Books, London.

Pitt-Rivers, A. H. L. F. (1892). *Excavations in Cranborne Chase, III.* Published privately.

Poidebard, A. (1939). *Un grand port disparu, Tyr.* Bibliothèque archéologique et historique, vol. 29, Paris.

Poidebard, A. & Lauffray, J. (1951). *Sidon: aménagements antiques du port de Saida.* Ministère des travaux publics, Beyrouth.

Pomey, P. (1973). L'architecture navale Romaine et les fouilles sous-marines. In Duval, P.-M. (ed.), *Recherches d'Archéologie Celtique et Gallo-Romaine,* pp. 37–51. Centre Nationale de Recherches Scientifiques, Paris.

Price, R. & Muckelroy, K. (1974). The second season of work on the *Kennemerland* site, 1973; an interim report. *I.J.N.A.*, **3**, 257–68.

– (1977). The *Kennemerland* site; the third and fourth seasons, 1974 and 1976. An interim report. *I.J.N.A.*, **6**, 187–218.

Prynne, M. W. (1968). Henry V's *Grace Dieu*. *Mariner's Mirror*, **54**, 115–28.

Renfrew, C. (1973). *Before civilisation*. Jonathan Cape, London.

Rice, W.McP. (1824). An ancient vessel recently found under the old bed of the River Rother in 1822. *Archaeologia*, **20**, 553–65.

Robinson, M. S. (1958). *The van der Velde Drawings. A catalogue of drawings in the National Maritime Museum*. Cambridge University Press, London.

Robinson, W. S. & Brainerd, G. W. (1951). A method for chronologically ordering archaeological deposits, and The place of chronological ordering in archaeological analysis. *American Antiquity*, **16**, 293–313.

Rochier, R.(1975). Note sur un des plus gros jas d'ancre antique connu. *C.A.S.*, **4**, 149–50.

Roghi, G. (1965). Spargi. In Taylor, J. du P. (ed.), *Marine archaeology*, pp. 103–18. Hutchinson, London.

Rostovtsev, M. I. (1926). *The social and economic history of the Roman Empire*. Oxford University Press, Oxford.

Rule, M. H. (1972). The *Mary Rose*; interim report, 1971. *I.J.N.A.*, **1**, 132–4.

– (1973). The *Mary Rose*; second interim report. *I.J.N.A.*, **2**, 385–8.

– (1976). An early gun-port lid. *Mariner's Mirror*, **62**, 184–5.

Sanlaville, P. (1972). Vermutus dating of changes in sea level. In UNESCO, *Underwater archaeology, a nascent discipline*, pp. 185–91. UNESCO, Paris.

Santamaria, C. (1972). Etude d'un site archéologique sous-marine situé à l'est du Cap Dramont. *C.A.S.*, **1**, 65–73.

Santamaria, C., Dumas, F., Benoit, F. & Sivirine, A. (1965). Dramont 'A'. In Taylor, J. du P. (ed.), *Marine archaeology*, pp. 93–103. Hutchinson, London.

Scranton, R. L. & Ramage, E. S. (1967). Investigations at Corinthian Kenchreai. *Hesperia*, **36**, 124–86.

Shaw, J. W. (1972). Greek and Roman harbourworks. In Bass, G. F. (ed.), *A history of seafaring, based on underwater archaeology*, pp. 88–112. Thames and Hudson, London.

Sheppard, T. (1926). Roman remains in North Lincolnshire. *Trans. E. Riding Antiq. Soc.*, **25**, 170–4.

Siegel, S. (1956). *Nonparametric statistics for the behavioural sciences*. McGraw Hill Series in Psychology, New York.

Sieveking, G. de G. (1976). Progress in economic and social archaeology. In Sieveking, G. de G., Longworth, I. H., and Wilson, K. E. (eds.), *Problems in economic and social archaeology*, pp. xv–xxvi. Duckworth, London.

Smith, R. A. (1907). The wreck on Pudding Pan Rock, Herne Bay, Kent. *Proc. Soc. Antiq.*, **21**, 268–91.

– (1909). The Pudding Pan Rock, Herne Bay, Kent. *Proc. Soc. Antiq.*, **22**, 395–414.

Sneath, P. H. A. & Sokal, R. R. (1973). *Numerical taxonomy ; the principles and practice of numerical classifications*. W. H. Freeman, San Francisco.

Stanbury, M. (ed.) (1975). *Batavia catalogue*. Perth Western Australian Museum, Perth, W.A.

Stenuit, R. (1972). *Treasures of the Armada*. David and Charles, Newton Abbot.

– (1974). Early relics of the VOC trade from Shetland; the wreck of the flute *Lastdrager* loss off Yell, 1653. *I.J.N.A.*, **3**, 213–56.

– (1975). Treasure of Porto Santo. *National Geographic*, **148**(2), 260–75.

Stevens, S., Philp, B. & Williams, W. (1976). A major discovery of Bronze Age implements at Dover. *Kent Archaeol. Review*, **43**, 67–73.

Swiny, H. W. & Katzev, M. L. (1973). The Kyrenia shipwreck; a fourth century B.C. merchant ship. In Blackman, D. J. (ed.), *Marine archaeology*, pp. 339–59. Butterworth, London.

Tailez, P. (1965). Titan. In Taylor, J. du P. (ed.), *Marine archaeology*, pp. 76–92. Hutchinson, London.

Tatton-Brown, T. W. T. (1974). Old Custom House. *Medieval Archaeol.*, **18**, 202–4.

Taylor, E. G. R. (1956). *The haven-finding art*. Hollis and Carter, London.

Taylor, J. du P. (ed.) (1965). *Marine archaeology*. Hutchinson, London.

Tchernia, A. (1969). Les fouilles sous-marines de Planier (Bouche-du-Rhône). *Comptes rendus de l'Académie des inscriptions et belles lettres (Inst. de France), 1969*, 292–309.

Tchernia, A. & Pomey, P. (1978). *L'épave romaine de la Madrague de Giens (Var)*. Supplément à *Gallia*.

Testaguzza, O. (1964). The port of Rome. *Archaeology*, **17**, 173–9.

Thomas, C. (1959). Imported pottery in dark-age western Britain. *Medieval Archaeol.*, **3**, 89–111.

Thompson, I. A. A. (1975). Spanish Armada guns. *Mariner's Mirror*, **61**, 355–71.

Thompson, M. W. (1967). *Novgorod the Great*. Evelyn, Adams and Mackay, London.

Throckmorton, P. (1969). Ancient ship yields new facts and a strange cargo. *National Geographic*, **135**(2), 282–300.

– (1970). *Shipwrecks and archaeology ; the unharvested sea*. Victor Gollancz, London.

– (1973*a*). Ships and shipwrecks; the archaeology of ships. In Blackman, D. J. (ed.), *Marine archaeology*, pp. 493–520. Butterworth, London.

– (1973*b*). The Roman wreck at Pantano Longarini. *I.J.N.A.*, **2**, 243–66.

Throckmorton, P., Hall, E. T., Frost, H., Martin, C., Walton M. G. & Wignall, S. (1969). *Surveying in archaeology underwater*. Colt Archaeological Institute monograph No. 5. Bernard Quaritch, London.

Toudouze, G. C. (1934). *Histoire de la Marine*. Paris.

Tylecote, R. F. (1977). Durable materials for sea water: the archaeological evidence. *I.J.N.A.*, **6**, 269–83.

Ucelli, G. (1950). *Le navi di Nemi*. La Liberia dello Stato, Roma.

Uhlig, H. H. (1948). *The corrosion handbook*. Electrochemical Society, New York.

UNESCO (1972). *Underwater archaeology, a nascent discipline*. UNESCO, Paris.

van der Heide, G. D. (1956). Archaeological investigations in new land. *Antiquity and Survival*, **1**, 93–120.

– (1976). *Archaeological research in the Zuider Zee*. National Maritime Museum, London.

van Doorninck, F. H. (1967). The seventh century ship at Yassi Ada; some contributions to the history of naval architecture. Ph.D. thesis. University of Pennsylvania.

– (1972). Byzantium, mistress of the sea; 330–641. In Bass, G. F. (ed.), *A history of seafaring, based on underwater archaeology*, pp. 134–58. Thames and Hudson, London.

– (1976). The fourth century wreck at Yassi Ada; an interim report on the hull. *I.J.N.A.*, **5**, 115–31.

Visquis, A. G. (1973). Premier inventaire du mobilier de l'épave des jarres à Agay. *C.A.S.*, **2**, 157–67.

Vrsalovic, D. (1974). *Istrazivanja i zastita podmorskih archeoloskih spomenika u SR Hrvatskoj*. Republicki Zavod za zastitu spomenika kulcture, Zagreb.

Wainwright, F. T. (1962). *Archaeology and place-names and history*. Routledge and Kegan Paul, London.

Wallace, P. F. & McGrail, S. (1976). Wood quay, Dublin. *IJNA.*, **5**, 180.

Ward, J. H. (1963). Hierarchical grouping to optimise an objective function. *J. American Statist. Assoc.*, **58**, 236–44.

Waters, D. W. (1958). *The art of navigation in England in Elizabethan and early Stuart times*. Hollis and Carter, London.

Weier, L. E. (1974). The deterioration of inorganic materials under the sea. *Institute of Archaeol. Bull.*, **11**, 131–63.

– (1975). A fourteenth–fifteenth century A.D. shipwreck at Sattahip. *I.J.N.A.*, **4**, 385–6.

Weinberg, G. D., Grace, V. R., Edwards, G. R., Robinson, H. S., Throckmorton, P. & Ralph, E. K. (1965). The Antikythera shipwreck reconsidered. *Trans. American Philosoph. Soc.*, **55**(3).

Wheeler, R. C. & van Gemert, R. C. (1972). Waterways open the New World. In Bass, G. F. (ed.), *A history of seafaring, based on underwater archaeology*, pp. 282–304. Thames and Hudson, London.

Wheeler, R. C., Kenyon, W. A., Woolworth, A. R. & Birk, D. A. (1975). *Voices from the rapids*. Minnesota Historical Archaeology Series, No. 3. Minnesota Historical Society, St Paul, Minnesota.

Wheeler, R. E. M. (1954a). *Archaeology from the earth*. Oxford University Press, Oxford.

– (1954b). *Rome beyond the Imperial frontiers*. George Bell, London.

White, L. (1962). *Medieval technology and social change*. Oxford University Press, Oxford.

Wignall, S. (1973). The Armada shot controversy. In Blackman, D. J. (ed.), *Marine archaeology*, pp. 463–77. Butterworth, London.

Wilkes, W. St J. (1971). *Nautical archaeology*. David and Charles, Newton Abbot.

Williams, P. F. de C. (1976). Roman harbours. *I.J.N.A.*, **5**, 73–9.

Wishart, D. (1969). An algorithm for hierarchical classifications. *Biometrics*, **25**, 165–70.

Witsen, N. (1671). *Architectura navalis et regimen nauticum . . . . scheeps-bouw en bestier*. Amsterdam. (Reprinted Graphic, 1970.)

Wright, E. V. (1976). *The North Ferriby boats*. National Maritime Museum, Maritime Monographs and Reports, No. 23, London.

Yorke, R. A. & Davidson, D. P. (1969). Roman harbours of Algeria. *Underwater Association Report, 1969*, pp. 8–21.

Yorke, R. A. & Little, J. H. (1975). Offshore survey at Carthage, Tunisia, 1973. *I.J.N.A.*, **4**, 85–102.

Yorke, R. A., Little, J. H. & Davidson, D. P. (1976). Offshore surveys of the harbours of Carthage; a summary of the 1975 season's work. *I.J.N.A.*, **5**, 173–6.

Zacharchuk, W. (1972). The Restigouche excavation. *I.J.N.A.*, **1**, 157–63.

Zenkovich, V. P. (1967). *Process of coastal development*. Transl. Fry, D. G. Steers, J. A. & King, C. A. M. (eds.), Oliver and Boyd, Edinburgh.

INDEX

Aberdaron, 148
Adelaar (1728), 108, 180
Admiralty, English, 3, 91, 95, 97
Advena (1912), 56
Agay wreck, 145
Adge wreck, 72
Albenga wreck, 60, 66, 75
Alberti, L. B., 11
Alexandria, 75, 83–4
algae, *see under* plants, sea-bed
amphorae
  dating of, 242
  indicators of trade, 71, 72–3,
    75, 143, 238, 242
  indicators of a vessel's size, 220
  indicators of wrecks, 16, 22, 66,
    126, 183, 187
  protecting ships' hulls, 65, 166,
    171, 183
Amsterdam (1749), 8, 19, 95, 224
analytical methods, *see under*
  individual techniques
Antikythera wreck, 12
Apollonia (Libya), 79, 83
Appian, 80
archaeology
  analysis in, 245–6
  chronology in, 56, 229, 242–5
  as a discipline, 4, 10, 22, 215–16
    226, 253
  evidence in, 56, 216, 231
  experimental, 7, 235–6
  rescue, 251
  rural, 228
  urban, 4, 228
arithmetic mean centre, 190–1
Artemision, Cape, wreck, 13
artemon (steering sail), 65
Arwad, 77
Athenaeus, 59
Athens, 3, 83
Athlit, 79
average link cluster analysis,
  see under group average
cluster analysis

backstaff, 120, 122–4, 125, 215
Baker, M., 91
Baltic
  region, 90, 99, 120, 134, 144
  special characteristics of water,
    17, 53, 134, 144, 170
Barker, P., 245
Barlow, E., 241
Barra, Outer Hebrides, 180
Basch, L., 68, 71, 217
Bascom, W., 150–4
Bass, G. F.,
  and archaeology under water,
    220, 248
  director of projects, 14, 16, 22,
    60, 192
  editor, 227
  and maritime trade, 71, 220
Bataiguier wreck, 145

Batavia (Dutch colony), 106, 108
Batavia (1629)
  investigations, 21, 186
  significance, 94–5, 108, 121,
    122, 125, 231
Bazan, Don Alvaro de, 98
Belle Île wrecks, 143, 238
Benoit, F., 63
Bermuda, 111, 114–15
Bevaix boat, 139–40
Binford, L. R., 249
Binisafuller wreck, 61
Björke boat, 85
Blackfriars
  boat I (Roman), 8, 17, 139–41
  boat III (seventeenth century
    A.D.), 139, 141
Blaeu, W. J., 123
Blundell, O., 11
Bremen cog, 133–4
Brigg 'raft', 128
British Association, 12
British Museum, 18
Bulbury Camp, 149
Bulgaria, 147
bullion, as cargo, 20, 106–8,
  111–14, 245
Bursledon ship, *see under Grace
  Dieu*
Byblos, 147
Byzantinos, G., 12

Caesar, Julius, 74, 149
Caesarea, 83
Caligula, 66
Canada, 20
cannons
  indicators of a vessel's purpose,
    114–15, 137
  indicators of wrecks, 22, 126,
    190, 192
  significance in naval warfare,
    93, 101, 102–4, 113
Carr, E. H., 226
Carthage, 79–82
Casa de la Contratación, 111
centroid cluster analysis, 211
Cheops boat, 62
China, 136–8, 145
Chretienne wreck A, 61, 62
Chuanchow Bay wreck, 138, 145
Clark, J. G. D., 3, 252
Clarke, D. L., 6, 224, 227, 228,
  246
clay pipes
  British, 57, 191, 223, 244
  Dutch, 57, 108, 200, 201, 213
CLUSTAN, computer package,
  207–12
cluster analysis, 207–14, *see also*
  individual techniques
coins, *see under* bullion
Colonna, Cardinal, 11
Columbus, C., 111–12

communication under water,
  40–2, 252
conservation, 35–6, 46, 167
Constantinople, 241
construction of ships, 61–9,
  84–92, 99–101, 127–41, 217,
  231–4
Cosa, 79
Council for Nautical Archaeology,
  19
Cousteau, J.-Y., 14, 22
crannogs, 12
Curaçao (1729), 121
Cyprus, 15, 61, 70–1, 147, 218

Dartmouth (1690)
  contents, 121–5, 213, 223, 237,
    244–5
  investigations, 46–7, 188–91,
    192, 217
  preservation, 53–5, 166, 177
  structural remains, 95–8,
    218–19, 231, 234
  wrecking, 166, 171–2, 174
Davidson, D. A., 78
Davis, J., 122
Deane Brothers, 11
Defense (1779), 20, 118
De Liefde (1711), 18, 106
Demarchi, F., 11
Denmark, 55, 85, 87, 88–90, 132,
  133, 234
dispersion, index of, 202
diving
  dangers in, 25, 36
  development of, 10–11, 14, 22,
    166
  performance during, 36–40
  techniques of, 24–6, 36–42
Dolley, M., 102
Dover, bronze age artefacts from,
  142
Dramont, Cap, 148, 170
  wreck A, 60
  wreck D, 16, 187
draughts, ships', 91–2, 217–18
dug-outs, *see under* log boats
Dumas, F., 14, 15, 160, 170
Dunkirk, 234
Dutch East India Company
  (VOC), 19, 21, 95, 106–10,
  125, 224, 240, 244

Eagle (1659), 115
Ealdred, Abbot of St Albans, 11
Egypt, 3, 62, 147, *see also under*
  Alexandria
Ellingaa boat, 132
Engelhardt, C., 11
ethnology
  as a discipline, 4, 6, 7
  maritime, 6, 7, 230, 234–5,
    241–2
Euclidean distance, similarity
  measure, 207–12

excavation under water
  organisation, 47–8
  strategy, 31, 50–1, 182, 245–6,
    250
  techniques, 28–31, 43, 49–50,
    245

Fiar Isle, 99
Ferriby, North, boats from, 8,
  127–8
finance for maritime archaeology,
  47–8, 250–1
Finley, M., 75
fishing vessels, 219
Fiumicino
  boats, 60, 66–7
  Roman harbour, *see under*
    Portus
Flemming, N. C., 79, 80, 83
Flinder, A., 146
Florida, 111, 114–15
France, 14, 16, 53, 60–1, 104, 115,
  117, 148, 187, 238
Frank, T., 69
Friarton, log boat, 128
Frost, H., 39, 67, 77, 146, 160
furthest neighbour cluster
  analysis, 210–11

Gagnan, E., 14
Gandolfo wreck, 73
Gelidonya, Cape, bronze age
  wreck
  cargo and bronze age trade, 15,
    70–1, 125, 127, 143, 218, 220,
    238
  site analysis, 183, 192, 221
  structural remains, 70, 127, 131,
    221, 233
  see also, 15, 218, 220
Girona (1588), 19, 99, 102, 104,
  121, 122, 245
Gokstad boat, 87, 90, 236
Grace Dieu (1439), 8, 91, 132
grain ships (Alexandria–Rome),
  3, 75
Gran Grifon, El, (1588), 99, 104,
  220
Grand Congloué wreck(s), 14, 56,
  60, 62, 72–3
Grand Ribaud wreck A, 16
grave boats, 8, 9, 84, 87, 91, 131
Graveney boat, 8, 18, 90, 132, 186
Gredstedbro boat, 85
Greece, 12, 171
Green, J. N., 21
Greenhill, B., 84, 231
Greenland, 90
group average cluster analysis,
  210,212, 213

Haiti, 112
Halsewell (1786), 110
Halsnoy boat, 85
harbours, 6, 13, 75–84
Hartley, B., 242
Hasslöf, O., 232, 234, 241
Hastings, Sussex, 95
Havant, D., 108
Hawkins, J., 98
Hengistbury Head, Hampshire,
  143
Henningsen, H., 241
Heraclea (1940), 171
Herculaneum, 56
Hiero II, of Syracuse, 59
history
  as a discipline, 4, 6–7, 228,
    229–30, 232–3
  maritime, 6, 7, 228, 232–4
Hjortspring boat, 128–30

Hollandia (1742), 108, 125, 175
Hornell, J., 231, 234
Huelva, bronze age artefacts from,
  143

Iceland, 90
India, 110, 135–6, 138
Indian Ocean, 135–6, 145, 149
Ireland, 52, 99, 134, 192
iron concretion, 34, 47, 52, 113,
  180
Israel, 20
Italy, 13, 60, 72–4, 99

Jaccard, coefficient of, 206
Jamaica, 112, 115
James Matthews (1841), 116
Japan, 21, 106, 138, 145
Jezirat Fara'un, 146
Jondet, G., 83
Jutholmen wreck, 46

Kalmar boats, 132
Kalnes rock carvings, 128–30
Katzev, M. L., 16, 42
Keller, C., 248
Keltridge, W., 95
Kenchreai, 79
Kendall rank correlation
  coefficient, 162
Kennemerland (1664)
  cargo, 108–10, 167, 196–214,
    220, 223–4, 244–5
  navigational instruments, 121,
    123–4, 215
  other wrecks on site, 56
  site analysis, 167–9, 183,
    196–214
  site description, 52, 159,
    177–80, 181
  site excavation, 50, 52, 196–7
  structural remains, 95
  wrecking, 159, 167, 172–5
Kenya, 20
Klastad ship, 87
Korea, 145
Kos, 71, 72
Kvalsund boat, 85
Kyrenia wreck
  investigations, 15, 61, 183, 187,
    217
  significance, 65, 71–2, 187, 217

Ladby boat, 87, 89, 236
Lance–Williams coefficient cluster
  analysis, 211
Landström, B., 135, 231
Lastdrager (1652), 108, 121, 122
laws, relating to maritime
  archaeology, 14, 20, 153, 251
lead
  as cargo or ballast, 72, 108, 172,
    200, 221
  sheathing, 65
  sounding, 120
Lebanon, 147
Lethbridge, T. C., 234
Lewis, M., 102
Liang-shan Hsien boat, 137
Limnoria lignorum, 53, 151
Little, J. H., 79
Ljubljana boat, 140
log boats, 84, 128, 138, 140
Lovely (1802), 175
Lyell, C., 11

Machault (1760), 20, 117
McQuitty's coefficient cluster
  analysis, 211, 212
Madrague de Giens wreck, 61, 64,
  75, 220

Mahdia
  harbour, 82
  wreck, 12, 62
Maria Juan (1588), 102
Marquis de Maulauze (1760), 117
Marseilles, 74, 80
Marx, R., 112, 150
Mary Rose (1545)
  investigations, 20, 43, 45, 217
  preservation, 171, 177, 232
  significance, 92–3, 132, 182, 231
Marzememi Bay, 56
mean square between blocks
  statistic, 213
median cluster analysis, 211
Medina Sidonia, Duke of, 101
Mercator, G., 120
mercury, 108
Messina, Straits of, wreck, 71–2
Mombasa wreck, *see under Santo
  Antonio de Tanna*
Monaco harbour wreck, 60, 64
Morrison, J., 64, 68
Motya, 82
Mövik harbour, 176, 181
Müller-Wille, M., 8
Mullion wreck, 218
museums, 18, 33, 88, 118–20, 241,
  252

Naples, 99
National Maritime Museum,
  Greenwich, 18, 120, 123, 236
nearest neighbour cluster analysis,
  209–10
Needham, J., 137
Neft, D. S., 191
Nemi Roman ships, 11, 13, 60,
  65, 149
Nesteroff, W. D., 160
Netherlands, 17, 99, 106, 132,
  159, *see also under* Dutch
  East India Company
Nicholas (1790), 125
Nieuw Rhoon (1776), 110
Norway, 85–7, 128, 132, 176
Nuestra Senora de Atoche (1622),
  114
Nydam boat, 8, 11, 85

Odyssey, 83, 233
Old Custom House, London, 134
Oseberg boat, 86–7
Ostia, Roman harbour at, *see
  under* Portus
Owen, D. I., 72

Pakistan, 135
Pantano Longarini, 60, 64, 66,
  184, 186, 218
Parker, A. J., 56, 70, 72
Pennsylvania, University of, 14
Phaselis, 79, 83
Philip II of Spain, 98, 99, 101
photography under water, 31–3
Piraeus, 80, 83
Pirenne, H., 144–5
Pitt-Rivers, F., 251
Planiers, Île de
  wreck III, 53, 61, 73, 170
  wreck IV, 72, 170
plants, sea-bed, 160, 163, 176, 181
Poidebard, A., 13, 76–8
Pollard, H., 11
Polybius, 80
Pompeii, 56, 149, 229
porcelain, Chinese, 101, 109, 110,
  114, 222, 224
Port Vendres wreck II, 72
portage sites in North America,
  20, 141

Porto Cheli, 79
Porto Longo, 171
Portugal, 72
Portus, 60, 66, 79, 82, 83
preservation of materials under
    water, 52–5, 165–9
product–moment similarity
    measure, 207–12
Pudding Pan Rock wreck, 11, 143,
    242
Punic warships, near Marsala in
    Sicily, 67–9, 232, 233

rams, ship's, 68–9
recovery techniques under water,
    33–4, 152–4
Red Sea, 135, 149
Reinach, S., 12
Rhodes, 71, 75, 187
Robinson–Brainerd index of
    similarity, 207
Roche Fouras wreck, 16, 46
Rome, 3, 12, 75, 82
Roskilde wrecks, 8, 88–90, 132,
    184–5, 217
Rostovtsev, M. I., 69
Royal George (1782), 170
Rui (1733), 114
runs test, 213
Rye (or Rother) boat, 11, 134, 139

St Andrews University, Institute
    of Maritime Archaeology, 20
St Helena, 109
Salcombe, bronze age artefacts
    from, 142
salvage operations, historic, 10,
    57, 159, 165–9
Samos, 71, 187
San Antonio (1621), 114, 116
San Esteban (1554), 113
San Jose (1733), 114
San Juan de Sicilia (1588), 99, 103
Santa Maria (1493), 112
Santa Maria de Iciar (1554), 112
Santa Maria de la Rosa (1588),
    19, 99, 100–4, 175, 231
Santo Antonio de Tanna (1697),
    20, 110
Sapphire (1695), 20, 115, 116
Sattahip wreck, 20, 145
Scipio Aemelianus, 81
Scotland, 11–12, 95, 159
Sea Venturer (1609), 115
search techniques under water,
    28, 42–3
sediments, on sea-bed, 26–31, 43,
    49–50, 151, 160–4, 175–82
Shetland Islands, 18, 110, 159,
    165, 235
Sheytan Deresi wreck (?), 181
shipworm, 65, *see also under
    Limnoria lignorum, Teredo
    navalis*, and *Xylophaga*
Sicily, 56, 67, 99

Sidon, 76–7
Sieveking, G., 229
simple matching coefficient, 206
simulation, computer, 214, 236
skin boats, 3, 84, 128–9
Skuldelev, wrecks, *see under*
    Roskilde, wrecks
Slot ter Hooge (1724), 106
Society of Antiquaries of London,
    11
South Edinburgh Channel wreck,
    182
Sozopol, 147
Spain, 70, 72, 74, 105, 106,
    111–15, 143
Spanish Armada (1588), 19,
    98–105, 121, 216, 220, 232,
    237, 245, *see also under
    individual ships*
Spargi wreck, 60, 160
spatial analysis, 187–95, 199–214,
    *see also under individual
    techniques*
Star Carr, 3
Stenuit, R., 122
Stockholm, 17, 85
Stonar, 238
stoneware, salt glazed, 50, 200,
    213, 242–4
Strabo, 143
Suecia (1740), 110
sundial, pocket, 108–9
survey techniques under water, 31,
    43–6, 250
Sutton Hoo boat, 8, 17, 85, 235
Swan (1692), 115
Sweden, 17, 85–6, 93–4, 122, 134
Syria, 71

Taillez, P., 14
Taormina, Cape, 64
Taylor, J. du P., 15
Teredo navalis, 53, 95, 151, 170
Texas, 112–13, 122
Thailand, 20, 145
Thapsus, 83
Thompson, I. A., 103, 105
Throckmorton, P., 15, 56, 65–6,
    171, 184, 216
tides, 162–3, 174–5, 176–80
Titan wreck, 14, 60, 62, 65, 72, 74
Tobermory galleon, *see under San
    Juan de Sicilia*
Torre Sgaratta wreck, 60, 65
Toudouze, G. D., 59
Tradelière wreck, 16
training
    for diving, 25–6
    for maritime archaeology, 37–8,
    39, 48, 252–3,
trend surface analysis, 193–5
Trial (1622), 110
Trinidad Valencera (1588)
    contents, 52, 101–3, 121, 220,

222–3, 237
    history, 99, 220
    investigations, 43, 45
    preservation, 52, 99, 177
    significance, 101, 103, 237
    site analysis, 192–5, 196
Tucker, E., 114
Tune boat, 87
Tunisia, 12, 79–83
Turkey, 14–5, 16, 60–1
Tyre, 13, 76–8, 81

Underwater Association, 26
UNESCO, 79
USA, 20, 22, 87, 117–18
Utrecht boat, 140

Valentine (1776), 110
van der Heide, G. R., 17
van der Velde, W. the Younger,
    96, 218
van Doorninck, F. H., 187
Vergulde Draeck (1656), 21, 108,
    244
Vermutus, 77
Verulamium, 11
Victory, HMS, 96
Virginia Merchant (1660), 115

Ward's method cluster analysis
    211–12, 213
Warwick (1619), 115
Wasa
    investigations, 17, 36, 183
    significance, 53, 93–4, 96, 170,
    232
wave motion, effect of, 176–80
Wendela (1737), 110
Western Australia, 21, 94–5, 106,
    110, 116
Wheeler, R. E. M., 4
White, L., 229
Winchester (1695), 115
Witte Leeuw (1613), 109–10
wood, 36, 46–7, 53–5, 92–8, 150
Wood Quay, Dublin, 134

Xylophagai 151–2

Yassi Ada
    fourth-century A.D. wreck, 46,
    64, 183, 187, 222
    seventh-century A.D. wreck, 64,
    66, 183, 187, 188, 221–2, 241
    wrecks, general, 15, 56, 60–1,
    170, 196, 217
Yorke, R. A., 78, 79, 83
Yorktown wrecks, 20, 117–8
Yugoslavia, 16

Zeewijk (1727), 21
Zuider Zee, wrecks within, 9,
    132–3, 144
Zwammerdam wrecks, 17, 139